Special Forces Pilot

Special Forces Pilot

A Flying Memoir
of the Falkland's War

Richard Hutchings

Pen & Sword
AVIATION

First published in Great Britain in 2008, and reprinted in 2009 by
Pen & Sword Aviation
An imprint of
Pen & Sword Books Ltd
47 Church Street
Barnsley
South Yorkshire
S70 2AS

ISBN 978 1 84415 804 1

A CIP catalogue record for this book is
available from the British Library

Typeset in 10pt Palatino by Mac Style, Beverley, East Yorkshire
Printed and bound in the UK by CPI Antony Rowe, Chippenham, Wiltshire

Pen & Sword Books Ltd incorporates the Imprints of Pen & Sword
Aviation, Pen & Sword Maritime, Pen & Sword Military,
Wharncliffe Local History, Pen & Sword Select, Pen & Sword Military
Classics, Leo Cooper, Remember When, Seaforth Publishing and
Frontline Publishing

For a complete list of Pen & Sword titles please contact
PEN & SWORD BOOKS LIMITED
47 Church Street, Barnsley, South Yorkshire, S70 2AS, England
E-mail: enquiries@pen-and-sword.co.uk
Website: www.pen-and-sword.co.uk

Epigraph

War is an ugly thing, but not the ugliest of things. The decayed and degraded state of moral and patriotic feeling which thinks that nothing is worth war is much worse. The person who has nothing for which he is willing to fight, nothing which is more important than his own personal safety, is a miserable creature and has no chance of being free unless made and kept so by the exertions of better men than himself.

John Stewart Mill

Contents

List of Maps and Figures   ix
Foreword by HRH The Duke of York   x
Preface   xi
Acknowledgements   xiii

Part 1 – The Road to War   1

Chapter 1   Will We, Won't We?   3

Chapter 2   The Passage to Ascension Island   13

Chapter 3   Task Force Reorganization at Ascension Island   37

Chapter 4   The Eve of War   40

Part 2 – Operations in the TEZ   63

Chapter 5   Arrival in the TEZ – Operation Sutton Commences   65

Chapter 6   HMS *Sheffield* – A Shattering Blow   80

Chapter 7   HMS *Yarmouth* – 'These Things Happen in War'   89

Chapter 8   The Narwal Incident   93

Chapter 9   Operation Sutton Continues   105

Chapter 10 Pebble Island   111

Part 3 – The Mainland Option   121

Chapter 11 'You're Never Going to Believe This'   123

Chapter 12 HMS *Invincible*   138

Chapter 13 A One-way Trip to Argentina   143

Chapter 14 Fog, Now What?   146

Chapter 15 'Chile, it's F****** Freezing!'   149

Chapter 16 Arrival at Useless Bay   152

Chapter 17 The Beach South of Punta Arenas   154

Chapter 18 Survival in the Hostile Chilean Countryside   158

Chapter 19 The Hill   167

Chapter 20 'Are you the Three British Airmen?'   171

Chapter 21 The Flight to Santiago, Courtesy of the RAF   174

Chapter 22 Santiago – 'It's a Small World'   177

Chapter 23 The Flight to London – What no Interpol?   182

Chapter 24 Arrival in the UK – 'We're Not Expecting You'   185

Chapter 25 The 'Safe House'   190

Chapter 26 The Aftermath   194

Epilogue   197

Glossary   200
Index   205

Maps and Figures

Map 1.   Special Forces Insertion/Extraction and Resupply Routes   119
Map 2.   Operation Plum Duff Insertion Route   156
Map 3.   Route Flown in Argentina and Chile   157
Figure 1. ZA 290 Flight Servicing Certificate   141

Foreword

Over the last 25 years, the conduct of operations during the Falklands War by sea, land and air has been comprehensively and, in some cases, precipitously analysed. Many books and countless articles have been written by participants, observers and journalists, which collectively form a body of knowledge and commentary on many aspects of operations during the conflict. Some of these accounts are widely acknowledged as accurate records of events at sea, on the ground and in the air and others, which purport to be definitive, do not withstand close scrutiny. What, for me, makes this book such an important addition to the bibliography of the conflict is that, to my knowledge, it is not just the first written account by a pilot who took part in Special Forces missions but also the only helicopter pilot's memoir from the war.

Richard Hutchings describes the operations undertaken by the crews of 846 Naval Air Squadron, who were trained to fly with Night Vision Goggles (NVG) in support of Special Forces. In 1982, binocular NVG was a new capability which was yet to be tested operationally. During the long but relatively quick passage to the Falkland Islands, a high priority for the Squadron was to familiarise selected aircrew with the goggles and to develop operational flying procedures, drills and tactics for their use. Furthermore, a cockpit modification scheme had to be designed, installed and tested to make the Sea King helicopters compatible with NVG flight. The procedures and tactics that were developed through trial and error were genuinely pioneering.

The tasks in support of Special Forces called for flying in atrocious weather conditions by day and at night, over enemy-held terrain, at just a few feet above the ground. During the early sorties in particular, the crews were effectively flying blind, not knowing where the enemy were. Equipped with their state of the art NVG, the aircrew were able to navigate accurately to and from target areas in what, to the naked eye, would have been total darkness. No British aircrew had flown helicopters in this way before. Those that flew these Special Forces missions during the Falklands War were as highly skilled and courageous as the men they carried.

In the final part of the book, the conduct of Operation MIKADO, the Special Forces mission to mainland Argentina, is described in detail. I personally felt proud to have been on hand, as 820 Squadron duty officer in HMS INVINCIBLE, to assist the Sea King crew as they made their final preparations for the one-way flight to Argentina. The account has been written following a period of careful reflection by the author, who, as a lieutenant in the Royal Marines, was the Captain of the Sea King which flew this most challenging of missions. This fascinating account benefits from the author having had access to Argentine and Chilean military sources. The result is a definitive record of events in the air and on the ground in Argentina and Chile.

I believe that all who read this very personal and moving story will feel immense pride in the professionalism and selfless courage of our Service personnel. It is a huge privilege to have been a member of such a team.

Preface

When describing Royal Naval Commando aircrew in his book, *One Hundred Days*, Admiral Sandy Woodward wrote: 'One way and another, the "Junglies" are a very special breed who perform a unique task under the most hazardous conditions.' During the conduct of operations in the Falklands War, the principal task of the 'Junglies' was to provide support to amphibious forces, in particular 3 Commando Brigade Royal Marines and the Special Forces teams of SAS and SBS engaged in reconnaissance and direct-action missions on and around the Falkland Islands, and on mainland Argentina. These tasks called for flying support helicopters in atrocious weather conditions by day and at night, over enemy-held terrain, at just a few feet above the ground. Flying with Night Vision Goggles (NVG) was a radical departure from the conventional night-flying operations which had been the bread and butter of the commando squadrons for a generation. En route to the Falkland Islands, the aircrew had to be trained, the aircraft modified and operational NVG procedures developed. The diversity of their range of skills and disciplines, which will be demonstrated throughout this narrative, demanded dedicated proficiency and courage in approaching their tasks. The 'Junglies' NVG operations during Operation Corporate were continually challenging, and at the cutting edge of night-flying capability and pioneering.

Since the earliest days of military aviation, the complements of Royal Naval squadrons have included a small number of Royal Marine pilots. Between 1979 and 1983 I was a member of 846 Naval Air Squadron and flew many operational sorties during the Falklands War. In this book I have set out to describe the operations undertaken by the crews of 846 Naval Air Squadron who were trained to fly with NVG in support of Special Forces. In the final part of the book I describe in detail the conduct of Operation Mikado – the ill-fated Special Forces mission on mainland Argentina. I have written the book as if I were telling my story to a close friend or relative, warts and all, and not as a formal historical record. In addition to describing my own experiences and thoughts as the war progressed, I have also attempted to capture my broader interactions with colleagues and communities within HMS *Hermes*. Recurring themes with positive overtones are the constructive attitude, professionalism, selflessness, courage and good humour of those with whom I worked and lived cheek by jowl. However, on occasions I was disappointed to observe that some officers were quick to cite the 'fog of war' as the reason for failure. More often than not it was a smoke screen to mask shortcomings in situational awareness.

Operating helicopters during war is a team effort. Without the round-the-clock hard work, professionalism, dedication and selflessness of the Squadron's engineers, maintainers, aircraft handlers and support personnel, the pilots and aircrewmen would not have had aircraft to fly. Tragically and sadly not all who deployed with 846 Squadron returned. This book is dedicated to 'Ben' Casey and 'Doc' Love.

Acknowledgements

In writing this book, I quickly came to realize how much I owe to other people: family, friends, colleagues and some sources who, because of the sensitivity of certain aspects of this book, must remain anonymous. To the latter group I am constrained to simply thanking you for having given me so much help.

To my wife Lorraine, I wish to say sorry for having caused you so much anxiety in 1982. To my two sons, Justin and James, I wish to say thank you for being such a tower of strength and support to your mother when she most needed it. To my daughter Kate I am most grateful for your patience and dedication in proofreading the manuscript.

I am particularly grateful to the following for reinforcing my own memory with their recollections, anecdotes, photographs and records from their flying logbooks and other sources: David Balchin, Alan Bennett, Simon Branch-Evans, John Cummins, Peter Imrie, Lyn Middleton, John Middleton, David Morgan, Nigel North, Bill Pollock and Simon Thornewill.

I would also like to express my appreciation to the following:

Edward Hamilton and Christine Cox for granting permission to reproduce the late John Hamilton's painting of the 'Pebble Island Raid' on the jacket to this book.

The MoD, in particular Rear Admiral Ian Moncrief, for granting permission to reproduce Admiralty Charts. The charts at Maps 1, 3 and 4 are reproduced by permission of the Controller of Her Majesty's Stationery Office and the UK Hydrographic Office.

The Press Association for granting permission to reproduce the photograph of my family during the Investiture at Buckingham Palace.

Professor Nigel West for granting permission to quote extracts from *The Secret War for the Falklands*.

Extracts from *One Hundred Days* by Sandy Woodward, 1992 are reprinted by permission of HarperCollins Publishers Ltd.

Part 1

The Road to War

CHAPTER 1

Will We, Won't We?

At 0430hrs on Friday, 2 April 1982, 150 men of the Argentine Special Forces landed by helicopter 3 miles south-west of the Falklands' capital, Port Stanley. This was the beginning of the Argentine invasion of the Falkland Islands and was followed by the landing of over 1,000 more specialist troops and marines. Five hours later, the eighty-man garrison of Royal Marines had surrendered on the order of the Island's Governor, Rex Hunt. The next day, the 22-man force of Royal Marines, which had landed from HMS *Endurance* onto South Georgia, some 800 miles south-east of Port Stanley, surrendered after a short but heroic battle. What became known as the Falklands War had started.

Meanwhile, in the UK on Wednesday, 31 March, intelligence and embassy reports confirmed that almost the entire Argentine fleet was at sea and that the invasion of the Falkland Islands was set for the early hours of 2 April. John Knott at once called the Prime Minister and a meeting was promptly arranged at her office in the House of Commons, also attended by Sir Henry Leach, the First Sea Lord. Henry Leach was given authority to make preparations. HMS *Hermes* and HMS *Invincible* would form the backbone of the maritime element of the Task Force. I was to learn a day later that *Hermes* would be my home for the next eight weeks. Later the following day, Mrs Thatcher ordered that troops be put on immediate alert for deployment to the South Atlantic. Within forty-eight hours, the Task Force was on four hours notice to sail.

The way that we, the British public, learned that our sovereign territory had been invaded did little to reassure us that the Government was in control of events.

By mid-morning on Friday, 2 April, Fleet Street was receiving news agency messages from Buenos Aires that Argentine forces had just landed at Port Stanley, which contradicted the MoD's understanding of events 8,000 miles away. Media communications channels were to prove more reliable and timely than official government communications channels on several occasions during subsequent operations. The relative effectiveness of these communication channels was to impact on me and my family just a few weeks later.

It is standard practice for military units to be at a specific notice for deployment, the usual peacetime notice for military units being seven days. When the notice is to be shortened it should be a step-by-step process within the overall timescale, so the earliest that the Task Force should have been deployable, in theory, was some time after seven days had lapsed from 2 April, i.e. not before 9 April. However, the first ships of the Task Force deployed on Monday, 5 April. How was this possible? The answer is simple: the Armed Forces have a 'can-do' attitude. Even if Foreign Office officials were not interpreting the signals intelligently, there were plenty of military planners who were. My own unit, 846 Naval Air Squadron, was at the time well dispersed with a detachment supporting the weapon training of a unit of 3 Commando Brigade, Royal Marines in north-west England, and another detachment had only just returned to our base having taken part in a maritime counter-terrorism exercise in the North Sea. Fortuitously, all squadron personnel and helicopters were due to be concentrated at the Royal Naval Air Station, Yeovilton, on or by Friday, 2 April, in time for a well-earned period of leave over Easter.

846 Squadron was first commissioned on 1 April 1943. Disbanded in 1945, the Squadron reformed in 1962 and this was when the commando squadrons earned the illustrious nickname of 'Junglies' from Army units whilst in Borneo. Flying Whirlwind HAS7s from HMS *Albion*, they were used in action against the terrorist Guerrillas, and the ground units were constantly impressed by their highly skilled jungle navigation. After disbanding again, 846 Squadron reformed, this time with the Wessex V, in 1968, as a commando helicopter squadron based at RNAS Culdrose, before relocating to RNAS Yeovilton in May 1972. In February 1979, the Squadron joined HMS *Bulwark*, and from December that year began a modernization programme with the Sea King IV.

In 1982, 846 Squadron was equipped with fourteen Sea King IVs, prior to which the Squadron had operated eighteen Wessex Vs, a well-tried and trusted workhorse. By contrast, the Sea King IV was unproven operationally. The Sea King IV, like all variants of the Sea King, was designed as a Naval Helicopter from the outset and had numerous features that made it well suited to embarked operations; these included powered folding rotor blades, a folding tail, a robust undercarriage, a telebrief system and construction from materials resistant to salt-water corrosion. The aircraft is a stable platform for Instrument Flying (IF) and in 1982 was fitted with a comprehensive suite of navigation aids including an Instrument Landing System (ILS), much the same as that found in civil airliners. The Sea King IV had clearance to fly in certain icing conditions. At the start of operations in 1982, the Sea King IV was not Night Vision Goggle (NVG) compatible. The Sea King also lacked the agility of the Wessex. On the plus side, the cabin was cavernous by comparison to the Wessex, with seats for up to twenty-seven troops, depending on equipment carried. The helicopter could carry heavy loads, underslung, over a very useful distance. With a full fuel load, the helicopter could remain airborne for six hours with up to ten troops embarked, depending on equipment to be carried. The Sea King IV was fitted with state-of-the-art communications, IFF and inertial navigation equipment.

Overall, a vast improvement on the Wessex V, but like the Sea Harrier (SHAR), it was yet to be battle tested.

Since 1962, the Squadron had supported units of 3 Commando Brigade during land-based and amphibious operations and exercises. Procedures and drills for the Sea King had been developed and regularly practised with units of the Brigade, HMS *Hermes* and HMS *Invincible*. The Squadron was, therefore, confident that it would acquit itself well in any operation. The only Achilles heal was the lack of a self-defence system or weapon, other than a GPMG, which could be fixed in the entrance of the cabin door and operated by either the aircrewman or, if needs dictated, one of the embarked troops.

Along with 845 Squadron, full command of 846 Squadron was exercised through the Fleet Air Arm chain of command to the Commanding Officer of the Royal Naval Air Station, Yeovilton. Operational command and control of the commando helicopter squadrons was delegated for operations and exercises to either Commodore Amphibious Warfare (Comaw) or Commander 3 Commando Brigade, as appropriate. This meant that, in reality, the Squadron had a foot in three camps when not operationally deployed. Such matters as change of readiness was communicated through Royal Navy command channels.

There was considerable excitement in 846 Squadron throughout the day on 1 April. The Squadron consisted of approximately 180 personnel who were highly trained to work together as a whole, or in smaller units, in any environment under operational circumstances. The bulk of the Squadron personnel were aircraft maintainers of various specializations who worked tirelessly to ensure that the Sea Kings were fully operational and ready for any task. Years of experience with this aircraft type, in a wide variety of theatres, allowed 846 Squadron to operate with a flexible, 'can-do' approach, something that has always been at the core of the 'Junglie' squadron philosophy. The general mood was, therefore, one of excited expectation and high morale, both, however, being deflated on more than one occasion during the day as the indecision of our politicians became apparent. It was clear that the Government still sought to avert the invasion through diplomatic channels, rightly so of course, but this was not the sort of news that servicemen 'champing at the bit' wanted to hear. The political and diplomatic vacillations were certainly felt at Yeovilton.

Throughout the day, an ever-changing stream of instructions was received. After the deployment had been stood down, it was revived again, but this time with only a small group from the Brigade and limited helicopter support. This disappointment did not suppress the determination of squadron personnel to do their duty, and if there was a potential opportunity to 'kick some Argentine butt', all wanted to be a part of it. To this end, aircrew who were due to leave the Squadron in the near future, were asking the Commanding Officer (CO), Lieutenant Commander Simon Thornewill, whether it would be possible to have their postings to new units delayed so that they could remain with the Squadron should it deploy to the South Atlantic. The CO did not let them down and after a few phone calls through the chain of command, he was able to announce that should the Squadron deploy to the South Atlantic, all aircrew who were due to leave it during the coming weeks and months would be remaining with the Squadron. One pilot, who had recently left the Squadron and started a training course to convert to the Lynx, was Alan (Wiggy) Bennett. 'Wiggy' and I were close friends and had trained together to fly the Wessex and subsequently the Sea King. The CO negotiated his immediate release from the training course and he rejoined the Squadron that day. I could not have known at the time that in a few weeks our lives were to become inextricably linked, through a mutual dependence for survival.

Throughout all of the excitement, order and counter-order of the day, the Squadron's Senior Pilot, Lieutenant Commander Bill Pollock, second-in-command, was trying to maintain some semblance of order and discipline – not an easy task with aircrew at the best of times, but now there was the added challenge of aircrew hell bent on 'kicking Argentine butt'! The CO and Senior Pilot had been quick to appreciate the possibility of the Squadron deploying to war and to this end, preparations had already been put in train over the previous couple of weeks. The servicing of the helicopters had been brought up to date and equipment packed. However, when squadron personnel returned home at the end of the day, most were convinced that nothing would come of it. That said, wives and girlfriends were left in no doubt that evening that the Squadron might be going to war in just a few days.

In Portsmouth, the ageing carrier HMS *Hermes* was about to begin a refit, was empty of stores and food, and covered in scaffolding. The somewhat newer, but smaller HMS *Invincible* had just returned from arctic warfare exercises in Norwegian waters, with her embarked Air Group, 801 Naval Air Squadron, with six Sea Harriers, later to increase to an Air Group of twelve. Work to prepare these ships started in earnest, with sailors and 'dockyard maties' working together around the clock, including working under floodlights at night, to ensure that no valuable minute was lost. Work on *Hermes* now had to assume a somewhat different priority if this venerable ship were to be ready to put to sea by high tide on the following Monday morning, just five days later.

The Defence Review of 1981 envisaged that the Navy, and consequently the Royal Dockyards, would play a small role in any future conflicts. It therefore called for a drastic reduction in the number of workers in the dockyard, the first rounds of redundancy notices being issued on 2 April 1982. Against this backdrop of redundancies, Britain went to war and once again the dockyard mobilized. The order received on 2 April was: 'Ships must sail by Monday morning!' The condition of HMS *Hermes* was of particular interest to many back at Yeovilton because 846 Squadron was the ship's designated commando helicopter squadron. 800 Squadron, with its Sea Harriers, also based at Yeovilton, would also be embarking as the ship's Air Group. In addition to the two Yeovilton-based squadrons, there would be a squadron of ASW helicopters embarked from RNAS Culdrose. It was clear from the outset that it was going to be a tight squeeze for aircraft, maintenance, briefing facilities and beds.

The morning of Friday, 2 April was to be a very early start for Simon Thornewill who was awoken by a telephone call at 0400hrs from the Captain of Yeovilton; the message was brief: 'You are to mobilize your squadron for sea immediately' – that was it, short and to the point! The message was relayed to a few key personnel within the Squadron through the well-tested recall system and all personnel were in the squadron lines by 0830hrs. The preparations of the past few days were now to pay dividends.

The squadron buildings were alive and buzzing with activity by the time I arrived at 0800hrs. The Squadron's Air Engineering Officer (AEO), Lieutenant Commander Richard Harden, and his team, were already well ahead of the game in getting the helicopters ready for embarkation. The buzz around the Squadron was that we were going to embark in *Hermes* either on Saturday or Sunday and head south towards the Falkland Islands on Monday, 5 April. The morning brief at 0830 that day was like no other. The CO told us as much as he knew at that time. There was clearly an issue over the state of the flight deck of *Hermes* – just the previous day it had been covered in scaffolding. There was also the issue of timings – there was a Harrier Air Group to embark, together with Sea Kings from our squadron, plus Sea Kings from another squadron, all of which had to be de-conflicted. The Harriers were to embark in several groups: eight on the Saturday, three the following day and the last aircraft after departure from Portsmouth. Another challenge was embarkation whilst the ship was alongside in the dockyard. Ordinarily, this was not permitted for safety and noise abatement reasons, but the nation was about to go to war.

'Bugger noise abatement,' said the CO, rather loudly. As the day progressed, final preparations and last-minute administrative matters were addressed.

'Have you all made your wills?' asked the Senior Pilot, with a wry smile on his face. It was apparent that some had not, but the Royal Navy has a form for just such an eventuality – but then the Royal Navy seems to have a form for just about every eventuality.

In terms of operational preparedness the Squadron was in good shape. We had supported amphibious training in Norway during February, so collectively and individually we were up to speed with ship-borne operations, troop drills and deck landings by day and night. The way in which I had personally joined the training and exercise in Norway was not altogether unusual: a four-stage transit flown over four days covering 1,500 miles. Embarkation in *Hermes*, in Norwegian waters, followed five days later. Long-distance transits were therefore commonplace for the Squadron, given its broad role. Experience of long-distance navigation was to prove invaluable during subsequent operations in the South Atlantic, where 200- or 300-mile transits over the sea at night were to become the norm for some of us. At the end of the day, embarkation in *Hermes* was confirmed for the following day.

On Friday, 2 April, the only personnel issue still to be resolved was the status of our foreign-exchange pilots. We had assumed from the outset that our Australian pilot, Ron Lawrence, and American pilot, Dale Johnson, would not be permitted to deploy, and confirmation was received later that day. The Task Force was to be a strictly British affair, which came as a major disappointment to Ron in particular, who without doubt was gutted.

'We have the same Head of State, for Christ's sake,' said Ron, but no one was listening. Ron was to remain at Yeovilton as the officer commanding the rear party, whereas Dale returned to the USA for the duration of hostilities.

In addition to resolving the issue of the non-British pilots, we learnt that there was also to be a potential addition to the Squadron's complement of pilots. On the Friday, the CO was contacted by Lieutenant Commander Mike Spencer and Lieutenant Peter Rainey with news that was to have a pivotal impact on the Squadron's subsequent operations. Mike was a test pilot working at the Royal Aircraft Establishment at Farnborough, and Peter was a test pilot working at the Aircraft and Armaments Experimental Establishment at Boscombe Down, who was to die tragically in a drowning accident in 2003. They made the CO aware of a significant development in the evolution of NVG. Earlier versions of NVG had significant limitations for flying operations because they covered part of the face, thereby restricting a pilot's ability to switch between flying with or without the aid of goggles. The new NVG were of a binocular design which facilitated quick and easy changes between flight, with or without them. It was clear that the new goggles had potential during night-flying operations in the South Atlantic, but from the Squadron's perspective they were an unknown quantity and needed to be evaluated. To this end, on the Sunday evening, the Squadron's Qualified Helicopter Instructor (QHI), Lieutenant Nigel North, together with the Helicopter Warfare Instructor (HWI), Lieutenant Bob Horton, our RAF exchange pilot, Flight Lieutenant Bob Gundy and Lieutenant Pete Rainey were to be driven to Farnborough to carry out a flying evaluation of the NVG in the establishment's Puma. It would therefore be another two days before we would know whether or not the goggles would be an addition to the Squadron inventory.

As the working day moved towards its close, the thoughts of most turned increasingly towards our loved ones and as soon as deployment was confirmed there was a mad scramble to find a phone somewhere so that calls could be made home to alert wives, girlfriends and families. Tonight was to be the last night that we would see our loved ones for an unknown period of time – as it turned out, it was to be the very last time for two of the aircrew.

That night at home we said our long farewells, for it was clear that the following morning there would only be enough time for the briefest of loving exchanges. At the time I had two young sons, Justin aged seven, and James aged four. Both were too young to understand fully what was about to happen, but grasped the essential fact that I was going to be away from home for quite a long time and that they, therefore, had to look after Mummy in my absence. Quite what families go through when their men, and increasingly these days also women, are away fighting for Queen and country can only really be appreciated by those to whom it has happened. During our absence in the South Atlantic, families were kept up to date as best as possible, within the constraints of operational security, through MoD information channels. However, on many occasions these channels proved to be considerably slower than the media – I shall return to this issue in a later chapter. Suffice it to say at this stage that servicemen and servicewomen, when deployed on operations, are always anxious to know that their loved ones back home are receiving accurate and timely information; regrettably on many occasions during the Falklands War this did not happen. Our fighting men and women are more effective if they do not have the unwelcome distraction of worrying about what is happening back home.

That night I packed my kit ready for embarkation. What to pack though? The military equipment was obvious, but what about personal items? I packed only two books, *Jonathan Livingston Seagull*, by Richard Bach, essential reading for all aviators, and *The Prophet* by Kahlil Gibran. I was somewhat amused to learn later, after embarkation in HMS *Hermes*, that one of the Harrier Pilots, Dave Morgan, had also bought with him a copy of *Jonathan Livingston Seagull*. Dave's career had been rather unusual, to say the least, in that he had transferred between the RN and RAF, and was later in his career to transfer back to the RN, but more of him later.

Saturday morning, 3 April, was an early start for everyone in the Squadron. With few exceptions, squadron personnel were driven to Yeovilton by wives or girlfriends and dropped off. It was with a heavy heart that I said farewell to Lorraine and the boys, and started to focus on the task ahead. It may seem to many that embarking a squadron of helicopters in a ship is an easy enough thing to do: just take off, fly to the ship and land – what could be simpler? To an extent that is exactly what happens, however, the helicopters need engineering and handling support the instant that they land on board, therefore embarkation has to be a staged evolution. A small party of maintainers, under the command of the Chief Artificer, Pat Garrett, had been dispatched to the ship the previous day to ensure that all was ready for the eventual arrival of the helicopters. Pat could always be relied upon to volunteer for an advance party if it meant that flying could be avoided, because in a previous squadron he had ditched in the sea whilst a passenger in a Wasp and barely escaped with his life. One advantage of being equipped with the Sea King is that it is possible to carry all squadron personnel and their kit in the aircraft if required during deployment. One hundred and eighty men with kit fit into fourteen helicopters easily. However, during amphibious operations the Squadron was often required to disembark in order to operate from a land-based Forward Operating Base (FOB), closer to the troops being supported, therefore vehicles and other heavy equipment were required to be embarked in addition to the helicopters and personnel, all of which took time and organizing.

Flight time to Portsmouth dockyard from Yeovilton, for the helicopters, would be just fifty minutes. Departures were staggered to ensure that the ship could cope with our arrival, as the last thing that HMS *Hermes* wanted was nine Sea Kings all arriving at the same time. Five Sea Kings were destined for a somewhat different means of deployment. A detachment of three Sea Kings, under the command of the Senior Pilot, deployed the following day to Portland to embark in HMS *Fearless*, while on 5 April, a Sea King taken from storage at Culdrose, was delivered to Yeovilton. By 7 April it had been repainted and assigned the call sign 'VW'. Later that day it was flown by Lieutenant Peter Spens-Black (Snatchblock) to RAF Lyneham, where it was stripped of its rotor blades and main rotor gearbox by a detachment of the Squadron's maintainers and placed carefully inside a Belfast Aircraft of the company Heavy Lift. The following day 'VW' arrived at Ascension Island and was hurriedly reassembled. Finally, on 26 April, 'VZ', a new aircraft, was flown onto HMS *Intrepid* as she passed the Lizard, arriving at Ascension Island on 5 May.

Our flight to Portsmouth was uneventful, but I could not help but take a somewhat more lingering and closer look at the English countryside as we flew over it on our way to Portsmouth; after all, none of us had any idea as to when we would be likely to see our homeland again. It felt strange landing on *Hermes*, on a Saturday, with the ship alongside the North-west Wall in Portsmouth dockyard. We were all supposed to be enjoying a well-earned Easter leave with our families and friends, but instead were about to set sail to take part in a war on the other side of the world. Any feelings of melancholy were brought to an abrupt halt shortly after we landed when we saw for the first time the amount of work being done to get the ship ready for sea. Not only was there scaffolding on the Island, there were also people carrying out what were obviously engineering works. But the sight that truly amazed me were the lines of sailors and officers lining the jetty, the ship's gangways and decks, passing boxes of provisions from one to another, in two enormous snake-like chains – a sight to behold. It was the first time that I had witnessed RN officers, with their sleeves rolled up, mucking in with ordinary sailors humping stores to provision a ship. This gave me a feeling of hope that for the coming weeks this demonstration of real teamwork at all levels would be sustained through subsequent operations.

Hermes was a familiar home to me and many other members of the Squadron. Just inside the Island, at flight-deck level, was the Line Office, very much the nerve centre of aircraft engineering operations. Having signed in my aircraft, I set off towards the wardroom. Aircrew are normally accommodated in cabins on 5 Deck, with the exception of the more senior officers like the CO, Senior Pilot and any other Lieutenant Commanders, who were accommodated on 4 Deck. The cabins on 5 Deck varied in size from single, through double to four berth, the one allocated to me being a single-berth compartment on 5S Deck

(5S10). Most of the other pilots in the Squadron were also accommodated on 5S Mess Deck. The cabin was small but comfortable. It had air conditioning of sorts – a rather noisy system, but one providing much-needed and welcome cooling air in what was otherwise a hot and stuffy place. This 10 foot by 6 foot compartment was to be my personal space, the inner sanctum, for the duration of my part in the operations to follow – a place where I could be alone with my thoughts. At the time, the significance of living on 5 Deck was not realized by any of us, but as we were to discover later, as the ship approached the 200-mile Total Exclusion Zone (TEZ) established around the Falkland Islands, 5 Deck was not a good place to be living.

I spent the rest of the afternoon wandering around the ship, refreshing my memory as to the shortest and quickest routes to the various places where, in the coming weeks, I would be spending much of my time when not flying. I was feeling pleased with myself for remembering the routes, but as I walked around the ship I remembered my first time on board, which had been a navigational nightmare!

To move from my cabin in 5S to the wardroom in 4T was a short journey up one ladder and aft one compartment – simple once you got used to it. In theory, armed with two sets of codes, start point and destination, it should have been possible to navigate to any part of the ship, however in practice it was not so simple. Some passageways had a habit of coming to an abrupt end just as you thought you were about to arrive at the destination, which required climbing or descending ladders in order to complete the journey. It was important to memorize routes so that we could move around the ship quickly when necessary.

During the evening it was customary for most of the embarked officers to meet in the wardroom for drinks, but this evening was to be an exception – it was time for a 'run ashore', naval speak for going out on the town. After a few beers and a bar snack, we headed back to the dockyard, pausing only long enough for each of us to make a phone call home; no mobile phones in those days, so it was an old-fashioned phone box that beckoned. With just two days remaining for phone calls I wanted to make sure that everything back home was as shipshape as possible. I did not find it easy to say any more farewells, so I focused on the practical rather than the emotional during our brief chat – apart from which, there was a queue of increasingly impatient friends outside waiting their turn.

Sunday, 4 April, was a day of frenetic activity aboard HMS *Hermes*. Once again the snake-like chains of naval ratings and officers appeared on the jetty, the gangways and ship's passageways, passing from one to another boxes of wide-ranging provisions to store the ship; this time there would be a lot more mouths to feed than usual. In various compartments and passageways, civilian and naval engineers and maintenance personnel were carrying out last-minute work to get the ship ready, working against the clock to ensure that *Hermes* was ready to sail on the morning tide the next day.

During this mayhem, the unlikely figure of John Knott appeared. The Secretary of State for Defence was paying a visit to the ships of the Task Force and the dockyard, having arrived by helicopter to visit the fleet. As he was about to board HMS *Hermes*, I saw him go up to a group of dockyard workers standing on the jetty and speak to them. There was no sign of the hostility that had greeted him a few months earlier during his last visit, and yet these were the very men whom he was putting out of work as a result of his Defence Review the previous year. Several had received their redundancy notices a few days before, but in spite of that, they'd all rallied round, working day and night; such was the mark of their quality as patriotic Brits. However, although he had been in the centre of a very emotional row about the future of the Royal Navy over the preceding six to nine months, and although there must have been a number of sailors on board *Hermes* who felt that he was responsible for having taken many wrong decisions, no hostility appeared to surface during the visit. The nation had a crisis and we just had to work together to put on a good show. It is a mark of just how much this country can come together in times of crisis and in a quite astonishing way.

By sunset, much of the mundane but important work of storing the ship had been completed and some of the passageways and spaces previously covered in engineering equipment and paraphernalia once again took on their customary ship-shape appearance. A few new faces appeared in the wardroom that evening. Not for the first time in modern warfare, activities of a Task Force were to be scrutinized first hand by members of the media. The BBC's Brian Hanrahan and ITN's Michael Nicholson were to sail with us the next day and remain with the ship throughout the conflict. It would be very interesting to observe how the RN were going to manage the journalists in an era of near-instant satellite communications capable of delivering reports to the people back home in almost real time. Such close and sustained contact with the media was a first for most personnel in the ship. That evening the two journalists were looked upon with a mixture of curiosity and suspicion. For some it would be a night for meeting and greeting, and guarding one's tongue, but for me and my like-minded friends it was the last opportunity for a pre-departure 'run ashore' – except for Nigel North, Bob Horton, Bob Grundy and Peter Rainey, all of whom had an appointment to keep with Mike Spencer and a Puma at Farnborough.

For the next few hours, whilst I was enjoying the delights of Portsmouth's night life for the last time, Nigel and his team flew the Puma around Salisbury Plain trying out the NVG for the first time. Under the instruction of Mike Spencer, each flew a 45-minute sortie to evaluate the potential of the goggles for our subsequent operations in the South Atlantic. Following a successful evening's evaluation, the team arrived back on board *Hermes* at 0300hrs on the Monday morning, clutching seven pairs of goggles. Six weeks later I was purposefully to destroy two sets of the goggles – but that's another story.

CHAPTER 2

The Passage to Ascension Island

The sailing of the carrier-led task force at 1045hrs on Monday, 5 April was to become indelibly etched on the national conscience. It was to be the biggest naval Task Force assembled since the Suez Crisis of 1956. It was a perfect spring morning, loading of stores had continued during the night and it seemed to me that the ship was now bursting at the seams. Hazy sunshine slowly warmed the decks of the waiting ships as they prepared for sea. On deck, Harriers and Sea Kings were ranged in readiness for the ship's departure. The ship's company was slowly taking up their positions lining the edge of the deck, ready for 'Procedure Alfa'. About 1,800 crew lined the ship's side as HMS *Hermes* slowly sailed out of harbour. There had not been a day quite like it since Suez just over twenty-five years earlier. Few members of the Task Force had experienced war fighting as such. Most of the Royal Marines, myself included, had experience of operations of many kinds, to include some war fighting, but we were pretty much the exception. Each man was to search his innermost thoughts at some stage in an attempt to understand how he would acquit himself. As the ship slipped her moorings I had no misgivings or doubts, but there were to be plenty of opportunities in the coming weeks when each man would return to this question – I, for one, certainly did.

I did not join any of the other members of the crew on deck for our departure from the dockyard, preferring to stay below deck and watch events from the comfort of the wardroom television room. It was a surreal experience to see the ship slowly moving out of the harbour with me sitting in one of the compartments watching events unfold. This was not to be the last time that I was to appear on television during the conflict, but the next time was not to be anything like as comfortable. From the television pictures, the send-off appeared tremendous. The record of Rod Stewart's 'Sailing' was being played from ashore, always a stir to the emotions of mariners. My thoughts moved quickly between what was happening on the ship, the scene outside and my family back in Somerset. I had managed to write a letter home and have it posted that morning, so I was able to express my thoughts and love to my family at what I knew would be a really emotional time for them.

Morale was at a peak, despite the news just received that Lord Carrington had resigned as Foreign Secretary. There seemed to be genuine surprise and upset at this news on board because Carrington was held in high regard by many and was considered to be a man of honour, let down by his team. There was equal surprise at the news that John Knott's offer to resign had not been accepted by Mrs Thatcher. Knott was the architect of a Defence Review the previous year, which if implemented in full, would have seen a significant reduction in the size and military capability of the Royal Navy. The most shocking aspect of his proposals was the loss of the Navy's specialist amphibious shipping and its aircraft carriers.

That day the media were full of news of yet more ships sailing to join the Task Force, not only warships, but also civilian ships taken up from trade, or STUFT, as we came to know them. Some of these ships had flight decks fixed to them in record time, another demonstration of the nation's resolve. Later in the operation, helicopters from my squadron were to be based on some of these ships.

News was received of the diplomatic initiatives being made to resolve the crisis peacefully. Most of us doubted that these initiatives would come to much, and I, for one, wanted to 'get stuck in' and do my bit to 'kick some Argentine butt'. I was not alone in this and engaged in war-fighting rhetoric with other like-minded chums during the day. Five tours of duty on the streets of Northern Ireland, important as they had been, were no substitute for real war fighting. But 'butt-kicking' was an activity for another day – today I had other duties to attend to. I was not due to fly until the following day which gave me an opportunity to prepare for my other role in the Squadron: Combat Survival Instructor (CSI), for which I had trained with the SAS at Hereford the previous year.

The Combat Survival Instructor (CSI) training course is an element towards the end of the SAS qualifying course and is thus attended by all SAS and SBS personnel, plus a small number of servicemen whose role requires them to operate behind enemy lines. Combat survival focuses on how to survive behind enemy lines and embraces skills in: navigation with the bare minimum of aids such as no map and/or compass; shelter using what nature provides and any equipment carried; the medical aspects of survival without access to medical personnel; trapping of animals; recognition of edible vegetation; preparing food for cooking and the various methods of cooking; camouflage and concealment; finding and purifying water; and last, but by no means least, escape, evasion and resistance to interrogation. It was my plan to deliver talks in each of these topics to the Squadron's pilots and aircrewmen over the coming days and weeks, so there was much to prepare.

As I was sitting in my cabin, my trip down memory lane was brought to an abrupt halt by 'Hands to flying stations' being piped around the ship. Just then one of the Squadron pilots, John Miller, a close and treasured friend, burst through the door, and, glancing at the notes and photographs spread over my bed, said, 'You can forget all of that crap. Get your arse in gear, Hutchings. Let's go and see who's doing the flying, then we have a flying programme to organize for tomorrow.' John and I had converted to the Wessex together in 1979 and the Sea King in 1981. He was an excellent pilot and a fine naval officer; together with 'Wiggy', two or three other pilots and myself, he was one of the Squadron's detachment commanders. Sadly, John died after a short illness during the time of writing this book.

We made our way to a small weather deck on top of the Island from where we could observe what was happening on deck. The ship was turned into wind to receive the final Harrier from Yeovilton. I did not recognize the pilot, but took note that he was from the RAF. I later discovered that he was Bertie Penfold, an exchange pilot, who, a few weeks later, I was to fly off the ship in rather sad circumstances.

From the 03 'goofing' deck, as it was known, John and I made our way to the wardroom ante-room and decided to make that our base for a while. As we were working on the next day's flying programme we were joined by Brian Hanrahan and Michael Nicholson. With their arrival we were careful not to discuss what we were doing, but instead introduced ourselves and made polite conversation about television, the news of the day – Carrington's resignation and Knott's survival – and wanted to know what Sue Carpenter, the news presenter, was like to work with: what red-blooded male wouldn't? They, for their part, wanted to know who we were, what we did, what the Sea King IV was like to fly, and so on. Fortunately much of what they wanted to know was already in the public domain and could be found in a copy of *Jane's*. We did not let on about this in case we appeared curt or dismissive, so we readily engaged them in conversation about the capabilities of the helicopter and how we operated in support of land forces. This free discussion certainly helped to break the ice and start the process of building mutual trust.

The wardroom main ante-room was a roughly rectangular-shaped compartment on 4 Deck, conveniently close to the pilots' cabins on 5 Deck. It had a bar along the length of one of the shorter sides and seating along the other three. The room was approximately 1,200 square feet, large enough to accommodate with ease the ship's complement of officers and the officers of one or two embarked squadrons. With two helicopter squadrons embarked and a larger-than-normal Sea Harrier Air Group, space was going to be at a premium. That evening there was a good party in the wardroom bar, plenty of mixing within groups, with an undertone of excited expectation and but one topic of conversation: the impending conflict.

Opinion was divided: some were of the view that the deployment to the South Atlantic was intended to be nothing more than a show of strength and resolve, and that ultimately, through this demonstration of deadly intent, together with international diplomacy, the Argentine Government would be coerced into withdrawing its forces from the Falkland Islands; others were not so sure. There had been widespread anti-colonialist sentiments among the popular masses in Argentina. Exploiting these sentiments, the military dictatorship of General Leopoldo Galtieri, Admiral Isaac Anaya and Brigadier Basilio Lami Dozo – names indelibly etched on the memories of all veterans of the Falklands War – ordered the military recapture of the Falkland Islands. This measure was supported by 99 per cent of the people, from whom the military dictatorship hid the most important reason for their action: their endeavour to perpetuate their dictatorship by giving it the prestige of recovering a portion of their country after 149 years of British occupation. Against this backdrop, it seemed inconceivable to most of the assembled officers in the wardroom that evening that General Galtieri would concede to international pressure for a withdrawal, thereby in effect consigning himself to ridicule at home and at best a future life in obscurity. The debate was remarkably well informed and sober, although by late that night few of the remaining stalwart drinkers were! Perhaps what best summed up the mood in the ship that night, and in subsequent days, was a short article which appeared in the ship's internal newspaper a few days later: 'Let us hope that any other ramshackle nation thinking of trying to tweak the old lion's tail will take note of what is hopefully about to happen to this particularly shaky dictatorship.' Revanchist sentiments indeed, which applied perhaps in equal measure to both sets of protagonists in the conflict, but with the UK Government's position underpinned by international law.

The rather serious tone of the conversation was brought to an abrupt halt by Brian Hanrahan, who had demonstrated his agility by climbing onto the bar and calling for quiet. Once he had his audience he announced, 'Gentlemen, for those who do not know me, I am Brian Hanrahan from the BBC. I would like to introduce my cameraman Bernard Hesketh and John Jockel, my sound man. We will be coming with you on *Hermes*. Now, I know that you are not very keen on the press, but I hope that as you get to know us you will come to trust us. In the meantime, I would like to buy a round of drinks.' The offer was followed by a cheer and a queue of the younger officers formed at the bar. No money ever changed hands across the bar. Drinks were signed for on chits and accounts settled when mess bills were produced once a month. Treating others to drinks was generally frowned upon in naval messes, but this was a rather special occasion, so eyebrows were kept firmly fixed down. I came to know Brian very well over the coming weeks and we chatted together often. Both he and Mike Nicholson seemed genuine in their desire not to compromise any aspect of the operation through inappropriate reporting. To this end, I and many others took them into our confidence whenever it was prudent to do so. During the operation, Brian in particular, and Mike sometimes, found themselves treading a knife edge.

Later that evening, the flying programme for the following day was confirmed and promulgated; I was to fly an hour's worth of Deck Landing

Practice (DLPs) with Michael (Doc) Love, one of the Squadron's only two Royal Marine aircrewmen. I was bang up to date with DLPs having spent some time on the ship during February and March, so I just needed to 'get my eye back in.' 'Doc' was blessed with a cheerful and jolly disposition and was a most able aircrewman. The role of the aircrewman is to control all that goes on in the main cabin of the helicopter, from ensuring that troops embark and disembark correctly and safely, through operating the winch when required, firing the GPMG when fitted in the main door, to assisting with navigation and operation of the aircraft systems and engine controls during certain emergencies. Over the coming days and weeks, 'Doc' and I were to be paired to fly many sorties and I got to know him well. Tragically, he was one of two of the Squadron's aircrewmen to be killed during subsequent operations.

I retired to my cabin earlier than had been the norm in the past. It was not unheard of for pilots to be the sole survivors after the bar had closed. During previous deployments, the wardroom bar had been the scene of much jollity, singing and mess games, but a sober reality was now descending over all of us. As the days progressed there was to be increasingly less scope for fun. I wrote a letter to Lorraine late that evening, because the following day was to be the last opportunity for mail to be taken off the ship as we passed by the Lizard Peninsular.

Tuesday, 6 April dawned with appalling weather. The ship was some 100 miles or so south-west of Land's End and steaming in a large circle waiting for more ships to join the Task Force. 'Doc' and I were briefed for our DLP sortie and made our preparations. In common with all the detachment commanders, I was self-authorizing for my flights when leading detachments, however, in keeping with wider Royal Navy practice, I was not permitted to authorize my own sorties when the Squadron was operating as a whole, embarked in a ship. The guiding principle is that the least number of authorizers the better to ensure tight control and consistency of standards. The final authority on a ship for launch of an aircraft is vested in the Captain, who sometimes attends the daily brief and approves the flying programme as a whole, or not, as the case may be. The outline details of each sortie are entered onto a flying authorization sheet, to include the aircraft registration number, the crew composition, take-off time, flight duration and an outline description of the task. The officer authorizing the sortie would only approve the sortie once he was satisfied that the crew selected for the sortie were competent, briefed and fully prepared. The aircraft Captain would then also initial the authorization sheet to indicate that he was aware of the scope of the authorization. When operating from Yeovilton, or from a FOB, pilots are not too concerned about achieving an exact take-off time. If an aircraft departs slightly early or late then the required arrival time at a destination could still be met by adjusting the aircraft's speed during transit.

Operating from a carrier, such as HMS *Hermes*, however, was a different 'kettle of fish'. Launch times, or 'Charlie' times as they are known, had to be met because a flight deck is a very busy place, with activity sometimes frenetic. Aircraft had to be brought to the flight deck from the hangar on one of the two lifts, ranged on their spots, manned and started ready for take-off. All of this activity needed to be reconciled with the often conflicting needs of the other squadrons, to include Harriers returning from sorties, sometimes low on fuel. We therefore launched at precisely the required time, to the second, or 'got it in the neck' from 'Flyco', the short form for Flight Control, a small team who worked in the ship's air department under the command of Commander Flying, also known as 'Wings'. During the Falklands War, 'Wings' was Commander Robin Shercliffe, a 'Junglie' of old, a good operator and a charming man who remained cool, calm and collected at all times; he was of immense value to the ship. However, none of us could afford to get on the wrong side of him because he could make life extremely difficult if he chose.

'Wings' was supported by a second-in-command, known as Lieutenant Commander Flying, or 'Little F', who managed the flying programme on a minute-by-minute basis throughout the day and night. 'Little F' would always be the first to 'get it in the neck' from the command if the flying programme was not running to schedule; he, in turn, was never slow to make his displeasure known to pilots, or aircraft handlers, if activities on deck were in danger of going awry. The flight-deck crew wore distinctive coloured shirts – yellow for marshallers and brown for handlers. All were under the control of the Flight Deck Officer (FDO) who was Lieutenant Commander Tony Hodgson, a most experienced FDO and all-round 'good egg'. Carriers are fitted with a deck-loop communications system into which the aircraft's telebrief system is plugged. This system enabled 'Flyco', the helicopter pilots and aircraft handlers and marshallers to talk to each other whilst the aircraft were on deck, without recourse to using radio; an essential capability during periods of communications silence. The Harriers were also fitted with this system, but it proved to be unreliable, therefore instructions were often passed to pilots through notes written on boards and held up so that the pilots could read them. This closed communications system enabled unfettered and frank exchanges between 'Flyco', pilots, aircraft handlers and marshallers, which would never be possible over live radio. On most occasions the communications were very much one way from 'Flyco' to either pilots or aircraft handlers who had incurred 'Little F's' displeasure. Later, during operations, the telebrief system was to prove a vital link in the navigation procedure used by the Sea Kings during the Advanced Force operations.

As anyone who has watched the film *Top Gun* will appreciate, the flight deck of a carrier is a very busy and dangerous place during flying operations. Harriers and helicopters would be operating concurrently – the noise level to unprotected ears would be literally deafening. Parked in front of the Island were vehicles and helicopters, while behind the Island were helicopters and/ or Harriers waiting to be moved onto spots for launch. Because the ship was proceeding to war, there was, unusually, live ordnance on the starboard side of the deck – an explosive mix of AIM 9L Sidewinders, 1,000lb bombs, ASW torpedoes and 2-inch rockets. The deck was not a place for sightseers (goofers). Every man had to know his place, his duty and be fully competent if a potential disaster was to be avoided.

Against this backdrop of pressure, I was determined that my sortie would launch on time. The lashings were taken off the aircraft, with the marshaller careful to count and indicate to me, as was the practice, that all four lashings had been removed. I was marshalled into a hover and off we went for an hour of DLPs. Nothing exciting in that, in fact rather monotonous during daylight, but it was an opportunity for 'Doc' and me to start working together, to gain each other's confidence and get used to each other's little foibles.

Whilst I was enjoying my flight, I kept one eye on the Harriers, never ceasing to marvel at how well the pilots coped with landing on the deck. Those guys did not have the luxury of an aircrewman in the back to give directions, the hover height was about 50 feet above the deck, so visual reference points were few and far between, and yet every time the Harriers were landed safely and in the right place, day and night. To this day the Harrier pilots have my admiration for their skill and courage, qualities that were to be proven time and time again during subsequent operations. To finish my hour, I took advantage of the low cloud base and poor visibility, and flew well out of sight of the ship to a position about 10 miles away. From here I called the ship and requested a Ship Controlled Approach (SCA) and flew my final approach under radar control. Having been flying over the sea, with few visual references, it was always reassuring to hear the voice on the other end of the radio, to see the wake of the ship and ultimately the ship appearing from out of the gloop – welcome back to 'Mother'. I landed in time to see Nigel manning an aircraft with Pete Rainey. Pete's background was in ASW flying and as such he was a competent pilot of the Sea King II. Nigel had the unenviable task of converting him to the Sea King IV with its different systems and role. Ordinarily such training would be undertaken in relatively slow time and at Yeovilton, but this was war and time was tight. There was no other option but simply to get on with it.

After lunch in the wardroom, I went to 03 Deck to observe several Sea Kings arriving from RNAS Culdrose, in Cornwall. The helicopters were a mix of Sea King IIs and Vs, both groups joining the Task Force, with other Sea Kings delivering last-minute stores, including cluster bombs for the Harriers. The returning Sea Kings took back with them to Culdrose the few civilian dockyard workers who had sailed with the ship from Portsmouth in order to complete last-minute repairs.

Now that the ship's Harrier and helicopter Air Group was complete, and the Task Force was assembled, with all but half-a-dozen of the non-combatants dispatched back to the relative safety of the mainland, the ship could continue its journey south in earnest. It was time to start passage across the often treacherous

Bay of Biscay towards Finisterre. The Bay is notorious for rough conditions and the next twenty-four hours were to be no exception. There was little mood for partying in the wardroom that evening, with the exception of a few 'salty old sea-dogs', prepared to risk their pints of beer being spilled over the bar; most aircrew opted for an early night. I, for one, did not wish to see the contents of my stomach being spilled anywhere where there was an audience, so I too hit the sack quite early. Being near the stern of the ship, 5S mess deck rose and fell quite a height as the ship crested each large wave. When lying down, the variation in acceleration was not too hard to bear, but when upright one's legs were frequently inclined to buckle at the knees when the stern suddenly rose 50 or 60 feet, a sensation not unlike riding a roller coaster. As I tried to get off to sleep I counted my blessings that I was not a member of the crew of one of the escorting frigates or destroyers.

The weather first thing in the morning of Wednesday, 7 April was a little less rough than it had been overnight but, nevertheless, was still uncomfortable. Conditions were far from ideal for flying. Although helicopters can operate in the very worst of weather conditions – many successful SAR sorties around the British coast are testament to that – there are wind strength limitations for engaging and stopping the rotors. During strong and particularly gusty wind conditions, before the rotor blades have time to either accelerate to their governed speed, or come to a complete stop, they are susceptible to a condition known as 'sailing', i.e. at intermediate rotor speeds there is insufficient speed to ensure the centrifugal force needed to keep the blades taut and horizontal, leaving the flying position of each blade at the mercy of the wind. Strong and gusty winds could very easily cause a blade to 'sail' far too high or low with potential for contact with either the deck or part of the helicopter. This had happened on board ships in the past, resulting in part of a rotor blade breaking off from the rotor system and hurtling across the deck at lethal speed. Anyone getting in the way would suffer serious injury or death. It is possible to manoeuvre a ship in such a way as to ameliorate or even obviate the effects of the wind so that rotors can be engaged and stopped safely. However, on this day the priority was for the Task Force to make good progress on its journey south, so only an urgent flying task would deflect *Hermes* from her Mean Line of Advance. Flying could wait for another day.

It was mid-morning when the CO called for all aircrew and the engineers to gather in the briefing room – at last Pete was to reveal his precious consignment of NVG and brief the curious audience. A small green rectangular shaped box, measuring 10 x 6 x 6 inches, made from Gortex-like material, was produced like a rabbit out of a magician's hat. Pete unzipped the box to reveal what appeared to be a small pair of binoculars.

'It's a pair of binos,' someone called out.

'It's a pair of Night Vision Goggles,' replied Pete. I had seen Passive Night Goggles (PNG) before; they had been around for a few years but were of a monocular design, covering half of the face, and with first-generation tubes giving a mediocre performance. These NVG were very different. Pete went on to give a thorough briefing covering the goggles' technology, development, capability and limitations.

In order to understand how any night-vision device works, try to compare it to a video camera, but one with an extremely high sensitivity to light. All night-vision systems provide the viewer with electronically enhanced viewing. When you see a night-vision scope, you are not actually viewing the scene before you, but instead you are viewing a video image of that scene. The heart of any night-vision system is an image-intensifier tube. The intensifiers are rated as either first, second or third generation. Image-intensifier tubes consist of a photocathode which converts light images to electron images (which in turn can be amplified) and a microchannel plate (in the second- and third-generation tubes) which converts the flow of electrons back to a light image. As a result one can see more light at the viewing end of a second- or third-generation tube for a given level of ambient light. Second- and third-generation tubes also generally exceed first-generation tubes in their ability to resolve detail, eliminate image distortions and they have longer useful tube life. Pete had brought with him from Farnborough seven sets of goggles, mostly second generation, but also two sets of third generation.

The briefing was brought to a rude halt by the sound of the ship's alarm – a cacophony of what sounded like car horns – followed by the pipe 'Hands to Action Stations, Hands to Action Stations, Assume NBC State One, Condition Zulu'. This was not the real thing, fortunately, but an exercise designed to test the ability of all on board to get to their nominated action station, wearing the correct kit and as quickly as possible. The correct kit for all on board included a life jacket carried on a belt and white fire-retardant, anti-flash hood and gloves, which were normally carried attached to the belt. On hearing this pipe the ship's passageways became a hive of activity with people rushing to their respective actions stations, ranging from the operations room, 'Flyco', the bridge and engine room, through to the ship's weapon systems, such as they were (two Sea Cat missile launchers and a few machine guns). The area assigned for aircrew was the briefing room, so we stayed where we were. The aim was to get to one's assigned Action Station as quickly as possible.

At first it took a long time – over thirty minutes – as people were getting used to finding their way around the ship. What did not help was finding all of the main hatches being shut and bolted down, leaving just a small 'kidney hatch' through which to scramble either up or down a ladder. Anyone with a waist measurement much over about 45 inches had a real problem and there were a few traffic jams caused because of the more portly chaps holding things up. Over the coming days the times decreased so that when we arrived at Ascension Island a few days later, Action Stations was achieved in under ten minutes. The ship's second-in-command, known as the Commander, was Commander John Locke. John lived in Dorset, not a million miles from my home in Somerset, so we knew each other long before this particular journey south. It was the Commander's responsibility to ensure that Action Stations was achieved quickly. At the end of the exercise he would make a pipe to debrief us on our usually pathetic efforts. John's voice was to become the best known in the ship over the coming weeks as our efforts during exercises progressed from abysmal to praiseworthy. More importantly in the weeks to come, it was to be John whose reassuring and authoritative voice was to keep us all informed of each incident and attack as they unfolded. The exercise on this day was brought to an end just in time for lunch.

That afternoon Pete delivered the rest of his NVG brief which was rather technical, so I have summarized a simplified version here. Night Vision Goggles are mounted on a pilot's helmet and sit approximately an inch from the eyes. This position enables pilots to look through the goggles outside the cockpit or under the goggles at flight instruments. Despite the advantages associated with NVGs, their application has limitations. Compared with optimal day vision, they are monochromatic, have a limited field of view (40°), and a lower visual acuity. In addition, the quality of the NVG image is variable depending on the operating environment. For example, the quality of the NVG image can vary depending on the amount of celestial illumination, the intensity of direct bright light, weather conditions, the height flown above the surface, the nature of the surface and speed of the aircraft.

In order to use NVGs safely, a Night Vision Imaging System (NVIS) is required of which NVGs form just one part. This is a comprehensive system, which includes cockpit lighting that does not degrade the NVG image. A NVIS may also include additional external lighting, other required aircraft components and equipment, initial and recurrent crew training, operating procedures and airworthiness requirements. The Squadron's leadership also needed to consider the resources required to support all of these elements. In 1982, we had just seven sets of goggles, some special filtered glass to cover the flight instruments in just five of the aircraft, plenty of 'Gaffa' tape and a determination to make it work – but not much time.

Loud sighs and mumbled conversations followed the conclusion of the brief – so much to take in and so little time in which to turn the theory into practice. The coming few days would be a hive of activity around the aircraft chosen for NVG modification. I borrowed a set of the goggles and took them away to my cabin.

Later that night, when it was dark, I went to the quarterdeck to try out the goggles. No helmets had been modified at this stage so I used them as one would look through a pair of binoculars.

'Wow,' I said out loud to myself – night had turned into day, well almost. After a few minutes I was joined on the quarterdeck by other pilots, each armed with a pair of goggles. There was universal praise for the goggles' potential and a desire to try them out whilst flying at night. This was to be the dawn of a new era for the Squadron and the beginning of a new and challenging chapter in my life.

The next morning the ship was 400 miles or so off Portugal and making steady progress south. The weather had improved with a slight sea, overcast, but with a reasonably high cloud base which the sun was attempting to penetrate – ideal conditions for flying. I was programmed with John Miller to fly a VIP taxi sortie, or 'Viptax' as it was better known. 'Viptax' involved flying a taxi service around the ships to pick up and drop off senior officers who were required to attend meetings on the Flagship. We flew the Sea King across to HMS *Invincible*, which was not too far away, and landed to collect our passengers. Into the aircraft climbed Jeremy Black (*Invincible's* Captain), Commander Sharkey Ward (CO of 801 Squadron), Commander Dusty Milner (*Invincible's* 'Wings'), Lieutenant Commander Ralph Wykes-Snead (CO 820 Squadron), Lieutenant Commander Rod O'Connor (*Invincible's* Air Operations Officer) and Flight Lieutenant Ian Mortimer (801 Squadron's Air Warfare Instructor (AWI)). We flew them to *Hermes* where our passengers were greeted on deck by the Captain, Lyn Middleton, an officer whom I had yet to meet, a situation that would be rectified several days later. The group left the flight deck and that was the last that we saw of them until later that morning when it was time to return them to *Invincible*.

Later that afternoon I was sitting in the wardroom when I was joined by the Squadron CO. I asked him what the meeting had been about that morning.

'A command planning meeting, with a lot of boring talk about how the Harriers were to operate and, oh yes, a lot of talk about beards,' he replied, clearly disdainful about aspects of the mornings proceedings.

'Beards?' I asked, curiously.

'Yes beards. When would our bearded brethren be shaving off?' Now I was really curious. Simon went on to explain that War Orders required that beards be shaved off because they were considered to be a hazard in action – something to do with respirators not able to make a perfect seal with the face. The ship was supposed to be a gas-tight citadel once all external doors were closed and sealed. A fine theory, but not one that I would wish to put to the test in a warship that had seen better days. As it turned out, there was no threat of attack from either chemical or biological weapons. In time, those who had shaved off their beards would re-grow them and many who did not have beards from the outset grew them as part of departmental or squadron beard-growing competitions.

During our conversation I explained to Simon that in 1976 I was to have been appointed to the position of second-in-command of the Royal Marines detachment on the Falkland Islands. Known as Naval Party 8901, it was this detachment that demonstrated such spirited resistance to the Argentine invasion force just a week earlier. However, in 1976, Lorraine was pregnant with our second son and I did not want to be away in the Falklands with my wife having to remain in the UK at such an important time, so Ron Crawford, the other Royal Marine pilot in the Squadron, and I swapped appointments – he went to the Falklands for a year and I went to the MoD. Ron was therefore about to return to very familiar territory. I agreed with Simon that from the next day I would run daily sessions of PT on the quarterdeck, each morning, for all Squadron officers and aircrewmen. This would have the triple benefits of keeping us all fit, bonding and also give the CO an opportunity to see at first hand just how the lads were coping overall. It also gave me another job in addition to combat survival talks, so there would be little danger of boredom.

That evening the weather improved. The sea was calm and there was barely any wind, other than that resulting from the ship still making around 20 knots, a welcome breeze now that the weather was warming up. There was flying scheduled for the Harriers that night, but in between day and night flying there was an opportunity for all crew to get on the flight deck for an hour, either for some serious exercise (the 'huffers and puffers'), a gentle stroll or just simply to appreciate the glorious sunset. Whatever thoughts were stirred in people by the calm blue sea and increasingly orange glow in the sky were brought to an abrupt halt by the ship's alarm and call to Action Stations; the Commander was certainly getting his money's worth. The timing of the drill was perfect though to get the flight deck clear in time for night flying and for the rest of us to get showered ready for dinner.

Earlier in the day, Pete Rainey had delivered the aluminium NVG plate for my helmet, so that night after sunset I returned to the quarterdeck to try out the goggles, this time wearing my helmet. After a period of adjustment, ably assisted by Pete, I looked around at the horizon and other ships in the vicinity.

'These things are fantastic,' I said out loud, forgetting that I was wearing the helmet and therefore shouting like some demented idiot wearing headphones whilst listening to music. What a berk, I won't make that mistake again, I thought, as I watched the now clearly visible grinning faces of my comrades. Later that evening, I was in my cabin to prepare notes for the following day's talk on survival navigation, little knowing that I would come to draw on all of my CSI experience in the not too distant future.

The next morning, the weather had taken a turn for the worse. There was a reasonable cloud base, but it was overcast and generally blustery. I was programmed for a one-hour sortie of troop drills with Petty Officer Aircrewman Kevin (Ben) Casey . 'Ben' and I had flown together on several occasions in the past and we had the measure of each other. He was a most able aircrewman, immensely likeable and irrepressibly cheerful. Our task that morning was to embark a stick of troops, fly a standard circuit and land back on the ship so that they could disembark and then go through the whole evolution several more times. The ship had a well-established procedure for moving embarked troops from their mess decks, onto the flight deck and then into the aircraft. From the hangar, the sticks of troops would be moved onto the aft lift, the lift raised to flight deck level and the sticks then led by their guides along the starboard side of the flight deck to the three o'clock position relative to the aircraft that they were to board. When the pilot was ready to embark troops, the guide would lead them to the aircraft and hand the aircrewman an embarkation card with details of the stick and their intended destination. This was a well-understood procedure, but one which needed to be practised many times to ensure that each man knew the assault routes and procedure. The starboard side of the flight deck was painted green to signify that it was safe for personnel to move within this area when the ship was at flying stations. Our stick that morning comprised sixteen Royal Marines from A Company 40 Commando Royal Marines, the only Royal Marines sub-unit embarked at the time. The troop drills went according to plan with the stick disembarking from the aircraft by several methods. The troop drills complete, I handed the aircraft over to another crew, on a rotors running crew change, and went below for lunch.

That afternoon I visited 03 Deck to watch the Harriers flying. The weather had improved with sunshine now gently warming the ship's superstructure. Some of the Harrier pilots were new to ship-borne operations so there was clearly scope for the unexpected. I was not to be disappointed and as I watched one of the aircraft being marshalled it drifted backwards towards the Island, which in due course it struck with its tail – I was in two minds whether to take cover or take out my camera! It was to be an afternoon of incidents and excitement. One of the Sea Kings of 826 Squadron, the ASW squadron, suffered a problem with its tail rotor which required the pilot to execute a running landing on the flight deck from the stern – nicely done too.

Following the end of the day flying programme there was an opportunity once again to use the flight deck for recreational purposes. Given our daily PT sessions on the quarterdeck, I felt that I could manage a gentle stroll in the warm sunshine with a clear conscience. There was an odd mix of activities for an hour or so, with some sailors working out hard, some, like me, enjoying a stroll, and others, still required to work, painting parts of the Island to cover up the myriad of rust marks. As I was enjoying the late afternoon sun, I could not help but wonder whether the painting was an activity designed to keep the lads occupied – idle hands etc. – or whether it was part of some cunning master plan. But of course not – this was, after all, the Royal Navy preparing for war!

Saturday, 10 April was a day without flying for me. The priority for the Squadron was to progress the work to modify the cockpit lighting systems of the five helicopters identified for NVG operations. It was delicate work. The special filtered glass that Pete had brought with him from Farnborough was of just sufficient quantity to cover the major flight instruments only, so the engineers had to work with considerable care to ensure that none was broken. The lights of other instruments would have to be disabled, with the instruments monitored by using filtered torches. The cockpits of the five NVG aircraft were starting to resemble the scene of an accident, with copious amounts of 'Gaffa' tape used to partially or fully cover various lights. Pete worked with the engineers for the next few days, anxious to ensure that we had at least two aircraft ready for flying once we arrived at Ascension Island, where the cockpit modifications and NVGs were to be tested in flight overland for the first time. As I watched them working, it occurred to me that if I was chosen to be one of the NVG crews for Advance Force Operations, then for me night would become day and vice versa. It was difficult enough sleeping at night sometimes, what with the relentless background noises, but to have to sleep during the day was going to be some challenge.

Later that morning it was announced by the Commander that a Harrier from HMS *Invincible* would be firing a Sidewinder missile in order to test the system. This offered an opportunity for 'goofing' on a grand scale, as many of the ship's complement as possible would want to see this. I didn't believe that anyone on the ship had witnessed a Sidewinder shoot before. The flight deck was packed almost to capacity as the first of two Harriers flew past the port side of the ship from aft to a position well forward of the ship. At this point the first Harrier dropped a flare. Even though it was a bright sunny day, the flare was clearly visible as it slowly drifted down towards the sea at about 1,000 feet. A couple of minutes later the second Harrier flew the same profile and when a couple of hundred metres forward of the ship it released a Sidewinder. At first the missile's flight path was straight and smooth, but after a few seconds it assumed the characteristic corkscrew flight pattern which gave the missile its name. It seemed like only a few seconds before the missile impacted with the flare. Like everyone else on deck, I did not know what to expect – in the event there was a small flash and that was it. The remains of the Sidewinder continued on for a few more seconds and then plunged into the sea; the show was over. The response of the assembled multitude was rather muted; what did they expect to see? Another aircraft being shot out of the sky? In the not too distant future that was exactly what we could expect.

As I was about to turn on my heels and leave the flight deck, a familiar voice said, 'It'll be our turn tomorrow.' I turned around to see the beaming face of Bob Horton, the Squadron's HWI. 'Tomorrow we get to fire our main armament, the mighty GPMG,' Bob exclaimed with his usual sardonic humour.

'Hmm', I said, 'I don't think that will give the "goofers" much excitement'.

Monday, 12 April was a busy day for the Squadron. The climate was now warming up nicely as we made steady progress towards Ascension Island. The island would be reached by the next weekend so there were only a few days remaining for the bulk of Squadron personnel to remain embarked in HMS *Hermes*. At Ascension we expected Squadron personnel to be redeployed, with an element remaining in *Hermes* and the remaining helicopters and personnel moving to the ships making up the amphibious component of the Task Force. Over the coming few days there was much to do, starting with the day's cabin gun exercise. I was programmed to fly a one-hour sortie with Nigel, Chief Petty Officer Aircrewman Terry Short and four other aircrewmen. Nigel and I were old friends and enjoyed flying together. In the weeks to come, Nigel was to make an important and pivotal contribution to the operation.

The GPMG could be mounted in the cabin door of the Sea King in a ground-fire suppression role. Fixed to a hinged mount that could be stowed either aft of the door when not in use, or deployed into its firing position, the gun was further modified with a two-handed trigger mechanism to replace the more familiar wooden butt. It is difficult for anyone firing the gun when airborne to observe the fall of shot in the vicinity of a ground target, so it was vital for the weapon operator to keep one eye on the tracer rounds and one eye on the target. A tracer round has a phosphorous base which, when fired, leaves a red glow behind it enabling the operator of the weapon to follow the trajectory of the rounds more easily, thereby being better placed to adjust the point of aim as necessary in order to hit the target.

We had an aircraft and, unusually on this occasion, several of the aircrewmen in the cabin, and a vast expanse of ocean into which to fire the weapon. All that was needed now was a target. *Hermes* duly obliged by towing behind her a splash target. The target was, to all intents and purposes, a metal pallet which could be deployed over the ship's stern from the quarterdeck onto the sea and towed behind the ship at any distance up to the length of the cable. Once airborne we manoeuvred the helicopter to a position about half a mile astern of the ship and flew a circuit at 500 feet in a race track around the splash target. The range of the GPMG is close to 2,000 metres, so we had to be careful to ensure that any stray rounds did not head in the general direction of the ship. Each aircrewman took turns to fire his allocation of rounds. The general principle when operating the gun is to fire short bursts of around three to five seconds each, but some of the aircrewmen clearly had difficulty counting, with several bursts well in excess of five seconds being observed. This enthusiasm was explained by the heat of the moment and determination to hit the target. All rounds expended, we duly returned to the ship.

Later that afternoon the flight deck was open for recreation. With temperatures now climbing into the 20s, there were lines of pale white bodies lying in rows along the edges of the deck, each man trying to 'soak-up a few rays' whilst there was still time. We all assumed that once the Task Force left Ascension that such opportunities would cease. All except for the few doubting Thomas's who remained convinced that after a few days of the Task Force anchored off Ascension, the Argentineans would pull out of the Falkland Islands and the Task Force would sail home again. Why not? After all, dispatching a submarine to the area during a previous period of tension in the mid-1970s had done the trick, so why not again? Surely a fully fledged Task Force that clearly meant business could have a far greater impact on the decision making of the Argentine Government than a solitary submarine. Such sentiments were understandable, but did not reflect the reality of a failing government desperate to cling on to power. When in England and champing at the bit, I could not wait for the opportunity to kick some butt, but as the likelihood of it happening grew ever closer, I started to have doubts about my bravado; I was not alone.

With any doubts about my motivation tucked firmly in the back of my mind, it was time to turn my attention to the night's flying task. It had become apparent that, following our arrival at Ascension, there would be a programme of cross-decking of personnel and stores to various ships, and a great deal of stores to be collected from Wideawake Airfield and distributed around the fleet. To this end, it was time to turn our attention to underslung load-lifting operations. The Sea King IV is fitted with equipment to enable loads to be carried underneath the aircraft, either in nets or directly via an arrangement of strops and harnesses. The procedure for lifting a load is straightforward, but needs regular practice to ensure that pilots, aircrewmen and load handlers on the ground or deck are working safely and in harmony. It is the responsibility of the aircraft captain to ensure that the load to be lifted is either cleared or authorized, safe to lift and land, and within the maximum payload of the aircraft. The aircraft's lifting equipment – a hook known as a SACRU, attached to an arrangement of steel cables – is controlled by a combination of the pilot and aircrewman, with both having access to release mechanisms to operate the hook. A load would be attached to the hook via either shackles attached directly to the load or an 8-foot or 16-foot-long strop. The lifting procedure was for the pilot to position the aircraft directly overhead the load under the guidance of the aircrewman, and for the load handler to first earth the hook by using a length of wire attached to a long insulated pole, with one end trailing on the ground or deck. This was an essential precursor to handling the hook because high voltages could build up in the hook due to static electricity generated during flight. The voltage could be lethal, so great care needed to be exercised by the load handler. With the load attached to the hook, the pilot would slowly increase hover height, ensuring that the load was plumb under the centre of the aircraft, and then gently transition into forward flight. Delivering the load was, in effect, the reverse of picking up in that the pilot would manoeuvre the aircraft to the spot for dropping the load, bring the aircraft to a hover and decrease the hover height until the load was on the surface, at which point the pilot would release, or 'pickle-off', the load from the hook by pressing the load release button on the pilot's cyclic control. In the event of a malfunction of the electrical load-release system, the aircrewman could release the load through a manual hook release mechanism. The major considerations for the crew when flying underslung loads are load stability and hover height – on more than one occasion loads have become unstable during flight, usually as a result of heavy-handed inputs on the cyclic, or excessive air speed. A lateral swing can build up to such an extent that the aircraft and load become unstable – if the pilot is unable to correct the instability then there is no alternative but to 'pickle-off' the load whilst still in flight.

I remembered witnessing such an event twenty-two years earlier during an exercise in Malaysia. 42 Commando Royal Marines was acting as enemy during a major amphibious exercise on the east coast of Malaysia. The unit had established a non-tactical base on the beach from which we operated throughout the exercise. Hygiene arrangements were basic, with the unit's engineers having constructed a rudimentary latrine, constructed of wood and corrugated steel, positioned over a deep pit. The latrine could accommodate about eight men at a time. It had a metal roof, was open towards the sea, but enclosed on the other three sides. In an attempt to provide a degree of privacy, sheets of hessian were hung between each sitting position. The unit CO clearly felt that the communal arrangements were inappropriate for a commanding officer, therefore he ordered the engineers to construct a single latrine for his exclusive use. The engineers did not have sufficient materials ashore for this task so they were lifted by Wessex to HMS *Bulwark,* which was operating a short distance offshore. The latrine having been duly constructed was then carried as a load underslung from a Wessex. Just about the whole unit was turned out on the beach to watch the approach and imminent arrival of the CO's latrine – I suspect that at this point you are way ahead of me! As the Wessex neared the beach the load became unstable and started a slow lateral swing. This rapidly deteriorated into a significant pendulum effect on the Wessex, at which point the pilot 'pickled' it off and the load plummeted to the edge of the beach and smashed into small pieces. The sight of the latrine plunging towards its inevitable destruction was greeted by roars of laughter and cheers by the assembled Marines, with the obvious exception of the CO who was observed to turn an interesting shade of scarlet and stomp off towards his tent.

With this image firmly in my thoughts, I prepared for my load-lifting sortie. I was determined not to make a spectacle of myself, because dropping a load would most certainly not be greeted with laughter and cheers; this was serious business. The day-into-night sortie flown with Martin Eales, one of the Squadron's younger, first-tour pilots, went according to plan. With the last load placed safely on deck, we flew one last circuit in order to get in a SCA for good measure and then put the aircraft to bed. This was my first session of night flying since embarkation, but I had no way of knowing that evening, as I returned to the wardroom, that for a few of us it was to become our way of life for days and weeks to come. Before turning in for the night, I visited 03 Deck to get a breath of fresh air and was in time to see Nigel, Bob Grundy and Dave Lord manning one of the Sea Kings on the first ship-borne NVG sortie, thereby starting the process of developing ship-borne NVG procedures.

Tuesday, 13 April started like most days, with a session of PT on the quarterdeck followed by one of my now regular talks on aspects of combat survival; today was a talk on the Geneva Convention, specifically one's rights and obligations.

I found it fascinating how, over time, the attention of the aircrew had become more focused with each lecture; they were hanging onto my every word. I had to ensure that all subjects were covered by the end of the week because once the Squadron had redeployed to other ships at Ascension there would be no further opportunity, so my talks were now a daily feature of the Squadron's programme. It was the CO's responsibility to ensure that every member of the Squadron was made aware of his rights and obligations under these conventions, and my job to deliver the briefings to this effect.

The subject of Human Rights was flavour of the month at the time of writing this book, however, in 1982 Human Rights was a little understood concept and rarely mentioned. International humanitarian law and international human rights law are two distinct but complementary bodies of law, both of which seek to protect the individual from arbitrary action and abuse. Human rights are inherent to the human being and protect the individual at all times, in war and in peace. International humanitarian law only applies in situations of armed conflict. Thus, in times of armed conflict, international human rights law and international humanitarian law both apply in a complementary manner.

If captured, members of the Armed Forces and accompanying non-combatant civilians, i.e. media, are required to be able to identify themselves to their captors in accordance with Article 4 of the Conventions. As such the information on the standard military issue ID card is in excess of the information required, so all members of the Task Force were required to hand in their ID cards for safe keeping and carry the ID card prescribed by Article 4. A copy is reproduced opposite.

This subject certainly grabbed the attention of all concerned, like no other, with each man keen to ensure that he knew his rights and at the same time the potential 'poo traps' and penalties for getting it wrong.

As the morning progressed the weather warmed up considerably, to the extent that the air-conditioning system in the ship was working at maximum capacity to keep the air inside the ship at a comfortable temperature. Every opportunity that I could find I went to 03 Deck to see what was happening on deck and to take advantage of the warm breeze. For the remainder of the day I was going to be very busy. Following the talk on the Geneva Convention, I was programmed for a one-hour sortie of troop drills with Nigel and Leading Aircrewman 'Topsy' Turner. As our QHI, it was Nigel's job to standardize all pilots to ensure that each flew the various types of sortie to a common set of procedures and drills, to the required standard and safely, so it was my turn to be put through the mill. The sortie went to plan, without incident, and afterwards I occupied myself preparing the following day's combat survival brief. I was also programmed later for my first night-flying sortie wearing NVGs, again paired with Nigel. It was to be a first for me, but Nigel's second NVG sortie, having flown one

---

Ident/189

If you are captured you are required, under the provisions of Article 17 of the Prisoner of War Convention, 1949, to give your captors the information set out below so that your capture may be reported to your next-of-kin. When you are interrogated, but not before, tear off the duplicate portion and give it to the interrogator. **GIVE NO OTHER INFORMATION.**

Once this card has been issued to you must carry it upon you at all times. In your own interest you must ensure that the particulars of your rank are kept up to date.

(Fill in your particulars in BLOCK LETTERS)

BRITISH FORCES IDENTITY CARD
(Issued in compliance with the provisions of
Article 17 of Geneva (POW) Convention, 1949)

SERVICE
NUMBER.....................RANK.....................
SURNAME...
CHRISTIAN/
FORENAME(s)..............................
DATE OF BIRTH..

BRITISH FORCES IDENTITY CARD
(Issued in compliance with the provisions of
Article 17 of Geneva (POW) Convention, 1949)
(DUPLICATE)
SERVICE
NUMBER.....................RANK.....................
SURNAME...
CHRISTIAN/
FORENAME(s)..............................
DATE OF BIRTH..

---

the previous night with Pete Rainey. That was still a few hours away, so I took advantage of the good weather and went onto 03 Deck.

The Harriers of 800 Squadron were busy flying dummy attacks against HMS *Invincible*, with her Harriers practising intercepts. There was not that much to see because, although the two ships were steaming within just a few miles of each other, the Harriers were starting their attack profiles from a long distance out to simulate having departed from a shore-based airfield. I was joined on deck by Dave Morgan from 800 Squadron. I asked him about the conduct of the sortie and he was very forthcoming in his analysis of just what was going on. It seemed that the command team in *Invincible* had placed a significantly higher priority to intercept training than the Flag staff team in *Hermes*, in particular Captain Lyn Middleton.

'The boys are getting rather frustrated,' he said.

'In what way?'

'Apparently Lyn Middleton is more concerned about the surface threat so we are spending more time training for that than intercept.'

'Are the skills and procedures that much different?'

'It's not that exactly, but now the Captain wants us to do some weapons trials, rocketing and toss-bombing etcetera, so it will be some time before we get around to intercepts.'

'Does that mean that you will be attacking the splash target?'

'Hopefully, if the Captain trusts us not to hit the ship,' he said with a laugh.

'Well at least that will give us something to look at to help pass the time,' I replied with a sigh.

'It will if we hit the ship,' he chuckled. With that Dave and I went our separate ways, both of us to prepare for our respective night-flying sorties.

I was night-deck qualified in general and current on *Hermes*, but this was to be my first night NVG sortie, for which re-qualification was needed. When operating at night, the flight deck is bathed in soft light by a number of floodlights fixed to the Island. The lights are controlled by rheostats in 'Flyco', therefore, light levels could be adjusted accordingly to reflect the ambient light levels. When wearing goggles, deck illumination would not, in theory, be required because the ambient light would normally be of sufficient level to give a reasonable view of things. However, the goggles are extremely sensitive to any source of artificial light and even though all deck lighting could be switched off and the ship darkened, the 'old lady' still leaked light from several places making goggle operations for launch and recovery difficult and potentially dangerous. Against this background, launch and recovery were to be executed in accordance with normal night-flying procedures, with the aircrew unable to use NVG.

I lifted the aircraft into the hover and transitioned into forward flight away from the ship as normal. Nigel was sitting in the left-hand seat and operating the Tactical Air Navigation System, or TANS as it is commonly known. In 1982, TANS was an inertial system, which could also receive information from Decca. However, there was no Decca coverage far away from the UK and, without an external source of position data, such as Decca or satellite fix, TANS had a tendency to drift. A number of positions over the sea, in latitude and longitude, had been programmed into TANS as waypoints, giving a box-shaped route for us to fly, eventually arriving back at the ship after an hour's flight. Over the coming nights, procedures would be developed to mitigate the drift of TANS, but for tonight the priority was for me to become accustomed to handling the aircraft whilst flying on goggles.

Well clear of the ship and established in flight at 500 feet, Nigel switched on his goggles and adjusted them to the flight position. The goggles could be placed in one of two positions, either stowed facing upwards, above the pilot's line of sight, or deployed down into the flight position. As soon as he was ready,

Nigel took control of the aircraft and it was my turn to switch on the goggles. I deployed the goggles into the flight position and looked around outside the aircraft. It was a clear night, just after a full moon and about half cloud cover, so the ambient light level was quite good. I could see the horizon clearly, there were more stars than I had ever seen before in my life and *Hermes*, now some distance away to our port side, looked like a large green light. I peered under the goggles towards the ship and could see nothing but blackness – back on the goggles there she was lit up like a Christmas tree for all to see.

Before setting out on the navigation exercise, we had a task to perform for the ship. Each helicopter carried a number of small boxes of chaff. Chaff are tiny strips of tin foil which, when deployed, form a small metallic cloud which, in theory, radar waves will not penetrate. The ship wanted to test the effectiveness of chaff to break the lock of the ship's Sea Cat missile system, so we flew a series of circuits at 200 feet and at varying distances from the ship. As soon as the Sea Cat had acquired the aircraft, 'Flyco' let us know by radio. At this point the aircrewman threw a box of chaff out of the back of the aircraft from the main cabin door. The last thing that we wanted was a cloud of fine metal strips being blown back into the aircraft, therefore, just before the box of chaff was thrown, a boot full of right rudder would be applied which had the effect of throwing the aircraft out of balance with the result that the natural movement of air was away from the starboard side of the aircraft, and the main cabin door. There were several grades of chaff carried in the aircraft, each optimized to be effective against radar systems operating in specific frequency bands. Our trial was successful, with lock being broken during all chaff deployments. Over time, the Squadron was to develop a procedure whereby a standard deployment of chaff would include one of each grade, just to be sure.

The trial complete, I now carried out some manoeuvres, first turning the aircraft to the right and then to the left. A climb was followed by a descent. Judging height was clearly going to be an issue. When looking straight down at the sea it was impossible to judge height looking through the goggles, so frequent reference to the flight instruments was as essential as during a conventional night-flying sortie. This proved simple enough, as the goggles being positioned about an inch in front of the eye enabled me to see below them and observe the flight instruments without difficulty. The Flight Control System (AFCS), or auto-pilot as it was also known, received feeds from the radio altimeter, or 'radalt' as it was commonly known, and the barometric altimeter, or 'baralt'. The 'radalt' controller could be adjusted to select a height at which the aircraft was to fly. Once engaged the auto-pilot would keep the aircraft flying at the chosen height without any further input from the pilot. When I wanted to descend the aircraft, the non-handling pilot, Nigel in this instance, would slowly adjust the height on the radalt controller and the aircraft would slowly descend to the chosen height.

As the sortie progressed, I became increasingly aware of the weight of the goggles and was grateful that the battery pack was on the back of the helmet helping to counterbalance the effect of the goggles on the front. The limited field of view of just 40° was, for me, less of an issue. I found that by frequently moving my head from side to side I could get as good a view of the outside world as I needed. The main flight instruments had been covered with filtered glass and were clearly visible, while the less important instruments were observed by use of torches which had been similarly modified. These gave sufficient light for map reading and ensured that the light from the torches did not interfere with the goggles.

After very nearly an hour of flying, we had navigated to a position approximately 10 miles from *Hermes* and called on the radio for a SCA. The ship was clearly visible and we could have flown back without recourse to the ship's radar, but we seldom missed the opportunity to fly an SCA. When we were a couple of miles from the ship, we followed the reverse procedure as we had for switching to goggles in order to revert to conventional night flying. Nigel stowed his goggles first and took control once his sight had readjusted to the darkness. A couple of minutes later it was my turn and Nigel handed control back to me. We were now plunged back into total darkness and continued to close with the ship as for a normal night approach. How easy this would be, I thought, if only we could fly approaches on goggles all the time, but it was not to be. I landed the aircraft and another of the pilots, 'Wiggy', took my place. It was to be a busy night for Nigel as he had three sorties to complete but for me, it was back to the wardroom for a well-earned pint.

Thursday, 15 April was to be like no other thus far. The first flying activity of the day was the CO, Nigel and Petty Officer Aircrewman Richie Burnett flying the short distance to HMS *Glamorgan* to pick up Admiral Woodward and his staff. From the moment that the aircraft touched down on deck with the Admiral, *Hermes* became the Flagship of the Task Force. The ship was now well and truly steaming through the doldrums, with not a breath of air, flat calm sea, clear blue sky and the temperature well into the upper 20s – the stage was set for an obscure and quaint spectacle, unique to the Royal Navy: King Neptune's visit to the ship. There would be no more flying before nightfall because the flight deck had to be readied for King Neptune's court. All morning there was feverish activity on deck close to the Island as a bunch of hairy-arsed sailors, mostly senior rates, set about constructing the stage for the afternoon's proceedings. Legend has it that whenever a ship crossed the equator (the line), carrying sailors who had never crossed the line before, King Neptune would rise up from the sea, visit the ship and carry out an initiation ceremony on the yet-to-be-initiated sailors. The apparatus for the ceremony comprised a stage, raised about 5 feet above deck, with a throne for King Neptune, suitably adorned with artificial palms and other foliage thought to be apt. Below the stage was a ducking pool constructed from scaffolding, presumably 'liberated' from the contractors during work on the ship in Portsmouth. The scaffolding was covered in heavy canvass and half-filled with water. The stage was now set for the afternoon's entertainment.

After lunch, the flight deck slowly filled with members of the ship's company all dressed for recreation, most not wearing tops – an opportunity to soak-up some rays would seldom be wasted. As soon as an audience of a few hundred had assembled, onto the deck stepped King Neptune and his entourage, greeted by a loud cheer and whistles. King Neptune turned out to be a well-built senior rating, dressed for the part wearing flowing multi-coloured robes, a large false beard, wig made from string, a crown and carrying a trident. He was accompanied by similarly attired senior ratings, but without crowns or tridents. Neptune's helpers were carrying buckets of white paste, a large pair of artificial scissors and a large artificial cut-throat razor. Once Neptune had taken his place on his throne a succession of officers, sailors and marines were dragged before Neptune and made to kneel before him.

Neptune was no respecter of rank, all being equal in his eyes! Once before him each man in turn was subjected to the humiliation of being made to drink soapy water from a large goblet. The drink was followed by being covered in a mix of flour and water paste, given a shave and haircut and, with great ceremony, thrown backwards into the pool of water. Each man was ducked several times to rapturous applause before being helped out of the pool and presented with a certificate. I have my certificate to this day, which reads:

A Proclamation

To all mariners and lubbers alike wherever they may be, be it known by his royal proclamation that His Gracious Majesty King Neptune, ruler of the Seven Seas and Six Oceans and all underwater terrains, did after all due consideration, admit to his realm one

Lt Hutchings RM

Who on the 15th day of April 1982 did sail across latitude 0 degrees.

In committing this offence the aforementioned mariner did undergo the penalties laid down and passing the same to the satisfaction of his Majesty and his court, did then pay homage and become a humble servant to His Majesty from that time on.

Neptunus Rex

SPECIAL FALKLAND WAR EDITION

The festivities completed, the flight deck was returned to a fit state ready for the night's flying programme. For most of the crew it was to be the last afternoon of recreation for months. Conditions in the ship were now uncomfortable by day, the sun beating down on the deck quickly warming it to such an extent that you could almost fry eggs on it. This heat permeated throughout the ship causing the air-conditioning to work overtime. The following day the ship would be within helicopter-flying distance of Ascension Island, so there was to be a mail run. That evening I wrote a letter home before experiencing a restless night's sleep due to the warm, sticky conditions.

Friday, 16 April was another day of glorious weather and flat calm sea. It was to be a busy day for flying; the Harriers were going to fly their first live weapon sorties and 846 Squadron had more practice 'Vertrep' sorties for those crews yet to be worked up. I was not on the flying programme so I decided to have a very early breakfast and go on to the quarterdeck to watch the Harriers' weapon sorties. A smoke float had been dropped astern of the ship and it was just daylight as the first aircraft ran in for weapon release. The first wave of aircraft were toss-bombing. To me this appeared to be rather like throwing darts at a board. When thrown, a dart never flies flat, but follows a flight path akin to a ballistic trajectory, with the dart first rising before it falls to its point of impact. Toss-bombing looked to be similar. The pilots flew their aircraft in level flight until, at an appropriate point, the pilot pulled the stick back and the aircraft started to climb. At this point, the bomb was released and travelled in a curved arc as it fell towards the smoke flare. Three Harriers made the run in quick succession, with all three scoring hits on or very close to the target. The next three aircraft dropped what appeared to be retard bombs with the effect of creating a much bigger splash than the first three armed with conventional contact bombs. There followed two more Harriers, each firing ripples of 2-inch rockets at the target with impressive results.

I thought that was it, but in the far distance I could just make out two more Harriers flying towards the ship at low level. The first Harrier pulled up and tossed something high into the air. I wondered what the hell it was – had something gone wrong? My doubts were assuaged a few seconds later as a flare burst into a bright light high in the air. At this point the second Harrier launched what was clearly a Sidewinder which closed the flare with its characteristic corkscrew flight path and duly impacted, albeit with a rather disappointing small flash. The show was over. 800 Squadron had demonstrated to all concerned that the weapons worked and that they had the skills to hit the target; my squadron was also well worked up. As I left the quarterdeck I had just one thought: all appeared to augur well for the hostilities that were just around the corner.

CHAPTER 3

Task Force Reorganization at Ascension Island

Any plan is bad which is incapable of modification.

Publilius Syrus

Saturday, 17 April was to be my busiest flying day since leaving Portsmouth twelve days earlier. The ship was anchored a couple of miles west of Ascension Island, within clear view of Wideawake Airfield. The small island of Ascension lies in the South Atlantic 750 miles north-west of the Island of Saint Helena and covers an area of 35 square miles. Ascension is a rocky peak of purely volcanic origin with its base just west of the mid-Atlantic ridge. The highest point (Green Mountain) at some 2,817 feet is covered with lush vegetation. The ocean surrounding the island abounds with many varieties of shark – not a good place to ditch! This, then, was to be home for the major part of the amphibious element of the Task Force for the next three weeks or so.

My first flight of the day was with Pete Imrie. We departed HMS *Hermes* for a 'round-robin' flight to all ships to collect mail. With an aircraft almost full to bursting point, we then flew to Wideawake Airfield to drop and pick up mail and the first of many underslung loads to be taken to the fleet, now all at anchor off Ascension. The sight that greeted Pete and me as we approached was extraordinary. Spread across the aircraft dispersal area were no less than 2,000 loads of stores, all to be flown to various ships of the Task Force. As I looked across this vast sea of stores, I could not help but marvel at the incredible amount of man-hours of effort that must have been expended in preparing the loads; clearly the team had not been idle! The priority was to take the stores to the ships that would be forming the Advance Force. On 17 April alone, helicopters were to carry 258 loads to various ships. The ground-handling team was not ready to hook up the first load so I landed the aircraft for a while. Bounding across dispersal was the familiar figure of Peter Spens-Black, one of the Squadron's pilots. As mentioned briefly in the first chapter, Peter had not embarked in

Hermes on 5 April, but instead had led the detachment of one Sea King to RAF Lyneham. There, along with four Wessex V of 845 Squadron, they were prepared by a small detachment of the two squadrons' engineers for airfreight in Belfast aircraft belonging to Heavy Lift, a civil air cargo company, and were flown to Ascension in advance of the Task Force. On arrival they had been rebuilt ready for immediate support to British Forces Support Unit Ascension Island (BFSUAI) and the Task Force on its arrival. Peter climbed into the back of the aircraft and plugged in his helmet to the intercom system, following which we exchanged pleasantries until my first load was ready for lifting.

With a marshaller waving frantically to get my attention, Peter climbed out of the aircraft and waved us off. I manoeuvred overhead the load, picked it up and set off out to sea to deliver it to HMS *Invincible*. The flying time between Wideawake and the ships was just a few minutes as most were anchored about 2 miles off the cost. We settled into the routine of lifting loads for nearly two hours. There were insufficient nets, strops and shackles for all 2,000 loads, so after delivering each load to its destination, we had to wait for either the load to be moved out of its net or for shackles to be removed, so that they could be returned to Wideawake for use on another load. It was set to be a long and tiring day, so every helicopter that was serviceable was pressed into service lifting stores, including the ASW Sea Kings. Two Wessex of 845 Squadron had already departed Ascension embarked in HMS *Antrim* on 12 April, bound for South Georgia, leaving just two others to act as 'Vertrep' workhorses.

As the squadrons settled into the routine of vertical replenishment, the Ascension-based Sea King flew a Viptax sortie, carrying Admiral Fieldhouse and his staff to *Hermes* for a high-level conference – the 'Council of War.' Brigadier Thompson and Commodore Clapp arrived from HMS *Fearless* which had steamed ahead of the rest of the amphibious shipping in order to attend the conference. The basic plan which emerged was simple: to blockade the Falklands with the nuclear submarines, recapture South Georgia, establish air and sea control with the advanced and carrier battle groups, carry out a landing from the amphibious group ships, and then retake the islands – clearly easier said than done!

After an hour's break on *Hermes*, I spent the rest of the morning flying a total of three hours of 'Vertrep' sorties, punctuated by further short breaks. My final sortie of the afternoon was a 'Viptax'. The 'Council of War' was over and it was time for the commanders to be returned from whence they came; this time it was the turn of Petty Officer Aircrewman Alfie Brennan and me to do the honours. The first sortie was to take Admiral Fieldhouse and his team back to Wideawake. Thereafter, the Brigadier and the Commodore were returned to *Fearless*, and other ships' captains and assorted commanders and operations officers were taken back to their respective ships. It was a long 'Viptax', in all taking very nearly two hours and thirty minutes to complete the 'round-robin', and was the culmination of six hours and thirty minutes of flying during the day, with yet more to come.

Our brief interlude at Ascension was to be the only opportunity for pilots to fly NVG over the land. The island was covered in fine dust, so the only place suitable for landing was Wideawake. It was not possible to fly a route around the island with intermediate landings, nor would there be time for every NVG-converted pilot to fly hands on. Instead, it was decided to fly just two aircraft and for each to have a number of non-handling pilots in the cabin looking out whilst other pilots did the flying. The selection of pilots and aircrewmen for the advance force would be determined as a result of their assessment by Nigel and the boss during these two sorties, together with each man's own appreciation as to whether or not he was comfortable flying with goggles. Today, most helicopter pilots are trained to fly with NVG, or similar systems, but in 1982 we were feeling our way and pioneering procedures in real time. Some pilots were not comfortable with this, some were; it was a personal choice. The CO could hardly force a man to take part in operations that were to require long sorties flying at night with NVG if he felt in any way uncomfortable or anxious about it; there could be no room for doubt. That night's sortie was therefore a pivotal moment for each man in deciding for himself whether he felt ready for NVG operations or not.

Conditions for flying that night were good: clear sky, plenty of starlight, but the moon, which was in its last quarter, had set during the afternoon. We flew around the island negotiating with relative ease the hazards and were able to fly at NOE levels, literally just above the tops of the few trees on the island. Navigation was straightforward and accurate, and there were plenty of places en route at which we could update TANS. As we flew overhead waypoints, with known grid references, we fixed our exact position in TANS, thereby correcting any drift. After two hours of flying around what was, by then, a very familiar island, the aim had been achieved of introducing each pilot and aircrewman to NVG flight over land, and with both the boss and each of us now better placed to judge who should be in the 'goggle-gang' for the next phase of the operation.

Having landed back on *Hermes*, we adjourned to the wardroom for some well-earned beers. There was much discussion within the group about how each pilot felt that the sortie had gone and what each of us felt about flying on goggles over the land. There was split opinion – some like myself, were very keen, others not so sure. The boss talked to each of us in turn about how we felt. Even before this sortie he had a good feel as to who would be going forward with the Advance Force group and who would be redeploying to other ships. It would be the following morning before we were to discover what fate had in store for each of us.

CHAPTER 4

The Eve of War

The programme for the morning of Sunday, 18 April started with the Squadron aircrew meeting in the briefing room at 0830hrs to be told the plan for redeployment. HMS *Hermes* was due to weigh anchor late morning and proceed south, thus there should have been ample time for those not remaining with the carrier group to pack their kit and leave the ship for Ascension in an orderly manner. But all hope of an orderly transition was brought to an abrupt halt at about 0900hrs as *Hermes* went to Action Stations for real for the first of what would be many occasions. It had been reported from one of the other ships in the group that a submarine periscope had been sighted close to the ships. A mad scramble ensued as *Hermes* made preparations for a rather hurried departure. ASW Sea Kings were scrambled to investigate the reported sighting and members of 846 Squadron, who were not remaining with the ship, rushed to pack their kit ready for a hasty departure for Ascension. After several minutes, four Sea Kings departed *Hermes* carrying the CO, and the remaining aircrew and maintainers to Ascension. Shortly afterwards another Sea King arrived from HMS *Fearless* carrying Bill Pollock, the Senior Pilot – it was all change.

The ASW Sea Kings were unable to confirm whether the contact was a submarine or whale, but the smart money was on the sighting being the periscope of a Russian submarine having a look at us. Whilst I was pondering the operational effectiveness of the Task Force ASW capability, Bill, the Senior Pilot, brought me back to reality by letting it be known to the assembled aircrew that there was still a busy 'Vertrep' programme to complete and that I was first to be programmed to fly a two-hour sortie with Pete Imrie. One of the ramifications of the plan, hatched during the 'Council of War', was that many of the stores that had been delivered during the previous day's flying programme were now on the wrong ships and needed to be relocated to their rightful destinations. This activity of redistribution was to necessitate many sorties, flown over several days and nights. The ASW Sea Kings were now engaged in a round-the-clock programme of surveillance so were not as available to assist in the movement of stores. My squadron was about to embark on a busy night-flying phase, so the 'Vertrep' programme was to become our daytime bread and butter activity for many days to come. This day, flying conditions could not have been better – clear blue sky and a calm sea. But during the days ahead, we knew only too well that weather conditions would deteriorate as our short stay at Ascension, with its tropical idyll, became a distant memory as *Hermes* made her passage south. All the more reason, therefore, for moving as many stores as possible over the coming few days.

With the sortie completed, I had time to reflect on the composition of the Squadron team for Advance Force operations. Simon had redeployed to HMS *Fearless* where he was best-placed to advise the Brigadier and Commodore on support helicopter operations, both during the Advance Force phase and the main amphibious operation to come. The Squadron group of five aircraft in *Hermes* was, therefore, under the command of the Senior Pilot. Over the coming days and weeks, Bill would find himself working closely with Colonel Richard Preston, Brigadier Thompson's liaison officer, assigned to the Admiral's staff for the purpose of coordinating Special Forces tasking during Advance Force operations. The Brigadier and Commodore needed information and intelligence to enable them to plan the amphibious landing and subsequent land battle; it was essential to have information on the Argentine troop positions and the suitability of the beaches and potential helicopter landing sites. To this end, patrols of Special Forces from the SAS and SBS would need to be inserted into the islands to glean the requisite information and intelligence. The targets for the Special Forces missions would be discussed by the Brigadier and Colonel Preston over a secure communications link on a regular basis, and then passed to the Special Forces commanders and Bill for detailed planning. The first insertions would be just thirteen days hence, in the meantime, the detachment had aircraft modifications to complete and tactical flying procedures to develop and work up.

The Special Forces group for Advance Force operations embarked in *Hermes* whilst at Ascension. There were two distinct groupings: G Squadron, 22 SAS and 3 SBS. There were also a few specialists from other arms in the Advance Force who were to work closely with Special Forces, most notably RAF Photographic Interpreters and Naval Gunfire Support Officers. The SBS detachment was under the command of a friend of several years standing; I'll call him Captain 'C'. Our friendship also proved beneficial in developing a working relationship with the SAS planning team, in particular the officer commanding, Major 'E'. Whereas the SBS and Royal Naval commando squadrons had worked together on many occasions over the years, helicopter support to the SAS had normally been provided by the RAF and the Army Air Corps Flight integral to the Regiment, so there was an operational relationship and an environment of mutual trust to be built. Captain 'C' played a pivotal role in this and was able to assuage any doubts that were in the minds of G Squadron as to the operational efficacy of 846 Squadron. Similarly, off Ascension, on HMS *Fearless*, Simon Thornewill was developing a sound working relationship with the CO of 22 SAS, Lieutenant Colonel Mike Rose, later to rise to the rank of General.

Although I had spent some time with the SAS at Hereford the previous year, I was far better acquainted with the roles and capabilities of the SBS. One of the roles of the SBS is to survey and reconnoitre beaches and shoreline prior to amphibious landings by the main forces (usually Royal Marines). Not only is information required by amphibious and landing-force commanders on the numbers and disposition of any nearby enemy, they also survey the approaches to the beaches to ensure that they are suitable for a landing. Special devices are used to measure the gradient of the beaches. The consistency of the sand is examined to ensure it can support the weight of the various landing craft and vehicles that will traverse the beach. SBS divers are skilled too in the use of explosives and demolitions, which gives them the capability to clear mines and obstructions from the shoreline and beaches.

When considering the SAS and SBS, I often hear the question: which one is the better unit? This question was on the lips of many in *Hermes* as we made our progress south. Although a juvenile and perhaps puerile concern, it hasn't dissuaded some former members of both organizations criticizing each other's competence in a series of books. I felt that the relationship was perhaps somewhat akin to the healthy rivalry that has long existed between the Royal Marines and the Parachute Regiment. However, such comparisons are becoming increasingly academic as the two organizations are less distinguishable than at any time in their history. They are now part of the same organisation (UKSF) and are often deployed on joint missions. But in 1982 there was a distinct rivalry and one which had to be understood by those required to work closely with both groups, myself included. Being a Royal Marine, I was careful never to appear biased.

During the day, as I moved around the ship and talked to more and more people, it became apparent that the mood in *Hermes* was now focused on the hostilities that lay just a few days ahead. Late that morning, Admiral Woodward addressed all on board. He said that the ship was now well and truly on its way to war and that we should all prepare ourselves for the coming conflict. There were a number of well-thumbed newspapers in the wardroom which had been the first opportunity for us to read what was happening on the international stage with General Al Haig's shuttle diplomacy, back home in Parliament and evolving public opinion. It appeared that the latter was hardening in favour of military action given Argentine intransigence and the stance of the UN. The results of an opinion poll taken on 12 April showed that four out of five people were backing the Government's policy and if the few dissenters did not want actual fighting, they were mostly pleased that diplomacy was at least backed by a formidable punch. The Falklands crisis had blown up literally overnight. For many people it appeared that it was a time not so much for patriotism, but a hunger for information from radio and television broadcasts, and by scouring the papers for details. In the Task Force we did not have the luxury of TV broadcasts, but had, instead, to settle for a few dog-eared and, by now, out-of-date newspapers, some videos of TV news footage delivered to the ship whilst at Ascension, and the BBC World Service bulletins. It was satisfying and reassuring to know that as we made our preparations for war the people were, in the main, supporting us.

Later that night, Nigel, Bob Horton and 'Doc' Love flew a two-hour, thirty-minute-long HDS sortie to Ascension Island and back. It was the first opportunity to practise a long-range NVG sortie over the sea and to test the accuracy of TANS. All went well and Nigel was to remark on his return that he had seen *Hermes* on his return journey long before the ship had detected the aircraft on its radar. The ability of the aircraft to fly below radar cover would prove to be a pivotal capability in the success of our subsequent NVG operations.

In sharing a briefing room with the Harrier Air Group, we were starting to appreciate the tensions and frictions developing between the *Hermes* Air Group and the Air Group embarked in *Invincible*. I never became totally privy to all of the reasons for the friction, but during the course of a few chats with Dave Morgan and Tony Ogilvy, it became apparent that there were differences of opinion between the two groups as to the most effective tactics and procedures for air interdiction and ground-attack profiles against potential targets on the Falkland Islands. It is not for me to add to this debate in any way but, in the context of attack profiles, the Harrier pilots in *Hermes* were, by now, well aware of our NVG and were keen to explore their potential for ground-attack sorties. Our engineers quickly manufactured some additional goggle mounting plates and these were fixed to the helmets of a small number of the Harrier pilots. The cockpits of some of the Harriers were temporarily modified to make them NVG compatible. Dave Morgan reported back that the definition that the goggles afforded was sufficient for the delivery of weapons. Attack profiles were developed over a couple of days for high-angle dive attacks with 1,000lb bombs, with the express aim of cratering the runway at Stanley Airfield. Very careful management of the goggles would be essential because we had just the seven sets. However, after a couple of days it became clear that high-angle attacks for the Harriers were off the menu. Intelligence had been received to the effect that the airfield at Stanley had formidable defences, including anti-aircraft guns, radar-guided Oerlikon guns, Roland SAM systems and shoulder-launched SAMs – all in all an awesome array of weapons. On learning this, it occurred to me that it would be advisable to steer well clear of Stanley if I had any Special Forces to drop off nearby.

With Special Forces insertions very much in mind, we spent much of the next two days discussing and progressing procedures for the mounting and conduct of our goggle operations. For several days, the Brigadier and Commodore had been feeding their intelligence requirements to Richard Preston, who in turn worked with the Special Forces planning team and Bill. It would be several days before *Hermes* would be in a position to insert Special Forces patrols; in the meantime, we had to work up our flying procedures. From the outset it was clear that there would be fairly long flights over the sea from *Hermes* to the various objectives inland. The Argentine Air Force did not have a night-attack capability, therefore the ship could afford to operate as close to the islands as 100 miles or so during the hours of darkness, with the proviso that she was at least 200 miles to the east of the islands by daybreak. During this relatively small window of opportunity, the helicopters had to be ranged on deck, loaded, execute the 100-mile or so transit to landfall, navigate from landfall to the objective and back to the coast, and return to the ship. This small window of opportunity would militate against singleton helicopter operations in favour of insertions by formations of two or more helicopters on most occasions. This would have the added advantage of navigation data share between the helicopters during flight so that any TANS drift could be obviated. On achieving landfall, the formation would split, with each helicopter completing its specific task, to return independently to *Hermes* on completion. This sounded straightforward, but flying in close formation on goggles at night had not been tried, nor had shared navigation, therefore there were several procedures to develop and practise over and over again in the next few days.

During Monday, 19 April, the Squadron continued its busy 'Vertrep' programme, but for me there would be no flying, affording the opportunity to prepare and deliver another series of talks on combat survival. The aircrew chosen for the Advance Force operations were in the category of military personnel required to operate behind enemy lines and therefore were prone to capture. I decided to repeat the series of lectures delivered to all Squadron aircrew prior to our arrival at Ascension, only this time I knew that I would have their undivided attention. My first lecture was survival navigation. The aircrew were all bright guys and I was confident that each would remember enough to be of use should the unthinkable happen. The irony in delivering all of the survival briefs was that in a few days time I would be relying on all of my experience as a Combat Survival Instructor, whereas no other member of the Squadron, and only one Harrier pilot, would find themselves in a situation of needing to fall back on this knowledge.

The night of Tuesday, 20 April was the first opportunity for the Squadron to try out the newly developed NVG formation-flight procedures. We were all rested during the day in preparation for the sortie to ensure that we were fresh. The plan was to fly a four-aircraft formation, with Nigel and Paul Humphreys in the lead aircraft, Pete and me in number two, Bob Horton and John (Stumpy) Middleton in number three and Bob Grundy and 'Wiggy' in number four. Bob Grundy was a very experienced aviator who was also our Instrument Rating Instructor (IRI). Like most of us longer-serving pilots, Bob had flown a tour with 846 Squadron on the Wessex prior to converting to the Sea King. 'Stumpy' had qualified on the same Wessex training course as I had and we were close friends. Bob Horton as the Squadron HWI, was experienced in helicopter tactics and weapons, and Paul was a first-tour pilot who had been with the Squadron for just a few months.

The stage was set for our first pioneering NVG formation flight, the launch time for which was dictated by a combination of two factors: the ship's general flying programme and the state of the moon. Firstly, the Harriers were flying just about every night in order to gain and retain night-deck currency, and the ASW Sea Kings were maintaining an anti-submarine screen around the ships through a system of maintaining one or two helicopters on station at all times – known as a 'ripple' of helicopters. The second factor was the level of light. The minimum safe light level for NVG flight was judged to be 5 millilux – the equivalent to hardly any moonlight and unbroken starlight. I'll attempt to put this into an easily understood context. One millilux is equal to 1/1,000 of a lux. The typical light level on a bright sunny day is 100,000 lux. The level at twilight is typically 10 lux, reducing by the end of nautical twilight to one lux. The light level with a full moon and no cloud is typically 0.1 lux, reducing to 0.01 lux with a quarter moon. A moonless night with clear skies is typically 0.001 lux, or one millilux. So as can be seen, 5 millilux is a very low level of ambient light. However, the goggles amplify this to a level sufficient for safe flight. As this was to be our first night formation flight, we were keen to launch when the light level was at its highest, but the moon was almost at the end of its last quarter and not rising until 0300hrs. This was not long before dawn so we had no alternative but to launch in starlight and accept the limitations of a reduced level of ambient light; accordingly launch was set for midnight.

By 2300hrs, the four aircraft were ranged on deck. Keen to ensure that we achieved our 'Charlie' time, the crews manned the aircraft in plenty of time. The launch was to be in accordance with standard night-flying procedures. Pete and I manned our aircraft early, together with our aircrewman, 'Doc' Love. We tested the goggles and cockpit NVG lighting, and started the aircraft as normal. Bill, the Senior Pilot, had agreed a procedure with 'Flyco 'whereby we would launch from an agreed position in latitude and longitude'. With all four aircraft now ready for departure and our launch time approaching, Nigel called 'Flyco' on the telebrief.

'Formation ready for nav update; check course and speed'.

'Present course is 190 degrees, speed is 15 knots, standby for nav update,' came the reply. As 'Flyco' read out the figures, I and my fellow co-pilots were entering the data into TANS in real time. After a pause of thirty seconds 'Flyco' spoke again.

'Standby for nav update. Position is south 22 degrees, 28 point 6; west 16 degrees, 25 point 5.' As 'Flyco' read out the figures I entered them into TANS and fixed our position. The four aircraft crews entered the data simultaneously, thereby ensuring a common datum for launch.

The four aircraft launched and departed HMS *Hermes* as practised during previous NVG sorties. The aircraft were about thirty seconds apart on launch.

Having departed the ship, each aircraft turned immediately onto the heading towards the first waypoint that had been programmed into TANS, climbing to 200 feet and increasing speed to 100 knots. At this stage the only lights switched on were the aircraft's navigation lights. Once well clear of the ship, Pete and I deployed our goggles using the procedure developed during the earlier flights. With its navigation lights still switched on, the lead aircraft was clearly visible. As we closed to formation distance, approximately five rotor spans apart, the navigation lights were switched off on each aircraft. The formation that we had chosen was a loose V-shaped formation, or 'Vic'. With the three following aircraft flying slightly higher than the lead, it was possible to fly in formation without difficulty. The tips of the rotor blades prescribed a bright green circle of light when viewed through the goggles. This circle of light was caused by the build-up of static electricity in the rotor blades as they were spinning. The combination of the light circle and heat plume from the engine exhausts made it possible to maintain an accurate position behind the lead aircraft.

Waypoints had been chosen that were approximately thirty minutes flying time apart, affording the opportunity to test our newly developed navigation procedure to obviate TANS drift. When navigating by TANS, a needle appears in the main Attitude Indicator (AI) which indicates the heading to be flown to achieve the selected waypoint. The three following aircraft were required to follow the lead aircraft irrespective of the heading to steer information indicated by TANS. Over time, a difference could develop in the TANS heading information and the heading being flown to follow the lead aircraft. At exactly the halfway point of the navigation leg, any difference between TANS heading information and actual heading was noted, and could be as much as 5 degrees. The following aircraft in turn signalled their respective TANS heading information to the lead aircraft. Given that it was essential to maintain radio silence during flight, we devised a method of communication by using Morse Code. The aircrewman in each aircraft signalled to the lead aircraft the bearing and distance indicated by TANS to the waypoint, by using a standard service-issue, right-angled torch. To reduce the amount of light from the torch, the lens was covered in 'Gaffa' tape, except for a tiny hole in the centre. This gave sufficient light for the Morse signal to be read when viewed through goggles. Armed with TANS information from all four aircraft, the crew of the lead aircraft, on this occasion Nigel, Paul and Petty Officer Richie Burnett, averaged the four headings and adjusted the heading of their aircraft accordingly. The new heading to steer was then passed by the lead aircraft aircrewman to the following aircraft using the same system of communication. Headings were adjusted and the degree of drift noted.

Having flown overhead the waypoint, we proceeded on the second leg of our route. Again a leg of approximately thirty minutes to allow sufficient scope for heading adjustment at the midway point. We passed heading information to the lead aircraft and made a heading adjustment as for the first leg. The third leg unfolded in much the same way as the other two. We were now on the final leg, with HMS *Hermes* clearly visible in the far distance. As we approached the ship, we followed the procedure for stowing the goggles and made our final approach in accordance with normal night-flying procedures. I remarked to Pete that I would not want to be flying low level over land in light levels any lower than we had experienced that night. Pete was in full agreement, stressing that 5 millilux was to be the absolute minimum level at which NVG sorties would be authorized.

Having put the aircraft to bed, we met in the briefing room to talk through the sortie. There was a consensus that it had gone well and that the procedures had worked as expected. Over the next couple of nights we would repeat the sortie profile, with the same crew configuration and the same aircraft, but changing the lead on each night – tomorrow it would be my turn with Pete and 'Doc' to lead the formation. It was now almost 0300hrs and time for some much-needed sleep. As I arrived in my small piece of personal space, I was blissfully unaware that sleeping arrangements for all of us on 5 Deck were going to change for the worse in the not-too-distant future.

The following morning, Wednesday, 21 April, I took advantage of a well-deserved lie-in following the previous night's activities. Late morning, I wandered onto 03 Deck just in time to see one of the Harriers scrambled.

'What's going on?' I asked Tony Ogilvy, who was standing beside me.

'The ship's radar has detected a contact at high altitude quite close by, so Simon Hargreaves is going to investigate.' There then followed a period of tense uncertainty while we waited for any news. It was clear that we would not discover anything by remaining on the deck, so we both ventured to the briefing room. The room was a buzz of excitement as the Harrier pilots were speculating as to the nature of the contact. Shortly after our arrival, 800 Squadron CO, Lieutenant Commander Andy Auld, walked into the briefing room, having returned from the ship's operations room, to report that the radar contact was an Argentine Boeing 707 painted in military livery. This was the first contact with the enemy and we all believed that there would be many more in the days ahead.

That afternoon, I was programmed for another of my combat survival talks: survival shelters. In most survival situations, four priorities must be addressed before any other needs are met. Finding or making shelter is one of the most important survival priorities because it allows a person to stay protected from the elements, thus hopefully, warm and dry. The environment in the Falklands at the time of year when we would be operating was cold and wet, so shelter would be a high priority for survival. I finished my talk by reminding everyone that the imperative for downed aircrew was to return to 'friendly' territory as quickly as practicably possible. Shelters should, therefore, be occupied for short periods only when either the weather conditions were extreme, or during periods of rest during daylight hours. With an enemy probably on the lookout for downed aircrew, no one could afford the luxury of a gold-plated shelter. Briefing complete, we were about to leave the room when we heard the pipe 'Launch the Alert 5 aircraft'. What's going on, we all wondered and rushed to 03 Deck to see what was afoot.

It took no more that a minute to reach 03 Deck from the briefing room. By the time we reached the deck, the Harrier was about to taxi from its Alert 5 position behind the Island on the starboard side of the flight deck, to line up in the centre of the deck ready to launch. I could see that the pilot was Dave Morgan. It became apparent that as a result of the morning's encounter with the Argentine 707, Admiral Woodward had decided to institute a policy of Harriers at five minutes notice to launch, round the clock. This required the pilot to be strapped into the cockpit and ready to start the engine – how tedious for the pilots, I thought, but yet another indication that things were slowly heating up. On this occasion it turned out to be a legitimate commercial flight, but clearly no chances could be taken.

That night I was programmed for another NVG formation sortie with Pete and 'Doc'. The sortie was planned to follow the same format as for the previous night, except for a longer flight over a greater distance which would keep us in the air for three hours, thirty minutes. The aim of this sortie was twofold: to test navigation procedures by flying legs that would be representative in distance of sorties that would be flown into the Falkland Islands; and to experience the effect of prolonged flight wearing goggles. This time Pete, 'Doc' and I were to fly the lead aircraft. We manned our respective aircraft in plenty of time to ensure that we launched at the required time, 'Flyco' delivered the navigation data and we launched into the darkness. We flew very nearly 350 miles in all and as *Hermes* finally came into view again she was a most welcome sight. We went through our familiar procedure for reverting to conventional night flying and I was once again amazed at just how dark it was in the real world. Prolonged use of goggles results in a condition known as 'brown-eye', which is similar to the residual effect on sight which results from looking at a very bright light for too long. After three hours, thirty minutes of looking through goggles, the 'brown-eye' effect was quite marked, making everything appear much darker than it really was, but this soon passed as we signed in our aircraft and proceeded to the briefing room. There was a consensus that the sortie had gone as planned and that TANS drift was within published limits. Tomorrow night there would be more of the same, but for now our only interest was for some much-needed sleep.

The day's excitement started very early on Thursday, 22 April when the ship's radar picked up another high-altitude contact – this time a Harrier from HMS *Invincible* was scrambled to investigate. It turned out to be the Argentine 707 from the previous day, back to have another look at the Task Force. ROE did not permit engagement, so the Harrier pilot flew very close to the 707 which persuaded its pilot to turn away from the fleet. I was blissfully unaware of all of this because I was enjoying a very deep sleep after the previous late night. Later in the morning I made preparations for what was to be the last of my combat survival talks; this time the subject was to be evading the enemy.

Meanwhile, on HMS *Fearless*, anchored off Ascension Island, the Brigadier and Commodore continued to make their plans for the amphibious landing and subsequent land operations. Targets for reconnaissance were now arriving on *Hermes* via the regular phone calls with Richard Preston, details of which were never passed to the pilots who were ultimately to fly the missions, for reasons of operational security. It would be possible for a target to be compromised by aircrew should an aircraft be forced down over land and the aircrew be captured. In any case, the actual target was of no interest to the aircrew – all that we needed to know was the location for drop-off and/or pick-up and any restrictions in route selection. However, the target locations enabled the Special Forces planning team of Major 'E' and Captain 'C' to discuss landing site options with Bill, the Senior Pilot, who was the only member of the Squadron group to be made aware of the reconnaissance targets. Bill, in turn, could identify suitable landing sites and potential routes and pass these to the aircrew. He had planned from the outset not to fly the operational sorties, other than in extremis, otherwise his contribution to the Special Forces planning team could have been undermined. As it turned out, Bill's input into the Special Forces planning process was to prove crucial.

It became apparent over time that the areas of interest that would require reconnaissance, as potential landing beaches, would be to the west side of East Falkland: San Carlos, Volunteer Bay and Berkley Sound. Similarly, vantage points overlooking these sites would need to be reconnoitred for enemy presence together with likely approach routes to Port Stanley, the obvious final objective for land forces. These areas of interest were likely to result in flights into three or four main areas of East Falkland in order to insert and extract Special Forces' patrols. In the context of operational security, the aircrew would not be able to mark their maps in any way which could compromise either landing sites or ingress and egress routes, therefore, each of us would need to become very familiar with the landscape. It would have been a very tall order indeed for each member of the aircrew to study and memorize the detail of the whole of East Falkland, so it was decided that the island should be divided into four sectors, with each helicopter crew dedicated to operating in just one quadrant.

As the aircrew were pouring over maps of East Falkland, we received news from Bill that the operation to recapture South Georgia, 'Paraquet', had been launched, but had got off to a disastrous start. The Task Group, comprising HMS *Antrim*, HMS *Brilliant*, HMS *Plymouth* and RFA *Tidespring* had arrived in the area of South Georgia the previous day, and a Special Forces patrol of SAS had been inserted on the Fortuna Glacier by the two Wessex helicopters of 845 Squadron.

Conditions on the glacier proved to be atrocious and, after only twelve hours ashore, the SAS patrol asked to be evacuated. In attempting to rescue them, the two Wessex helicopters crashed in 'white-out' conditions leaving just the Wessex III of HMS *Antrim* to recover the aircrew of the downed helicopters and the SAS patrol. This was not an auspicious start to the operation with both Special Forces and all but one of the helicopters proving not to be up to the job. 'We must clearly do a great deal better' was the sentiment in our crew room that day. The news about Operation Paraquet reminded me that I was not the only member of my family deployed in the South Atlantic. My brother, David, was embarked in HMS *Endurance* as the Weapons Engineering Officer (WEO). With thoughts of him, the topography of East Falkland and crashed helicopters firmly in the forefront of my mind, I delivered the last of my talks on combat survival: evading the enemy, the introduction for which had been handed to me on a plate!

With this salutary lesson foremost in the minds of all the aircrew, we made early preparations for the night's NVG sortie. It was the very last vestiges of the moon, thus we would probably not be able to fly again for at least three nights until the new moon had risen. With planning behind us we had dinner and a few hours of sleep because launch would not be until 0430hrs. After an early dinner and some well-deserved sleep, each crew made their way to the flight deck to man their respective aircraft. The aircraft were started and on cue the now familiar voice from 'Flyco' delivered the navigation data. With our position firmly fixed in TANS the formation launched into the darkness of the South Atlantic.

The length of that night's flight was to be one hour and thirty minutes. Bob Horton and 'Stumpy' were in the lead aircraft, with Nigel and Paul in the number two position, Pete, 'Doc' and I in the number three slot and Bob Grundy and 'Wiggy' bringing up the rear. This way, over the three sorties, all but one crew had taken a turn at lead, position two, position three and position four. We flew what, by now, had become a standard navigation pattern of waypoints away from the ship. Once we were established in formation, lights off and all flying on goggles, we descended to fly at a height of 50 feet above the surface. The previous two sorties had been flown at 200 feet, but now we needed to become practised in flying at what was to be our operational height for insertion: 50 feet above the surface when flying over the sea and even lower when flying over the land. The sortie was conducted without incident and we all felt that we were making excellent progress – navigation procedures were working well, formation keeping was accurate, relatively long duration flight had been achieved and each crew was working well. After one hour, forty minutes of flight, we landed back on *Hermes* and put the aircraft to bed, satisfied that thus far all was going according to plan. The following day was to be busy for some of the crews continuing the 'Vertrep' programme, so with a feeling of satisfaction at our progress, I took to my bed at 0630hrs on Friday, 23 April, blissfully ignorant of the series of events that would unfold, leading to tragedy later that day.

I awoke late in the morning and went to the wardroom for coffee, where I was to learn that the ship had moved to action messing and that there was to be no more sleeping below the waterline. Ordinarily officers would be waited on by stewards for all meals, but under the action messing arrangements, a self-service system became the norm which proved to be popular. On the other hand, the new sleeping arrangements were not at all popular. Admiral Woodward's staff had assessed that there was a potential threat to the ships of the Task Force from Argentine submarines – they had two older ex-British boats – hence the order being issued to all ships of the Task Force that there was to be no more sleeping below the waterline. This meant that anyone whose cabin or mess deck was on 5 Deck or below had to make alternative sleeping arrangements. For those of us who did not count ship's officers amongst our close friends, hot-bunking was not an option. For us the sleeping arrangement from now on was to be a camp bed on the floor of the wardroom main ante-room. What had previously been a space for the officers in which to relax and have a well-deserved pint now became a combination of a dormitory of several camp beds and a bar. Over the coming days this arrangement proved to be an irreconcilable and a curious mix of frustrating inconvenience, punctuated by moments of great hilarity. Meanwhile, I was curious as to how others on the ship were coping, so I went for a walk around the various passageways. Everywhere sailors were putting down camp beds; some were even trying to sleep in corners whilst the day-to-day activities of the ship were carrying on around them. I had a vision of tripping over a sailor in the middle of the night as he was trying to get some no doubt well-deserved sleep and I was trying to make my way back to the wardroom in the early hours after yet another NVG sortie – time would tell.

It was now well into the afternoon and weather conditions were starting to deteriorate. The sea state was a lot higher than it had been at any time since leaving Ascension, the sky was overcast and it was getting cold. In these conditions it was acceptable for the flying programme to continue as single-pilot sorties. In 1982, the Sea King IV was a single-pilot, but two-crew aircraft. However, for NVG operations, conventional night flying and flight in IMC, two pilots were required. With the weather on the turn for the worse, Bill warned me that I might be required to continue flying the 'Vertrep' programme into the night, but that he would let me know in due course. I decided to see for myself and went to 03 Deck for a look at the weather. By then, late afternoon, there was about a 20-foot swell, cloud base of around 1,000 feet and a wind just short of gale force. In these conditions, single pilot sorties were still safe, but with conditions deteriorating, I started to prepare mentally for a conventional night-flying sortie. I decided to have an early dinner and prepared my kit should I be required to fly.

After dinner, I went into the briefing room and Bill informed me that I would be flying with 'Stumpy' and 'Doc', but that Bob Grundy, who was flying a day into night sortie with 'Ben' Casey as aircrewman, had radioed the ship and advised that we went to two-pilot manning for night flying because, as it was getting dark, visibility was deteriorating. Bob had been ordered to return to *Hermes* so that Bill could fly with him and assess conditions for himself. With that, Bill left the briefing room and went to 'Flyco' so that he could talk to Bob by radio if necessary.

Several minutes passed before Bill returned to the briefing room at about 1715hrs. Looking ashen, he told the few aircrew who were in the room that Bob had ditched his aircraft and that an ASW Sea King of 820 Squadron, from HMS *Invincible,* that had been taking part in the ASW screen, had picked up the distress signal from his Sarbe , diverted to the source of the signal, winched Bob up from the sea and that he was on his way back to *Hermes* where he would be checked over by the doctors. There was, sadly, no news of 'Ben'. We were all shocked at this news and were unsure as to how to react or what to do next. Bill went to the sick bay to talk to Bob and the rest of the Squadron aircrew set about speculating amongst ourselves as to what might have happened. We considered the obvious possible causes of mechanical failure or pilot error. Bob was one of our more experienced pilots, was outstanding when flying on instruments and was one of a small number of the Squadron pilots who was competent to be authorized for flying day into night sorties. When this sort of tragic accident happens, part of you hopes that it is not a mechanical failure because of the obvious ramifications for continued flying operations. On the other hand, part of you hopes that it is not pilot error because of the immediate impact on the mental well-being of the pilot concerned: an irreconcilable dichotomy.

Later that night Bill gathered all aircrew together to let us know the outcome of his talk to Bob and what the plan was for searching for 'Ben'. Admiral Woodward had ordered that HMS *Yarmouth*, RFA *Resource* and RFA *Olmeda* search the area until one hour after dawn, at which time they were to rejoin the Task Force. Survival time in the sea in current temperatures was only a few hours, but could be several days if 'Ben' had been able to get into the aircraft's dinghy. With three ships and a helicopter searching, a dinghy could be found if it had it not drifted outside the search area.

When talking to Bill, Bob explained what had happened. The aircraft had picked up an underslung load from one of the RFAs and proceeded to *Hermes* to deliver the load. As he was part-way to the ship, Bob considered that conditions were now too bad to continue the flight with an underslung load and so returned to the RFA to drop the load. He then proceeded towards *Hermes'* last known position, at which point 'Ben' was in the vicinity of the cabin door, the normal station for the aircrewman during 'Vertrep' sorties. It was now dark and visibility had decreased markedly. Bob had seen a red light to the port side of the aircraft, but was unable to identify the ship, so he asked 'Ben' to move to the front of the aircraft from where he would be able to assist with lookout. As he was walking forward, the aircraft impacted the water. Bob instinctively evacuated the aircraft as trained and regularly practised during drills. When in his dinghy he looked around in the swell and could see no sign of 'Ben'. He noticed that the aircraft had broken in two, laterally, immediately behind the pilots' seats, with the tail section of the cabin still afloat. On seeing this, Bob swam from his dinghy to the tail section, diving down inside to see if 'Ben' was trapped inside, but to no avail. It was at this point that the ASW Sea King arrived on the scene and winched Bob into the aircraft.

On hearing this account, we were all deeply shocked and saddened that 'Ben' had not been recovered. As the night wore on, conditions were judged to be unsuitable for night flight other than in radar-equipped aircraft. The 'Vertrep' programme was therefore put on hold until the following day. It was with a heavy heart that I returned to my camp bed in the wardroom, the occupants of which were understandably in a very subdued mood. In the meantime the ASW Sea Kings continued to scour the area for any clue as to 'Ben's' fate.

Saturday, 24 April was a day of mixed news, some good, some bad. I was awoken in my new sleeping quarters by the sound of the Commander on the ship's tannoy, informing one and all that we had made significant advances in the South Georgia operation, which included inflicting serious damage to one of the Argentine submarines, the ARA *Santa Fe*. Apparently, the boat had been spotted on the surface about 5 miles distant from Grytviken by Lieutenant Commander Ian Stanley. Ian had been the pilot of the Wessex III which had only recently rescued the SAS and aircrew from their disastrous venture on the Fortuna Glacier. Ian attacked the submarine with a combination of machine gun and depth charges and was able to keep the boat from diving until help arrived in the form of a Wasp helicopter flown by Lieutenant Commander Tony Ellerbeck. Tony attacked the submarine with AS12 missiles, a marinized version of the SS11 anti-tank missile, scoring a direct hit on the boat's fin. Eventually the ARA *Santa Fe* limped into Grytviken harbour and was to take no further part in hostilities.

Whilst this drama was unfolding, the bulk of the Royal Marine force, M Company, was some 200 miles away in RFA *Tidespring*, at least ten hours steaming time away from being in a position to make a landing onto South Georgia. The Land Force commander, Major Guy Sherridan, was keen to exploit the Argentine set-back and land a force immediately in the vicinity of Grytviken where the bulk of the Argentine force was located. His request was approved by the Naval Task Group Commander, and with an ad hoc landing force made up of elements of M Company, SAS, SBS and the Royal Marine detachments from HMS *Plymouth* and HMS *Antrim*, the force was landed using a combination of ASW helicopters from HMS *Antrim*, HMS *Brilliant* and HMS *Plymouth*, under cover of naval gunfire support from *Antrim* and *Plymouth*. As the landing force advanced on the Argentine position at Grytviken, naval gunfire support was creeping forward slowly towards the Argentine position. When rounds were falling within a couple of hundred metres of the Argentine position, a white flag was seen and the Argentine force on South Georgia surrendered. This was fantastic news and was greeted by a rousing cheer from the officers in the wardroom ante-room, all of whom, like me, were getting ready for the day's operations after a nightmarish few hours of enduring mass snoring and other unsavoury noises! This was to become the norm – it was like being back at school in a dormitory of badly behaved schoolboys.

Later that morning I went to the briefing room to check on the flying programme for later in the day. I walked into the room to see the very familiar, but unexpected face of Sharkey Ward who was deeply engrossed in talking Harrier tactics with Tony Ogilvy, SAVO and another couple of the 800 Squadron pilots. I was not at all interested in their conversation, for it was none of my business, but my ears pricked up when I heard Sharkey mention that HMS *Invincible*'s Captain had interpreted the order for the new sleeping arrangements with an apparent healthy degree of common sense. On *Invincible* the new sleeping arrangements were introduced on a discretionary basis which left me wondering just which captain might in time be proven to be the more astute. With this hot news, I quickly made my way back to the wardroom to spread the news about J.J. Black's enlightened interpretation of orders. I had been away from the ante-room for about an hour and was, therefore, amazed at the scene which greeted me on entering the compartment. I had been fortunate to claim my sleeping space when I did, for where there had been just a handful of camp beds an hour earlier, there were now about fifty laid out in four neat rows running from the bar back towards the main door, with just sufficient room between the rows for people to be able to walk to the bar if needs be.

Early that afternoon there was a memorial service for 'Ben'. The search overnight had not revealed any clue as to his fate and so the worst was assumed. The ship's small chapel was crammed to capacity with Squadron personnel, Harrier pilots and members of the ship's company, each wanting to pay his respects and share the Squadron's feeling of loss and deep sadness. Later that afternoon, I was programmed for up to two hours flying a HDS sortie around the ships of the Task Force with Richie Burnett as aircrewman. HDS is essentially a 'round-robin' flight to all ships delivering papers, small items of stores and taking passengers to and from other ships. After the morning's exciting news from South Georgia, this flight felt like an anti-climax and almost an embarrassment. However, the routine day-to-day business of the Task Force had to continue and it was my turn for a share of this mundane but, nonetheless, important task.

That evening, as we gathered in the wardroom, we were able to hear for ourselves the latest news from South Georgia via the BBC World Service. The reports of earlier in the day were confirmed and more detail of the operation emerged. The ASW Sea King pilots were cock-a-hoop with the news about the crippling of ARA *Santa Fe* and we few Royal Marines were immensely proud of what our small force had achieved against overwhelming odds. The ROE had been changed allowing the Harrier pilots to harass the Argentine 707 should it return, so they too were in euphoric mood. However, my joy was constrained by thoughts of 'Ben' and the realization that by now his next of kin, Elly, would have been informed of his probable death.

As each day arrived, with it came increasingly worse weather. It was now Sunday, 25 April and the good news was that the moon was in its first quarter, so NVG flights could resume. The bad news was that moon rise was early in the day, setting at 1930hrs, one hour and thirty minutes after sunset. Launch time was, therefore, set for 1900hrs, thereby ensuring sufficient ambient light throughout the sortie. With no flying planned during daylight hours, I started a detailed map appreciation of likely ingress and egress routes for our forthcoming Special Forces insertion and extraction sorties. With the loss of one Sea King we were now down to four aircraft, so our initial plan to sector East Falkland into quadrants had to be revisited. After careful consideration, three sectors were decided on. Pete, 'Doc' and I would execute all flights into the sector to the south and east of the island, encompassing Stanley, Fitzroy, Goose Green, Darwin and Bluff Cove. Another crew would cover the areas around Teal Inlet, Douglas and all areas to the north, with the third crew concentrating on the western part of the island encompassing, Ajax Bay, San Carlos and coastal areas to the west. All crews would cover West Falkland. With these dispositions confirmed, the crews could now get on with some serious map study.

With our first insertion of Special Forces into the Falklands less than a week away, it was decided to up-arm the Sea Kings. The decision was made to remove the rear cabin window on the port side of the aircraft to cater for an additional GPMG, thereby being able to put down fire from both sides of the aircraft simultaneously, should it prove necessary. The aircrewman would man the GPMG in the cabin door as per established procedure and one of the Special Forces troops would be able to man the other gun. Simon 'Radar' Branch-Evans, now OC of the engineering detachment in *Hermes*, did not disappoint and within twenty-four hours a trial installation was ready for inspection. The mount for the gun had to perform two functions: to be securely attached to the aircraft but removable when not required; and be fitted with stops to restrict the arc of fire of the gun to safeguard against an over-exuberant gunner shooting off parts of the aircraft. 'Radar's' aircraft modification satisfied all requirements – all that was needed now was to test fire the new installation; this would have to wait until the following day.

Later than night we manned our aircraft for the first NVG sortie in three days. With the time for launch approaching, the now very familiar voice from 'Flyco' delivered the navigation data. With our position fixed, we launched and disappeared into the darkness. The sortie was conducted at 50 feet throughout, with Nigel, 'Wiggy' and Petty Officer Aircrewman Colin Tattersall flying the lead aircraft in our now well-practised, loose formation. Pete, 'Doc' and I were in the second aircraft with Bob Horton and Paul Humphreys bringing up the rear. Following an uneventful one-hour, thirty-minute flight, we returned to *Hermes* and put the aircraft to bed. As I walked into the wardroom at 2100hrs, I was greeted by the sight of officers wrestling with the new arrangement of the compartment doubling as a bar and its new status of being a large dormitory – not easy bedfellows.

Monday, 26 April dawned with miserable weather which was to last all day. The sea was very rough, there was a gale blowing, the cloud base was low and visibility poor, in light rain. One advantage of flying on days such as this was the opportunity to get off of the ship. Although a large ship, *Hermes* moved around a lot in heavy seas, with waves breaking over the flight deck on occasions. When airborne it was possible to escape the relentless roller-coaster ride. 'Doc' and I launched late morning and flew to a position a mile or so astern of the ship from where we could test 'Radar's' new GPMG mount. After a twenty-minute flight, we returned to the ship, job done. With the flight deck rising and falling as much as 80 feet in all, it was essential to pick the right moment to land. For a helicopter this is not too difficult and as the deck reached the top of a wave I landed. I could see the Alert 5 Harrier over to my right parked just behind the Island, with the pilot strapped in the cockpit. How the hell do the Harrier pilots manage to land in conditions like these? I wondered. As soon as they commit to landing there is no going back, no facility for rising and falling to match the deck motion; I made it my business to find out. With the aircraft returned to the hangar I set off to the briefing room in search of a Harrier pilot. There I found Dave Morgan, who delivered a somewhat tongue-in-cheek description of landing a Harrier on a heaving deck. I took with a pinch of salt his description of it being 'quite easy really', sensing that there was considerable understatement in his description.

That afternoon I worked with Pete and 'Doc' studying maps of our sector of East Falkland. The topography appeared to be not unlike Dartmoor in relief and height. There was no obvious sign of trees, except in Stanley, and we would not be going there in a hurry; a few rivers and possibly dried-up river beds appeared to offer possible low-level routes. It would be essential to fly at ultra-low level to remain below radar coverage. Information on Argentine radar positions had been made available to The Royal Signals & Radar Establishment, Malvern – in return we were told that we could expect radar intervisibility traces to be delivered a few days later to help in our route selection and height planning. For now the priority was to memorize as much of the terrain in our areas as possible as we would not be able to mark our maps with routes during the Special Forces missions. We set about selecting a route to a notional drop-off point with each of us studying one leg of the route. After an hour or so we took turns to describe the route from memory, to include a general description of the terrain and features that would be seen ahead of the aircraft and to both sides. We were pleased with how it went after one attempt and decided to try the same exercise the following day with a different route.

As I was about to leave the briefing room, one of the Harrier pilots, Tony Ogilvy, entered. He was in a particularly ebullient mood.

'The ROE have been changed,' he announced with a broad grin. 'We can now shoot down the 707 if he gets too close to the Task Force again.'

'How fantastic it would be if the Sea Kings had a weapon capable of shooting down an aircraft,' I said. 'Any more developments?'

'Just trying to figure out a way of dispensing chaff if we need to. How do you guys do it?' I then explained how the aircrewman threw a handful of the boxes out of the back and that Nigel and I had trialled it a couple of weeks earlier against the ship's Sea Cat system. I also extolled the brilliance of 'Radar' at delivering bespoke solutions to the little problems that we fed him from time to time.

'We have our own boy wonder, Phil Hunt – if anyone can sort it out, he can.'

'Good luck,' I said and with that walked back into the ship and down to the hangar.

In the hangar, 'Radar' was supervising the work to fix the additional GPMG mounts to the remaining aircraft, now just four in number since the loss of Bob Grundy's aircraft three days earlier. Bob was also in the hangar – it was good to see him again after his ordeal. Apart from a few cuts and bruises, he looked OK physically. He was preparing for a back-in-the-saddle trip, flying with Pete Rainey and Pete Imrie. I wished him well and told him that I hoped that his trip would work out all right, although I knew that it would be a few days before he would be night flying again. It was also encouraging to see the aircraft now ready in all respects for the NVG operations that were to start just five days hence. The cockpits looked remarkably professional given the liberal application of 'Gaffa' tape. The additional GPMG mounts would also all be in position within a day.

'Radar' explained that the Squadron would be adopting War Scheduled Maintenance. I queried this, to which he explained that normal peacetime servicing would be suspended. During peacetime the aircraft were serviced at set times to reflect hours flown or lapsed time. Any snag, no matter how small, had to be recorded in the MoD Form 700, investigated and fixed. Resolving snags could be time consuming and, given the expected heavy flying programme that was to come and our reduced number of aircraft, we could not afford to have a single aircraft grounded for more than an hour or so. To this end, it would become the norm for aircraft to become crew dedicated, that is to say, each NVG crew would be assigned an aircraft and normally fly only that aircraft. That way, snags would be noted, but not recorded in the MoD Form 700 unless either immediately life-threatening, or having developed to such an extent that repair could not be delayed any further. To appreciate fully the extent of a problem, crews had to be dedicated to specific aircraft. War Scheduled Maintenance was set to commence on 28 April, in time for the commencement of Special Forces operations, just two days later.

Tuesday, 27 April was a day of equally miserable weather. Perhaps this was to be the norm from now on, I thought. I was programmed for a plane-guard sortie. When the Harriers launched, it was SOP for a helicopter to be airborne in the vicinity of the ship – in the unlikely event of a Harrier ditching, the helicopter could fly to the scene in just a few seconds and winch up the pilot. Ordinarily, the ASW Sea Kings on the screen would fulfil this commitment, but as we were getting closer to the Falkland Islands, there were to be two ASW Sea Kings on the screen at any given time and, with 826 Squadron aircraft serviceability suffering from their heavy flying programme, our squadron was to help out for a while. Plane-guard, although important, is just about the most mundane task that a pilot can be asked to fly – over two hours of loitering within the vicinity of the ship on the off-chance that a Harrier may ditch. The last thing that I wanted to see was a Harrier ditch, but if one had it was at least comforting for the Harrier pilots to know that we would be on the scene to effect a rescue in no time at all. Just over two hours later the task was complete and I was able to return to the ship.

'Never again,' I sighed, as I signed the aircraft back in.

Following lunch, I embarked on some more map study of East Falkland. That afternoon we received the radar intervisibility traces that we had been expecting. Drawn to a scale of 1:50,000 inches, they were a perfect fit over our maps. Armed with this information it was now possible to plot the radar coverage on our maps and mark the heights above which we would be unable to fly without detection by Argentine radar. In some areas it would be possible to fly at heights of up to 200 feet above ground; in other areas we would need to fly at below 50 feet. The only health warning was, of course, that the radar type and location information used in producing the traces might not have been accurate. We had no way of confirming radar locations before Special Forces were inserted, therefore the lowest risk option would be to fly all sorties over the islands at below 50 feet. Route selection could now begin in earnest.

Later that evening we received the news that a Total Exclusion Zone (TEZ) of 200 nautical miles radius would be established around the Falkland Islands with effect from 0800hrs on 30 April. This caused a buzz of excitement in the wardroom where the general mood was one of optimism, with morale high. I was left wondering, however, just how much of the banter was bravado and how much was genuine professionalism. Behind it all I saw a few worried faces in the wardroom that night.

Wednesday, 28 April dawned with the weather as miserable as ever. As I sat eating my breakfast, it dawned on me that with the deteriorating weather, tonight's programmed NVG training sortie might be the last opportunity for a NVG flight before the real thing in just another three days. Today would therefore be a day for tying up loose ends, double-checking all systems in the aircraft and some more serious map study. During the morning we received news through the BBC World Service of the outcome of a crucial meeting of the Organisation of American States (OAS) which had taken place two days earlier. OAS, I thought, and immediately had a vision of the film, *The Day of the Jackal*. Was a hit-man about to assassinate General Galtieri? No such luck of course. The meeting had produced a resolution offering qualified diplomatic support to Argentina, called on Britain to cease hostilities immediately, appealed to both governments to seek a diplomatic solution and deplored the EEC trade ban. On hearing this I thought, bloody cheek, British hostilities; what hostilities?

The conflict appeared to be producing some strange bedfellows among the Latin American countries. Chile was alone in having a territorial dispute with Argentina over the Beagle Channel and wanted in no way to be seen to condone the Argentine precedent. In as little as three weeks' time, Chile's hostility to Argentina's actions was to work to my advantage in a way that I could not have imagined.

Moonrise was early afternoon, therefore, to take advantage of what little moon there was, we would need to launch not long after nightfall; launch was set for 2000hrs. Three aircraft would be flying in the formation, with the crews as for the previous NVG sortie. The exercise of ranging the aircraft on deck from the hangar, manning and being ready for launch was now well worked up and achieved in a total of thirty minutes. As we were manning our aircraft, I could not help but sympathize with the Harrier pilot who was strapped into his cockpit at Alert 5. Poor sod, I thought, he must be freezing his nuts off. 'Flyco's' navigation data was delivered bang on time and at 2000hrs we launched into the darkness for a two-hour sortie. Again the flying was conducted at a height of 50 feet with navigation legs around thirty minutes each to ensure plenty of practice with the navigation procedure. Our collective Morse skills were now well up to speed, with the pilots competing with the aircrewmen to see who would be first to translate the signal from the lead aircraft into the new heading. The sortie was uneventful and, as we approached the ship and were about to land, it occurred to me that the next time that we saw this sight at night it would be having inserted Special Forces. It felt scary – just how scary we would soon discover.

The advantage of an early flight was the opportunity to get back to the wardroom in time for the bar to be still open. There was a decent-sized gathering in the wardroom that night, but those who were drinking were in the main having just one or two pints and calling it a night. For the Harrier pilots waiting for their turn at Alert 5, alcohol was soon to become a distant memory. Dave Morgan told me that the Harrier engineers had managed to find a solution for a workable chaff dispenser using wires and string, so the Harriers were now all set. The Air Group as a whole, therefore, seemed to be in good shape and good spirits for the battle that lay ahead: aircraft of both types had been modified and armed; aircrew were day and night deck qualified, and competent in procedures and tactics; and the maintainers and aircraft handlers were providing a sterling service to keep us in the air. What could possibly go wrong?

On Thursday, 29 April, some useful additions were made to the Task Force. HMS *Brilliant* joined us from South Georgia, together with some most welcome passengers: in all, ninety Special Forces personnel from D Squadron 22 SAS and 6 SBS, a handful of gunners and one or two RAF specialists. As I moved around the ship during the following day, I came across Special Forces marines and soldiers squeezed into corners of passageways trying to sleep, whilst hopefully not tripping up the ship's company and Air Group who were still going about their daily tasks. The NVG crews and aircraft were now prepared for the first missions that were just thirty-six hours away. The SAS patrols of G Squadron and SBS teams that we would be flying into the Falkland Islands were busy studying their maps, preparing equipment and trying to get some much-needed sleep. The ships of the Task Force were now established in an operating box 200 miles to the north-east of East Falkland, well out of range of fighter cover from the Argentine mainland. The weather had assumed its by now usual characteristics of grey skies, cold blustery conditions and a rough sea. The Senior Pilot spread the word amongst the aircrew that we would be briefed the following morning on the plan for 1 May. In the meantime, the priority was map study, personal admin and sleep.

There was no change in the weather on the last day of April. The carrier group continued its operations in a box to the north-east of the Falklands in a heavy sea and bitterly cold wind. Mid-morning the Squadron's aircrew and engineers gathered in the briefing room for Bill's brief on the following day's operations.

Offensive action was to start tonight with naval gunfire onto targets on Stanley airfield. During the early hours there would be a high-altitude bombing attack on the runway by a Vulcan based at Ascension. At the time of the Vulcan attack, the first helicopter insertions of Special Forces would take place, and finally, at dawn, the 800 Squadron Harriers would attack targets on Stanley Airfield and the small airstrip at Goose Green – action at last! Timing the Special Forces insertions to coincide with naval gunfire and the Vulcan attack was designed to enable the helicopters to fly to their landing sites well to the west of Stanley whilst the Argentine force was distracted by the attacks on Stanley airfield. We would be flying into the islands without any information about possible Argentine positions outside of Stanley and Goose Green. For all we knew, we could be flying directly overhead Argentine positions; the diversion was therefore most welcome.

The rest of the day was spent studying maps, planning, memorizing routes and preparing equipment. The aircrew also spent time listening to audio tapes of the electronic signature of Argentine radars. Between all of the NVG helicopters, we had just one hand-held Radar Warning Receiver (RWR). The 'Omega' device was a rectangular-shaped box measuring about 12 inches long by 6 inches deep and 4 inches wide, with a 6-inch long pyramid-shaped cone to one end, controls and switches on the opposite end, and a pistol grip handle attached at one end underneath. The RWR could be used in one of two ways: the pilot not flying the aircraft could unplug his helmet from the aircraft's intercom system and plug in to the RWR; or the RWR could be spliced into the intercom system via a splitter box so that both pilots and the aircrewman could hear the signals from the RWR whilst remaining in contact with each other. There were pros and cons for both options. Three heads were better than one when identifying a radar transmission; on the other hand, the radar signal could be a distraction at a time when the aircrew might need to pass important or urgent information to each other. The initial Special Forces insertion sortie was to be flown with the RWR kept separate to the intercom system and carried in the lead aircraft.

The RWR was sensitive to the frequencies of the transmissions of different types of radar. When a radar signal was detected, the pilot would rotate the RWR slowly through 360° until the strongest signal was received; this would give an indication of the bearing of the radar from the aircraft. By tuning the controls on the receiver it was possible to determine the Pulse Duration (PD), Pulse Recurrence Time (PRT) and Pulse Recurrence Frequency (PRF). Armed with this information the radar type could be identified, i.e. short-range target acquisition and fire-control radar or long-range surveillance radar. The nature of the signal would change when the aircraft had been illuminated by the radar and locked on. The RWR would prove to be invaluable, but with just the one, radar warning information would be available to only one aircraft per sortie, except when flying in formation during the insertion phase of the operation. Each member of the aircrew studied the radar recognition tapes intently during those final hours before commencement of operations. All pieces of the jigsaw were in place: aircraft prepared, NVG operating procedures developed and well practised, aircrew trained. All that we needed now was reasonable weather and some luck.

Part 2

Operations in the TEZ

Chapter 5

Arrival in the TEZ – Operation Sutton Commences

War is mainly a catalogue of blunders.

Winston Churchill

As I walked out onto the flight deck at 2100hrs on 30 April, the weather had improved. Gone were the gale-force winds and heavy seas of the past few days, and in their place all seemed eerily calm and peaceful. The moon, in its first quarter, was low in the night sky and there was about a quarter cloud cover – good light conditions for NVG operations. Ranged before me were the three aircraft on their spots ready for our first mission into the Falkland Islands. As I started my pre-flight walk around the aircraft, the first group of SAS arrived, followed a couple of minutes later by the second team. They busied themselves loading their equipment through the cabin door. I had never before seen such heavily loaded bergens and 'Doc' needed to use most of his muscle power to help lift their kit into the back of the helicopter. As I watched him struggling to load the aircraft, I wondered whether or not Pete and I had made sufficient allowance for the total weight of equipment when calculating the aircraft's payload; we would know soon enough. With our passengers firmly ensconced in the cabin, the engines were started, rotors engaged and the systems switched on-line in plenty of time for our 2130hrs launch. On cue 'Flyco' delivered the navigation data as practised many times during our training sorties, but this time it was for real. I fixed our position in TANS and all three aircraft launched into the darkness. Operation Sutton was underway.

Operation Sutton was the code word chosen for the land operations, to include the Special Forces intelligence and reconnaissance missions conducted prior to the amphibious landings. That night the Squadron inserted a total of four 4-man Special Forces patrols, a mix of both SAS and SBS teams, into East Falkland, with two 4-man patrols in my aircraft. Within five minutes of launch we had settled into our, by now, well-practised formation, at 100 knots and 50 feet. The distance to landfall was 80 nautical miles, which at 100kts and against a now stiffening westerly breeze, was to take very nearly one hour and fifteen minutes. After fifteen minutes of flight it was time for our first procedural navigation check. At precisely the halfway point I checked the TANS data which, in turn, 'Doc' signalled to Colin Tattersall, the aircrewman in the lead aircraft; the other aircraft quickly followed suit. After a couple of minutes there was no signal back from the lead aircraft which meant that the navigation was good, so we pressed on. After thirty minutes of flight it was time for the second navigation check and it was at this point that we caught our first sight of East Falkland. When looking under the goggles, outside the aircraft, it was pitch black – this was reassuring because the island was clearly visible through the goggles and, at that moment, I had an awful feeling that we must surely be visible to anyone on the island looking out to sea in our direction. In effect, we were flying blind. Although we had the RWR in the lead aircraft which would indicate contact by Argentine radar, we had no way of knowing whether or not we would be flying close to any Argentine positions. As we approached landfall I could feel the tension within the aircraft.

'It's now or never,' exclaimed Pete, a poignant remark which was met with a muted response. In a way, Pete had hit the nail on the head. We had only four Sea Kings with which to insert the Special Forces patrols – if we lost any of them and/or the aircrew, on Day 1 of the operation, it would have had a devastating impact on the conduct of future operations.

As the formation made its planned landfall at Concordia Rock, I fixed our position in TANS and noted that there were only a couple of degrees of drift. After a sea transit of 80 nautical miles this was reassuring and I thought it augured well for subsequent missions. Having made landfall the formation split, with each aircraft proceeding separately towards its destination. In my aircraft, Pete descended to fly at about 20 feet above ground level as we headed south across Bombilla Hill in an anti-clockwise route towards our first landing point, 20 miles to the west of Port Stanley and roughly north abeam Fitzroy. The hours of painstaking map study now bore fruit and I was able to describe the route to Pete with considerable accuracy as we made our way south and east. The route was predominantly low lying and grass covered, which looked remarkably like snow, and in places was rocky. Navigation was not difficult and all that stood between us and arriving in one piece at our destination were potential Argentine positions. I was acutely aware, as were all of us in the aircraft, that we could be discovered and shot down at any moment. We reached our destination after what felt like a lifetime, but was, in fact, just another twenty minutes of ultra-low-level flight and prepared to land the aircraft – so far so good. The ground was covered in short grass and with a few small rocks scattered about the area. Contrast through the goggles was not very good so I monitored the 'radalt' and called out our height as Pete slowly and carefully landed the aircraft.

Within seconds 'Doc' called out, 'I'm just unplugging for a second.' Suddenly it went eerily quiet in the back of the aircraft. A few seconds later the intercom burst back into life. 'Back on,' said 'Doc'.

'Where have you been?' asked Pete.

'I just went to grab a small rock as a memento and to prove that I was the first member of the Task Force to set foot on the Falklands.'

'Where's the SAS team?' I asked.

'They're long gone', replied 'Doc'. The first SAS patrol, led by Captain Aldwin Wight, had rapidly exited the aircraft, with 'Doc' helping to lower their heavy bergens to the ground.

Within a minute of arrival, the aircraft was transitioning forward towards our second destination, a position 20 miles to the north-west of Bluff Cove. Flight time was less than ten minutes and, like the first leg, was flown at about 20 feet over similar terrain. At the landing site I again called out the aircraft's height as Pete carefully landed. The patrol, led by Sergeant Joseph Mather, departed the aircraft with breakneck speed, clearly not wanting to be near a noisy helicopter any longer than necessary. Taking the hint, Pete transitioned into forward flight, turning north-west to clear the area of the two landing sites as quickly, but safely, as possible. We remained at around 20 feet until coasting out at a position approximately halfway between Cape Dolphin and Teal Inlet. When clear of the land the aircraft was climbed to 50 feet and we set heading back to 'Mother.' For most of the return journey I flew the aircraft and looked after the navigation, giving Pete a much-needed respite after the intense concentration of flying at only 20 feet over the island.

That night, in addition to the two SAS patrols that had been inserted in my aircraft, Special Forces patrols were inserted by the other two aircraft to locations from which the western approaches to Port Stanley could be observed, and the area around Port San Carlos. As soon as each aircraft had left the vicinity of its landing site, the patrols moved under cover of darkness towards OP positions from which their target areas could be observed. Distances covered on foot varied, but were up to approximately 20 miles. Following insertion, there were nine hours or so of darkness remaining during which time the patrols had to 'yomp' carrying 100lb bergens towards their destinations. As it was impossible in this time to cover such a distance and prepare an OP position before first light, the priority for the first night, therefore, was to move away from the helicopter landing sites as quickly as possible and cover a reasonable distance before finding a suitable location in which to lay up during daylight hours, with the objective of completing the move to the OP position over the following one or two nights. To achieve concealment, the patrols dug shallow scrapes into the Falkland's topsoil to a depth of about 18 inches or so. Any deeper and either granite or water would be encountered, such was the nature of the terrain. The shallow scrapes were covered with either camouflage nets, grass and soil, or chicken wire, grass and soil depending on personal preference. In these shallow scrapes the patrols had to remain concealed from the enemy throughout daylight hours, remaining as dry and warm as possible and eating as best they could, until moving on the next night. The selection of sites for the OPs was based on the meagre intelligence available from the Royal Marines of Naval Party 8901, repatriated after the Argentine invasion, and from civilians who chose not to live under occupation, but instead had travelled to the UK at the outset of hostilities. Each patrol's precise landing site had been chosen by the team's leader after discussion with either Major 'E' or Captain 'C', as appropriate, together with Bill and the aircraft captains. Given the age of the information, there was a degree of risk in OP and landing-site locations and insertion routes. During this first night we had to trust to luck and hope and pray that the enemy was nowhere near where we were.

Approximately thirty minutes after flying out from the coast, I could see HMS *Hermes* on the horizon. When looking under the goggles, it was to all intents and purposes pitch black, but the ship's inability to remain completely darkened turned her into a small green dot which was clearly visible from over 50 miles away. As we approached the ship we went through the goggle drill to revert back to conventional night flying, and I handed control back to Pete for the final approach and landing. Of the three aircraft, we had flown the longest distance that night, and so were the last aircraft to land back on HMS *Hermes* at just after midnight. As we walked away from the aircraft towards the Island, the other two Sea Kings were already on their way to the hangar via the aft lift, and twelve Harriers were lined up on the starboard side of the deck. In just over six hours, it would be their turn to see some action.

I made my way to the ACRB, now open twenty-four hours a day and had a much-needed hot drink. Most of the aircrew were there and, unsurprisingly, we talked about how we thought that our sorties had gone, without referring to the specifics, before moving into the briefing room, one crew at a time, for a formal debrief by Bill and Richard Preston. 'According to plan' and 'without incident' was the report made by Nigel and Pete. 'Wiggy' confirmed that the RWR had not detected any Argentinean radars; there was a consensus that the navigation had gone well and that TANS had been accurate. It was at this point that Bob Horton informed the group that having dropped off his Special Forces team, he had had an encounter with an Argentinean aircraft. It had not been possible to identify its type – it could have been a helicopter or a Pucara – but crucially Bob had managed to evade the aircraft. We were somewhat stunned by Bob's news which engendered an atmosphere of apprehension amongst the crews. After the formal debrief I returned to the ACRB for another coffee. It was now approaching 0200hrs and I was acutely aware that there were to be several more such nights, starting later that night, so I was keen to get into a routine of sleep by day and being awake at night. The Harriers would be launching for their attacks on Stanley Airfield and Goose Green airstrip in just over four hours, so I decided to do some more general map study to kill time before the Harriers' launch.

At around 0530hrs the Harrier pilots started arriving in the briefing room in time for a 0600hrs brief. They were all keen to know how the sorties had gone. By now I was the only member of the Squadron aircrew still up and about, so I briefed them on the generalities, without mentioning specifics like routes and locations, to maintain operational security. The Harrier pilots seemed to be generally amazed at what we had achieved, inserting a total of twenty-four Special Forces personnel into enemy held territory, apparently without detection and all before breakfast! I sensed that the Harrier community on *Hermes* were developing a healthy degree of respect for our small team – in fact, Tony Ogilvy was to say as much to me a few days later. Like many of the helicopter pilots in *Hermes*, I sensed from the outset, either rightly or wrongly, that compared to the Harrier pilots, we were regarded by the ship's air department and the Admiral's staff as very much second-class citizens. This feeling was exemplified from the outset in Portsmouth when each Harrier pilot, having landed on the ship for the first time, or after a period away from the ship, had been whisked away within a few minutes of landing to meet 'Wings' and shortly afterwards the Captain – no such courtesy was extended to the helicopter pilots. On the other hand, I never detected any such arrogance from the Harrier pilots themselves, but after this night I sensed that our relationship had moved to a higher plain.

I left the briefing room to 800 Squadron for their sortie brief and returned to the ACRB for yet more coffee. It was 0615hrs when I left the comfort of the ACRB and went up to 03 Deck to watch the Harrier pilots making their final preparations before manning their aircraft. Some of the aircraft were lined up along the ship's centre line, others were parked on the starboard side of the flight deck. As I watched, the first hint of dawn appeared on the distant horizon to the east. The blackness on deck was interrupted by the light of the pilots' torches as they were walking around their aircraft, and the blackness of the sky to the east was punctuated by subtle hues of yellow and pale orange as the sun struggled to make its first appearance on the distant horizon. The wind had freshened to a fairly stiff westerly since I had returned from my early morning jaunt, while the deck had more motion than earlier, but conditions were not uncomfortable and with the exception of one or two voices, the flight deck was eerily quiet. At about 0630hrs the pilots started manning their aircraft having first carefully checked the integrity of their weapons.

Ten minutes later the silence was broken by the sound of the Harriers' engines cranking into life. First the whine of the engines accelerating, followed a few seconds later by the unmistakable sound of the high-energy igniter units cracking into life. It was time to put on my ear muffs as the sound would soon be deafening. One by one the Harriers taxied from their parking spots on the starboard side of the deck towards the stern before turning to face the ski-jump at the far end of the deck. One of the Harriers appeared to have a problem on starting, so the other aircraft carefully taxied around it. After a few moments, the pilot managed to get the aircraft started, so all was well. With all Harriers ready for launch, the ship turned to the west to give maximum wind over the flight deck for launch, essential because the aircraft, being fully armed, were heavier than for previous sorties. Chocks and lashings were removed from the Harriers and everything was set for launch. At exactly 0650hrs the pilot of the lead aircraft applied full throttle and the aircraft launched into the dawn light. One by one the other aircraft took their turn and after just two minutes all twelve aircraft had launched and were rapidly disappearing to the west. Once again the flight deck returned to its previous eerie quiet, but this welcome tranquillity was soon broken by the sound of the aircraft handlers dragging the lashing chains across the deck before dumping them in the 'green' in readiness for the Harriers' return. As I watched I hoped that after the raid, all twelve sets of lashings would be needed.

It had been nearly four hours since I had landed back on HMS *Hermes*, at which time the ship had started to move further away from the islands, so that by the time of the Harrier launch, *Hermes* was approximately 250 nautical miles north-east of Stanley. Flight time to Stanley would be about an hour for the Harriers, so I had plenty of time for a hearty breakfast before returning to 03 Deck to watch the aircraft recover. The plan for the Harriers' attack was simple: the first wave of aircraft were to attack targets on Stanley airfield, the second wave were to attack the runway, whilst simultaneously, the third group were to attack the small airstrip at Goose Green. Throughout this time, the Harriers of 801 Squadron from HMS *Invincible* would be providing a number of aircraft on Combat Air Patrol, or CAP as it was commonly known. These aircraft had provided cover earlier in the morning for the Vulcan attack and then provided top cover for the attack by 800 Squadron. Later Sharkey Ward was to report that, although the aircraft on CAP had made contact on more than one occasion with Argentine Mirages during the attacks by 800 Squadron, their pilots appeared to have no appetite for a fight and scuttled for home on every occasion that the slower Harriers attempted to close with them for engagement. How frustrating for them, I thought, I bet they wished that the Harrier had supersonic performance.

It was a couple of hours later that I returned to 03 Deck to watch the return of the Harriers. To my amazement, I was the only person there which made me wonder if perhaps many of the ship's company were still in bed. Slowly but surely, in dribs and drabs, the aircraft started to arrive back from the raid, with one Harrier holding off to the port side of the ship and flying a few circuits. I wondered if he had a problem. After a few minutes, eight of the Harriers had landed and been hurriedly moved to their parking spots on the starboard side of the deck. With the flight deck now clear, the last Harrier made its approach, but, unusually, from directly astern of the ship and at a higher speed than had been the norm. As the aircraft approached, all deck marshallers and handlers beat a hasty retreat towards the nearest cover. The aircraft continued its approach and made a fast and firm touchdown by 6 spot, about 50 feet forward of the aft edge of the deck and came to a complete stop just short of the ski-jump – the first, and as it turned out, only running landing by a Harrier that I ever witnessed on a ship. I was curious to go to the flight deck and see what the fuss was all about, but there were still three more Harriers to account for, so I bided my time and waited where I was. About five minutes later the remaining Harriers appeared to the south-west: one, two, three, that's it, all twelve safely back.

After the last Harrier had landed I decided to go to the flight deck to see what all the fuss had been about with the running landing. As I started to move I was joined on 03 Deck by Brian Hanrahan. We had a brief conversation about the Harrier raid during which I was reluctant to discuss the number of aircraft that had taken part in it. However, I agreed with him that it would be true to say they had all been counted out and all counted back again. With that Brian smiled and I left 03 Deck, heading to the flight deck via the briefing room to grab my flying helmet.

When I arrived on the flight deck, something of a small crowd had gathered around the tail end of the Harrier and some were pointing at the fin. As I approached, a fairly large hole in the tail fin became apparent. That solves that mystery, I thought, promptly left the flight deck and made my way to the wardroom for an early lunch. By now I was very tired and desperate for sleep. After a light lunch I settled into my sleeping bag in the hellhole of the wardroom dormitory for what I hoped would be six hours of uninterrupted sleep. Sleep – how naïve can one be? I must have been dreaming! Although in 1982 the British Armed Forces had a 24-hour-a-day war-fighting capability, it appeared that the majority of people in *Hermes* were still very much day warriors, plus the usual eclectic mix of watchkeepers. I managed six or so hours of fitful rest before I was awoken by the very familiar voice of the Commander, John Locke, using the ship's broadcast system to inform us all that two of the ship's Harriers on CAP had been attacked by two Argentine fighters, type unknown, and that in the ensuing engagement one of the enemy aircraft had been seen to be destroyed. With that there was a loud cheer by those in the wardroom. Time to get up, I said to myself, time to start planning the coming night's mission.

As the afternoon turned into evening, details started to emerge about the engagements of the Harriers and the offensive operations of some of the escort ships which had been operating close to the north-east of the islands throughout the day. A group of escorts, led by HMS *Glamorgan*, had been bombarding Stanley airfield and nearby targets since just after the early morning Harrier raid. Not far away from this group another two of the escorts, HMS *Brilliant* and HMS *Yarmouth*, had been conducting ASW operations, supported by ASW Sea Kings from *Hermes*. It was whilst these operations were underway that Argentine aircraft made their first concerted attacks against the escorts. The Harriers on CAP in the area from both *Hermes* and *Invincible* had been kept very busy, with a number of 'dog-fights' resulting in the destruction of four Argentine fighter aircraft and no British losses. What a transformation, I thought, as I looked down on the hive of activity on the flight deck from my position on 03 Deck. The Harriers had been operating in pairs on CAP with two aircraft relieving two on station before returning to the ship to rearm, refuel and for the pilots to be debriefed. Just ten hours earlier the flight deck had resembled a 'sleepy hollow', now it appeared to be the busiest place in the South Atlantic. How long can we sustain this level of activity? I wondered.

As day turned into night, the level of activity on the ship slowed to a more comfortable pace. With the day's operations behind us, it was time to turn our attention to the detailed planning for the night's Special Forces insertions. It felt as if it had been only a few hours earlier that we were about to launch into the darkness on our first mission. Somehow all concept of time seemed to have disappeared. It is often said that time flies when you are having fun – well, we were certainly not having fun, but during an action-packed first day, the time had flown by. That night a total of five patrols were to be inserted into East Falkland – three SAS and two SBS – to be flown in three Sea Kings. The crews were to be Nigel, 'Wiggy' and Colin Tattersall in the lead aircraft, Pete, 'Doc' and me in the second and Bob Horton, Paul and Richie Burnett in the third. Under the cover of darkness and with the risk of air attack against the Task Force reduced, *Hermes* moved closer to the Falkland Islands in preparation for the insertion of the patrols.

As the night wore on, the weather improved. The moon was a little bigger and brighter than the previous night, so light conditions were still favourable for NVG flight. The ship moved to a position 100 nautical miles north-east of East Falkland in time for the launch, which again was set for 2130hrs. This launch time was ideal in many respects. The round-trip distance to be flown from ship to shore, with the number of troops to be carried, was easily manageable in a three-hour time window and would give the patrols enough hours of darkness to make reasonable progress from the landing sites towards their objectives. Ambient light levels were at their optimum, facilitating low-level flight and, following recovery of the aircraft, the ship had sufficient time to steam a reasonable distance to the north-east before daylight.

With the aircraft manned and the Special Forces patrols on board, 'Flyco' delivered the navigation data on cue. We launched into the darkness, quickly settling into our loose formation at 50 feet and set heading towards Cape Dolphin. We were aware that ASW Sea Kings from *Hermes* would be operating fairly close to the coast, so we aimed to go around them to the north, giving them a wide berth. Flight time would be similar to the previous night so we had nothing to look at outside the aircraft other than the sea for the best part of an hour. This gave us plenty of time to think about the task in hand and the risks compared to the previous night's operation when we had enjoyed the element of surprise. After Bob's close encounter the previous night, we were less confident of not being detected. It was clear to us all that the Argentine forces would be more alert and probably more trigger happy than before. At the quarter, half and three-quarter points we checked navigation and signalled our TANS data to the lead aircraft, followed shortly afterwards on each occasion by the third aircraft. Unlike the previous night, the lead aircraft signalled back a slight heading adjustment of 3°. Nearing landfall we caught a glimpse of some of the escorts making their way back to the Task Force from their earlier positions quite close to the coast. We gave them a very wide berth to the north and continued towards landfall. The possibility of being detected by their radar was remote because of our very low height, but it was a tense few minutes for us.

As we neared the coast, the waves breaking against the rocks became visible. At any moment I was half expecting the aircraft to be fired on from positions ashore but, as if by the grace of God, we had managed to remain undetected. As we flew over Concordia Rock I fixed our position in TANS and we set heading to the south towards our first landing site to the north of Darwin. Pete flew the aircraft at about 20 feet until we intercepted a dried-up river bed enabling us to descend even lower, so that to an observer on the ground the aircraft would have only just been visible above the surface. After approximately twenty minutes of white-knuckle flying, we arrived at the landing site. I called out our height to Pete as he slowly and carefully landed the aircraft. The SAS patrol of four men shot out of the cabin with breakneck speed despite carrying very heavy bergens. Within a minute of landing we were once again airborne and heading east towards our second landing site, to the north-west of Fitzroy. Flight time was less than ten minutes and after dropping off the second SAS patrol we set heading north-west towards our coasting-out position, a few miles to the east of Cape Dolphin. Having fixed our position as we coasted out, Pete handed control to me and we set heading back to 'Mother.' With about 50 miles to run, *Hermes* came into view through the goggles, a reassuring and welcome sight. A little over two hours, thirty minutes after launch we touched down on the flight deck: it was good to be home.

Once again my aircraft was the last to be recovered so the other crews were waiting for us as we made our way to the ACRB for coffee. In turn, each crew was debriefed by Bill and Richard Preston, 'according to plan' and 'without incident' being the consensus. How long can this good luck last? I wondered as I made my way to the wardroom. That night I was determined to get into my sleeping bag whilst it was still dark. It was now 0230hrs as I slipped into a deep sleep, blissfully unaware of the dramas which were developing at sea to the north and south of the Falkland Islands.

I had a rather rude awakening late in the morning of Sunday, 2 May. I was deep in sleep when at midday I awoke with a jolt as a result of a naval officer accidentally kicking the end of my camp bed whilst he rather clumsily made his way to the bar. As I struggled my way to the top of the sleeping bag and managed to extricate myself and sit up, I was greeted by the sight of a very sheepish-looking Lieutenant Commander, who said, 'Terribly sorry, 'Royal', can I buy you a beer?' Not wishing to appear in any way ungracious or churlish, and recognizing that I would not be flying for another twelve hours, I duly accepted his kind offer and sat in bed enjoying a pint of lager. This gave cause for much merriment amongst the officers who were in the wardroom at the time, with several of them offering to change places with me. Having enjoyed over eight hours sleep and a pint, I struggled out of my sleeping bag and went to my cabin to get ready for lunch and the day's activities.

As I ate lunch, the wardroom dining room was abuzz with rumours of the entire Argentine fleet being at sea and split either side of the islands. There was talk of the ASW operation during the early hours by the ASW Sea Kings of 826 Squadron searching for an Argentine submarine close to the north-east of East Falkland. Their three aircraft had dropped several depth charges and torpedoes, but it was never established whether or not they had been prosecuting a submarine or had been the first British subjects to be in contravention of the international whaling convention. Their operations had been supported by the escorts HMS *Brilliant* and HMS *Yarmouth* throughout the hours of darkness, only breaking off their support in order to rejoin the Task Force at around daybreak. I was curious as to how the Sea Kings managed to refuel from ships that had flight decks too small to accommodate such a large helicopter – I was to find out for myself just a week later. For now there was more exciting news to digest. One of the Sea Kings had detected a surface contact in the early hours of the morning and, as it closed to investigate the contact, the helicopter was fired upon by a small Argentine Patrol Vessel, the ARA *Alferez Sobral*, which, as we discovered later, had been searching for the crew of a Canberra which had been shot down by a 801 Squadron Harrier earlier in the day. The Sea King crew requested support and, in due course, two Lynx helicopters from HMS *Coventry* and HMS *Glasgow* attacked the vessel with Sea Skua missiles, badly damaging her. Hmm, I thought, an awful lot of activity in the area at around the time that I had been flying not too far away. I considered myself fortunate that my aircraft had not been detected by the patrol boat – or perhaps it had been, but was out of range. The RWR had certainly not detected any radar transmissions, so maybe it was simply a matter of timing.

Later in the afternoon I went to 03 Deck for a breath of refreshing, cold, South Atlantic air. The sea was calm, there was no wind and the sky was grey and overcast. Two Harriers were about to launch on CAP, otherwise there was an air of calm about the flight deck. Nothing here for me I decided, so I went below to the briefing room to start planning that night's insertion of Special Forces. Several of the Harrier pilots were also in the room and there was much discussion about the emerging threat at sea. A Harrier from *Invincible* had detected several surface contacts at about 200 miles to the north-west much earlier in the day, which had been interpreted by Admiral Woodward's staff as the Argentine Carrier Battle Group. Reports had also been received from the submarine HMS *Conqueror*, to the south-west of the islands, that the Argentine cruiser, ARA *General Belgrano*, was moving slowly to the east, whilst remaining just outside the TEZ. The Task Force was presented with an enemy force of considerable firepower, approaching from either side in a pincer movement. That will put pay to our operations tonight, I thought. *Hermes* could not possibly move closer to the islands to launch our aircraft with this developing threat just over the horizon. How would this situation unfold, we all wondered. Admiral Woodward let it be known later that he had anticipated an attack at around dawn, 0700hrs local time, but it never materialized. Thank God for that, I thought at the time – I was asleep then and would have hated to have missed the action!

During the afternoon, Harriers from *Hermes* and *Invincible* conducted searches to the north of the islands in an attempt to confirm the position of the Carrier Battle Group, but to no avail. The contacts of earlier in the day were no longer in the area. As darkness descended on the ships of the Task Force, I was in the briefing room making final preparations for the Special Forces insertion, together with several of the Harrier pilots who were similarly engaged in planning. At about 2000hrs, John Locke announced to those present that the *General Belgrano* had been sunk to the south of the islands. The announcement was greeted initially by a few seconds of stunned silence, followed by the loudest cheer I think that I had ever heard in such a confined space. The walls of the briefing room displayed pictures of various Argentine ships and aircraft. On hearing the announcement, Dave Morgan casually strolled to the photograph of the *Belgrano* and drew a cross through it with a red chinagraph pencil: two down, several more to go.

There were only two Special Forces teams to be inserted, so the crews of the other two aircraft were stood down. Launch time for insertion was set for 2230hrs, three hours before the moon set. At 2200hrs, Pete, 'Doc' and I manned the aircraft in readiness for launch. As I sat in the cockpit punching numbers into TANS, it occurred to me that with the sinking of the *Belgrano*, the Argentine Navy could, at this very moment, be conducting SAR and ASW type activities close to the islands. The ship had been sunk well to the south and west of the islands, and we would be flying to make a landfall to the north-east, so hopefully our activities would not conflict. At midnight 'Flyco' delivered the navigation data and we launched into the darkness, heading south-west from our position 120 nautical miles to the north-east of East Falkland. There was discernibly more tension in the aircraft that night than there had been during the previous two nights. With sea transits of well over an hour in length each way, there is little to do other than keep a good lookout, check navigation, fly accurately and talk about whatever enters one's head – normally a series of witty anecdotes about the day's events and minor mishaps. But tonight was different and there was no chit-chat, the focus being very much on the task in hand, together with thoughts of Argentinean sailors fighting for survival in the freezing cold waters of the South Atlantic, and the possibility of our detection either on the way in or back. Pete handed control to me for the rest of the transit until we reached landfall, this time on the coast, due north of Port Salvador. At this point I handed control back to Pete, fixed our position in TANS and we set heading south-west towards our chosen landing site across Falkland Sound to a position south of Port Howard.

We descended to 20 feet and dropped into the valley due south of Bombilla Hill. The terrain was open, low lying and barren with few landmarks close by for navigation. Instead I had to focus on more distant, high-terrain features which were clearly visible through the goggles on this light night, to confirm our navigation. After fifteen minutes we were flying south-west over the mouth of Brenton Lock, well away from the settlement of Darwin, and so low at this point that the aircraft was almost touching the water. Having flown over the southern bank of the loch, we followed a track parallel with the coast as we continued our route south-west towards a position on the coast due east of Fox Bay. The route across Lafonia was more undulating than the previous leg, so it was necessary to hug the contours to ensure that we remained below the skyline with the aircraft rising and falling like a big-dipper ride. From time to time I glanced outside the aircraft from underneath the goggles; it was still reassuringly pitch black. As we flew over the west coast of East Falkland, I updated our position in TANS. We headed due west to a position 20 miles north-east of Fox Bay, well out of sight of the settlement, skimming the tops of the low waves as we flew at 120 knots to cover the water gap as quickly as possible. Having arrived at the coastline of West Falkland, we turned north-east flying a route parallel with the coast towards our final destination, a position 15 miles south-west of Port Howard. Another uncomfortable roller-coaster of a leg. After just over thirty minutes of flying over the islands, Pete brought the aircraft to a hover and I talked him down for our fifth landing on the islands in only three nights of operations. As soon as the wheels were on the ground, the SAS patrol shot out of the aircraft like greased lightning and huddled in a clump by the wheels. Without further delay, we transitioned into forward flight turning 180° and set heading to retrace our route.

The journey back to the ship was uneventful, with no sign of enemy on the ground or at sea. I flew the aircraft most of the way on the return route and managed the navigation giving Pete a well-earned rest after the rigours associated with flying for a long time at such a low level. After about 50 miles transit over the sea, the welcome sight of *Hermes* came into view. Twenty-five minutes later, at 0130hrs, we were moving sideways over the deck and landing after a sortie lasting three hours, our longest yet. The aircraft was signed in and we made our way to the briefing room for the usual debrief by Bill and Richard. Immediately on entering the room Bill was quick to question whether or not we had made any contact with the enemy because one of the ASW Sea Kings on the screen had been fired upon by a surface vessel at around the time that we were flying on our return leg over the sea. Assuring him that we had made no contact, Bill left the briefing room to go to the ship's operations room to find out what was going on in the vicinity of where our aircraft had been just thirty minutes earlier.

With that, Pete, 'Doc' and I adjourned to the ACRB. After a few minutes, Bill returned with a look of satisfaction and an unusually broad grin, to report that two Lynx from HMS *Coventry* and HMS *Glasgow* had followed up the Sea King's report of a surface contact and had engaged an Argentine Patrol Boat with Sea Skua missiles, apparently sinking it. The news was greeted with yet another rousing cheer. Is this how we are supposed to react? I asked myself. The response to such news was probably quite normal and healthy, but it felt somehow inappropriate. Another ship for Dave to put a red cross through in due course. Rather than feeling euphoric, I went to the wardroom with mixed feelings – on the one hand the Task Force was undoubtedly experiencing a period of success, on the other hand, so many Argentine dead, each of them a mother's son. My feelings of doubt and melancholy were brought to an abrupt halt on entering the wardroom to the sound of snoring, coughing and flatulence. This is iniquitous, I thought, there must be a better solution to the sleeping arrangements than this. Later in the day I would make it my business to find alternative accommodation, but for now the sandman beckoned. It was with a feeling of satisfaction that I settled into my sleeping bag, realizing that during the last three nights the Squadron had managed to insert into the islands a total of fifteen Special Forces teams, without significant incident.

I awoke later that morning in time for an early lunch. *Hermes* was an old ship and therefore had scuttles, often incorrectly referred to as portholes by ignorant landlubbers. Looking out of one of the wardroom scuttles I could see that the ship was in thick fog, but unusually for foggy conditions, there was also something of a swell. After lunch I went to the briefing room where I bumped into Nigel.

'This weather's set for the day, so I don't think that we'll be doing any flying tonight,' he said, clearly disappointed. I shared Nigel's disappointment. There were more Special Forces patrols to be inserted and it was, therefore, frustrating that we would not be able to do our job that night. This lucky break gave me the opportunity that I was desperately looking for to start searching the ship for alternative sleeping arrangements. Over the next couple of hours I searched high and low, but to no avail. I was back in the area of my camp bed around teatime, when I was approached by an unusually cheerful looking 'Stumpy' Middleton.

'I think I've found us somewhere else to sleep,' he said very quietly, gesturing with his head that I should follow him out of the wardroom. He led the way aft to a door in the port after quarter of the ship.

'Look in here,' he said. I opened the door and looked with amazement into a large compartment that was obviously a cabin. There was a bed made up with pristine clean sheets, comfortable chairs, a coffee table and a writing bureau. Through a connecting door was a bathroom. The two rooms were airy, air-conditioned and quiet; we had stumbled upon the Captain's day cabin. Since the ship had moved to Defence Watches, the Captain had moved to occupy his sea cabin, a small compartment near the bridge and operations room from where he was better able to command. The day cabin was, therefore, empty and likely to remain so for the foreseeable future.

'Dare we?' I said. It was a rhetorical question for I had already made up my mind that this was to be my home for as long as I could get away with it. Without further ado, 'Stumpy' and I returned to the wardroom to collect our kit.

It was now early evening and the wardroom was quickly filling with officers taking advantage of the bad weather and hell bent on having a beer or two before dinner.

'We'll have to wait until this place quietens down, otherwise some folk will be wondering what we're up to and will follow us to see what's going on.'

'Agreed,' replied 'Stumpy'. 'There's room for more than just us two,' he added.

'Yes, but whoever we invite to go with us can't be snorers, agreed?'

'Definitely.' We then set about drawing up a short list of who would be in, who would be out. Definitely no 'Pingers', we agreed. 'Pinger' was the name by which ASW aircrew were known by the 'Junglie' fraternity, on account of the characteristic pinging sound made by the ASW Sea King's sonar. It was not that we didn't like 'Pingers', but we considered that their routine of 'rippling' aircraft on the screen twenty-four hours a day, with aircrew getting up and going to bed at all hours, would be incompatible with our working pattern. Finally we decided to take Paul Humphreys and Bob Horton, Dave Morgan and two other Harrier pilots into our confidence and share our little secret. Six would be an ideal number to occupy our new luxury accommodation. The die was cast. 'Stumpy' and I would move in late the next morning when the wardroom was normally at its quietest, thereby arousing the least curiosity and suspicion.

In the midst of what to some must seem to be frivolity, I was brought back to the reality of operations with a bump. We received news that one of the SAS patrols in the vicinity of Berkley Sound, just north of Stanley, had been surrounded by Argentine forces and had requested Harrier air support to strafe the Argentine positions closest to them. The request presented a problem to Admiral Woodward and his staff because to launch such an attack in the dense fog that was now engulfing the ship would have put the Harriers at considerable risk. In the end it was decided that the balance of the quantum of risk to the SAS patrol, versus the potential sacrifice to the Task Force in terms of the potential loss of two Harriers and their pilots, militated against providing air support. This was my first taste of the harsh realities of war-fighting decision making. It left me wondering how the Admiral managed ever to get a good night's sleep with such decisions on his conscience. I settled into my sleeping bag that night with mixed feelings. On the one hand I was feeling a sense of relief and smug satisfaction that I had resolved my future sleeping arrangements; on the other hand, at that very moment in time, there was a SAS patrol living in a squalid little hole in the ground, in atrocious weather conditions, within spitting distance of the enemy and in fear for their lives – and I was concerned about my sleeping arrangements. A rapidly developing sense of perspective swept over me as I drifted off to sleep.

It is said by many that ignorance is bliss and this was to prove an apposite description of my forthcoming domestic arrangements. From the following day, I and my friends were to enjoy many days and nights of uninterrupted sleep in the most comfortable, luxurious, peaceful, airy, spacious and air-conditioned accommodation in the ship. A few days later we were joined by Dave Morgan and another couple of Harrier pilots. It was not until some months later, after the war had ended, and when back at Yeovilton, that I was to discover that my new sleeping arrangements offered the potential of being killed. John Locke left *Hermes* shortly after the ship's return to UK and was appointed as the Commander of RNAS Yeovilton. In the wardroom bar one evening I recounted to John the events leading up to my decision to move from the wardroom into the Captain's day cabin. After I had finished regaling him with my tale of initiative and derring-do, he looked at me intently and announced, 'You and your friends were prats!'

I was lost for words as the wind was taken from my sails and my ego destroyed by those six simple words. 'Please explain,' I asked.

John then went on to describe the procedure enacted on each occasion that the ship was threatened with a potential attack, particularly on those that an attack by Exocet was assumed. *Hermes* would turn away from the direction of attack, deploy chaff and present the port after quarter to the direction of attack because this was the one part of the ship which, if hit, would sustain the least amount of critical damage. Therefore, for several days in my case and several weeks in the case of my friends, we had been sleeping in the most dangerous place on the biggest target in the South Atlantic, blissfully unaware of the danger that threatened our lives on an almost daily basis. But that night, as I settled deep into my sleeping bag, my thoughts were of the better domestic arrangements that lay ahead.

CHAPTER 6

HMS *Sheffield*, A Shattering Blow

Be not ashamed of mistakes and thus make them crimes.

Confucius

In the early hours of Tuesday, 4 May there was a second attack on Stanley airfield by a Vulcan based on Ascension. As for the first attack, the Harriers of 801 Squadron provided CAP cover in the unlikely event that Argentine fighters might attempt to interdict the Vulcan. After a journey of 3,500 miles, the Vulcan dropped its load of twenty-one bombs from 12,000 feet. All bombs missed their target and impacted harmlessly to the west of the runway. Why harmlessly? Because someone on the Vulcan had failed to arm the bombs before their release. The calculation by the Harrier pilots was that 137,000 gallons of aviation fuel had been wasted by the combination of the Vulcan and its supporting Victor tankers – enough fuel for the Harriers to have been able to mount 260 sorties into the islands delivering 1,300 bombs. It was a lamentable waste of fuel, ordnance and assets after the many hours of planning, preparation, teamwork and skilful flying to get the aircraft to its target.

After the fog of the previous twenty-four hours, the day dawned with a clear blue sky, a calm sea and a light breeze. Ideal conditions for flying and, therefore, ideal conditions for the Argentine Navy and Air Force to continue their attacks on the ships of the Task Force, now without its protective blanket of fog. I was up and about in time for breakfast and to ensure that, as the wardroom emptied of officers, I was ready to take up my bed at short notice and move to my new quarters without any prying eyes watching my every move. By mid-morning I was firmly ensconced in my new quarters. Having laid out my sleeping bag on the Captain's bed, I made my way to the briefing room to check on the day's flying programme. There were no Special Forces insertions planned for the coming night and no day flying tasks planned, so at this time I had a fairly quiet day in prospect – or so I thought.

It was at around 1100hrs when I bumped into Bill in one of the passageways.

'Get your kit on, *Sheffield* has been hit. I've authorized you for a SAR sortie with 'Wiggy'. Get airborne ASAP.' I did not need to be told twice. Within five minutes, 'Wiggy' and I were manning the aircraft and within another five minutes we were ready to launch. For this sortie, 'Wiggy' was co-pilot and navigator. As he was setting up TANS he asked 'Flyco' for a position for HMS *Sheffield*.

'You don't need one', came the reply, 'as soon as you launch head to the south-west, you'll see the smoke on the horizon.' Just before I was about to lift the aircraft into the hover, several sets of fire-fighting equipment and breathing apparatus were hurriedly loaded into the back of the aircraft. Without further delay I lifted the aircraft into the hover, transitioned across the deck and turned towards the south-west. When the aircraft was steady on heading, we could see the smoke on the distant horizon and closed the gap at best possible speed, wondering just what lay ahead. As the distance to the ship closed, I could start to make out the shapes of ships and other helicopters in the vicinity.

We were soon upon HMS *Sheffield* and the sight that greeted us was awesome in many respects. The ship was dead in the water with smoke pouring out from a large hole above the waterline, roughly amidships. The area around the bows and stern appeared undamaged. Alongside on her starboard side was HMS *Yarmouth*. I could see sailors of all rates making their way from various parts of the ship onto her weather deck, from where they scrambled over the ship's side onto the weather deck of *Yarmouth* where they were given a helping hand by the ship's crew. A short distance off *Sheffield's* port side was HMS *Arrow*, a Type 21 frigate. *Arrow* was playing her fire hoses onto *Sheffield's* burning hull. I called *Sheffield* and told them that I had fire-fighting equipment for her.

'Lower it onto the forecastle,' came the reply. I manoeuvred the aircraft over the bows and, once in a steady hover, 'Doc' lowered the equipment down to the deck on the winch. After four loads were delivered *Sheffield* advised that we remain well clear because the fire was moving towards her Sea Dart magazine.

With no immediate task, I decided to fly a sweep of the area within half a mile of the ship just in case there were any survivors in the water. The search bore no fruit, so it was a safe assumption that all 'hands' were either still on board *Sheffield* or making their way onto *Yarmouth*. As we scoured the area the extent of activity became apparent. There were several ASW Sea Kings with their dipping sonars in the water and Lynx helicopters from the nearby escorts engaged in ASW operations. At one stage I saw the unmistakable shape of a Mk 46 torpedo skimming through the water. Hmm, another poor unfortunate whale about to get a pounding, I thought, but better to be safe than sorry. Although the cause of the damage to *Sheffield* was obviously from a missile attack and not a torpedo – it gave the 'Pingers' some practice. The eeriest sight of all was of a Gemini inflatable boat, which I assumed had come from *Sheffield*, with no persons on board, cruising in a circle of about 10 metres radius. Round and round it went as if it had a ghost at the helm – something of a *Marie Celeste* moment. I considered recovering it to *Hermes* as an underslung load, but to what purpose? The idea was quickly abandoned.

After very nearly one hour and thirty minutes flying in the vicinity of *Sheffield*, watching crew members scrambling over the ship's sides onto *Yarmouth* and *Arrow*, which by now had joined *Yarmouth* immediately alongside, *Sheffield* released my aircraft and I flew back to *Hermes*, with the image of a burning warship foremost in my mind. Having signed the aircraft back in, I went to the briefing room in which a number of aircrew from both squadrons had already embarked on a post-mortem of the *Sheffield* attack.

The attack which damaged *Sheffield* was an extremely skilful and well-planned operation which found the weak spot in the Task Force's defences. The Super Etendards had flown low and thus avoided early detection. About twenty-five minutes after *Sheffield* was hit, a third Exocet was reported being fired at the Task Force. *Yarmouth* reported sighting this missile and fired her Corvus chaff rockets, apparently deflecting the missile – spotters aboard HMS *Alacrity* thought they saw the missile fall into the sea. After the war it was discovered that the Argentine pilots had sighted two contacts on their radars, one large and one small and had fired two Exocets at these targets. These echoes were presumably *Sheffield* and *Hermes*. In the final analysis all warships have to be expendable and the escorts are more expendable than most. *Sheffield*'s primary task that day was to protect the two carriers and if her eventual sinking kept the flagship out of harm's way then she had achieved that purpose. The attack was also a sobering, expensive and timely reminder of the risk posed to the amphibious landings, just two weeks hence. An assumed relative immunity to Exocet attack was a major factor in the choice of San Carlos as the main landing site.

Five hours after the attack on *Sheffield*, Captain 'Sam' Salt gave the order for the remaining crew to abandon ship. Word of this quickly swept through *Hermes*. The mood on board was serious and sombre. We were shocked into a realization that we were engaged in full-scale war and that we were certainly not invincible. As the afternoon turned into night, more details of the attack on *Sheffield* emerged. That morning, she had relieved her sister ship, HMS *Coventry*, from defence watch. The first anyone knew that something had happened to *Sheffield* was when *Coventry* received the message 'Sheffield is hit.' *Arrow* and *Yarmouth* were ordered to investigate. It was only when *Sheffield*'s Lynx helicopter unexpectedly landed on the deck of *Hermes* that any specific information was gathered. The Lynx carried *Sheffield*'s Operations Officer and Air Operations Officer. They confirmed that a missile had hit the ship.

Sheffield was fitted with the Type 965 radar system, an old system that was due to be upgraded to the Type 1022 system. As with so many ships in the Royal Navy, *Sheffield* had been designed with the cold war very much in mind. The 965 radar was capable of picking up aircraft flying at reasonable altitude and missiles launched from a reasonable height, neither of which happened with

. HMS *Hermes* ready for 'Procedure Alpha'. *(David Morgan)*

. HMS *Hermes* departs Portsmouth on 5 April. *(Peter Imrie)*

3. 'Huffers and Puffers' on HMS *Hermes*. (*David Balchin*

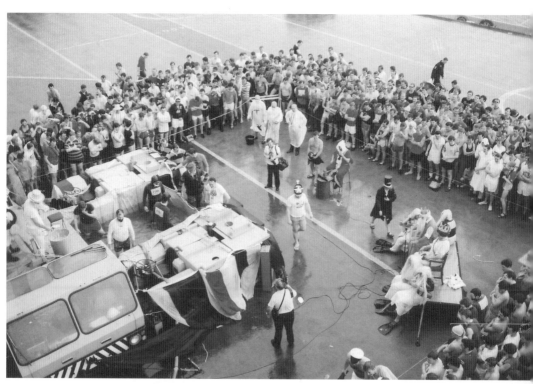

4. King Neptune's visit to HMS *Hermes*. (*David Balchin*

Wideawake Airfield, Ascension Island. *(Richard Hutchings)*

Preparations for Vertrep Wideawake. *(David Balchin)*

7. Vertrep Operations Wideawake. (*David Balchin*

8. HMS *Hermes* off Ascension Island. (*Richard Hutchings*

ANVIS Night Vision Goggles. (*Richard Hutchings*)

). The view through Night Vision Goggles. (*Richard Hutchings*)

11. HMS *Sheffield* Exocet strike. (*Peter Imrie*

12. HMS *Sheffield* ablaze. (*Peter Imrie*

3. Runway at Port Stanley showing little damage. (*David Balchin*)

4. The author flying a Sea King. (*Richard Hutchings*)

15. 'Victor Charlie'. *(Richard Hutchings*

16. Tierra del Fuego. *(Richard Hutchings*

7. Area close to the SAS drop-off. *(Richard Hutchings)*

18. Perimeter of Rio Grande Airbase. *(Richard Hutchings)*

19. AN/TPS 43 Radar.
(*Richard Hutchings*)

20. Sierra de Carmen
Whistles.
(*Richard Hutchings*)

1. Looking south from the hill at Punta Arenas. (*Richard Hutchings*)

2. 'Victor Charlie' wreckage at Agua Fresca. (*Richard Hutchings*)

23. 'Victor Charlie' burial of wreckage. (*Richard Hutchings*)

24. The lucky Sea Eagle. (*Richard Hutchings*)

5. The crew with Captain Marcos Torres. (*Marcos Torres*)

6. Crew with Lieutenant Colonel Haroldo Carrasco and Lieutenant Cesar Moran. (*Marcos Torres*)

27. The press conference, Santiago.   (*Richard Hutchings*)

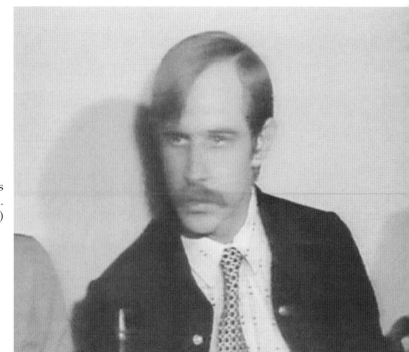

28. The statement is
      delivered.
(*Richard Hutchings*)

29. Safe house near Santiago Airport. (*Richard Hutchings*)

). 846 Squadron's arrival at Yeovilton.   (*David Balchin*)

31. The investiture.
(*Press Association*)

32. Souvenir from
'Victor Charlie'.
(*Richard Hutchings*)

Sheffield. The Exocet missile that hit her had been fired from a Super Etendard, the pilot launching it when only 6 miles from *Sheffield* – to all intents and purposes, this represented point-blank range. The rule of thumb was that an Exocet would be launched at a ship from 45 miles away and from a reasonable height, which a 965 radar would pick up. But this Exocet was launched and flew just above sea level and was not picked up by radar until it was too late to react. The Sea Dart missile system was also generally not overly good at picking up sea-skimming missiles. The crew had just five seconds warning that a missile was incoming. The Exocet caused great damage to *Sheffield*, hitting 8 feet above the water line and tearing a gash in the ship that measured 4 feet by 10 feet. The missile's burning rocket motor set fire to the ship and sufficiently damaged her electricity generating systems to prevent anti-fire mechanisms from working effectively; her water main had also been ruptured. The combination of lack of electricity and water meant that there was no way that the fires could be contained. A process of evacuation was initiated with the burns casualties being taken off first. In the immediate aftermath of the attack, there was little chance of the ship sinking so the crew who were not injured simply had to wait their turn on deck to be rescued. The injured had been evacuated in ASW Sea Kings from the screen, thus there were no members of the crew to be taken off in my aircraft.

In the briefing room the atmosphere was decidedly gloomy. Late in the morning three Harriers had carried out a raid on Goose Green; tragically only two returned. One of the Harriers, flown by Nick Taylor, had been shot down by Argentine anti-aircraft artillery fire. One of the surviving pilots, Gordie Batt, described what happened during the raid. As he was leading the raid and approaching the airstrip, his RWR detected that an Argentine radar had locked on to his aircraft, so he immediately turned away from the direction of attack and deployed chaff. At this point the radar locked on to Nick's aircraft which had been immediately behind the lead aircraft. His Harrier was hit by a 35mm high-explosive round which caused a large explosion immediately behind the cockpit. There is a kindred spirit amongst aircrew, regardless of aircraft type flown or squadron. That day we all shared in the grief of 800 Squadron. Later we were to learn that the Argentine forces at Goose Green had recovered Nick's body and accorded him a funeral with full military honours. A few weeks later, for reasons that will become apparent later in this book, I was the first member of the Task Force to return to Yeovilton. I had been back only a day when Nick's widow, Claire, came to see me. That conversation with Claire was one of the most difficult moments in my life – what does one say to a recently bereaved widow? Obviously devastated by the news of his loss, Claire and I were to talk about Nick, the type of missions that he had been flying and what life had been like on the ship during the war. I was able to tell her that Nick had been a popular and respected pilot, and always a cheerful member of the crew room.

At the end, he had been shown respect by the Argentine forces and accorded a military funeral with full honours.

There was a wake for Nick in the wardroom that evening in *Hermes*. The Royal Navy has a tradition whereby, when an officer is killed in combat, the wardroom mess members honour him and drink to his memory by using his mess number until the end of the night. The deceased officer's mess bill is then written off. Our thoughts that evening were very much of Nick and the poor souls who were killed or injured in *Sheffield*. Later that night, a decision was taken that, in due course, *Sheffield* would be towed away from the Task Force to South Georgia. There was a realization that the proximity of so many ships that were assisting *Sheffield* might be too tempting a target for the Argentine Air Force. But for now, out on the distant horizon, abandoned by her crew and in total darkness, except for the light of her fires, *Sheffield* cast a lonely and tragic figure as what little life and spirit that remained were slowly and surely extinguished whilst she continued to burn from stem to stern. There was pretty much a consensus in the wardroom that the day had been one of errors and miscalculation. Harriers from both ships had been tasked on a series of pointless surface searches; the Harrier attack on the airstrip at Goose Green had served little purpose because there were no targets there of any significance; and perhaps worst of all, *Sheffield* had been unnecessarily exposed to a threat by redeploying the Harrier CAP from a station in the vicinity of her to look for spurious surface contacts elsewhere. Lessons had to be learnt if the Task Force was to survive long enough to sustain the land operations which were still two weeks away. The events of the day resulted in *Hermes* being too far to the north-east of the Falkland Islands to contemplate any Special Forces insertions, which were therefore postponed until the following night.

The following morning there was something of a subdued atmosphere in the ship. With thoughts of *Sheffield* and Nick still foremost in our minds, we had to regain our focus and press on. There were lessons to be identified and learnt from both the *Sheffield* attack and Nick's death. It transpired that Nick had been flying without the benefit of a RWR in his aircraft because it had been removed some weeks earlier when the aircraft was being used for trials of the new Sea Eagle anti-ship missile installation. Following the trial, the RWR had not been refitted, so Nick had been flying without any ESM capability in his aircraft. His loss was, therefore, quite easily explained, although the decision to attack Goose Green in the first place was undoubtedly based on tenuous assumptions. *Sheffield*'s loss, on the other hand, was to prove a somewhat more complex issue to analyse. One of the procedures instituted as a result of the Exocet attack on her was that, in future, when an attack was suspected, chaff rockets would be fired by all ships at risk. A pattern of manoeuvres was to become the norm. When radar contact had been made with a suspected Argentine aircraft or missile, the ship would first go to action stations. A minute or so later John

Locke would inform us of the nature of the threat, typically something along the lines of: 'Radar contact 230 degrees, 30 miles, possible low-level aircraft.' At the appropriate juncture, the ship would turn sharply to present the port after quarter to the threat and a few seconds later the distinctive sound of the chaff rockets being fired would reverberate throughout the ship. The only occasions when I did not hear any of this was when soundly asleep during the day in the Captain's day cabin and unable to hear any of the ship's pipes – on occasions ignorance was bliss!

The weather on 5 May was a change from the previous day. Gone was the clear blue sky and good visibility, and in their place were low-level stratus and patches of fog. The go, no/go decision on Special Forces insertions planned for the Squadron would have to be made later in the day because *Hermes* was still a long way to the north-east of the Falkland Islands and the weather was marginal. The Harriers continued their round-the-clock CAP sorties to the west of the Task Force even though the two carriers were well outside the range of any fighters based on the mainland. I had considerable sympathy for the Harrier pilots because it was nigh on impossible for them to get a decent amount of sleep. If they were not on CAP, then it was Alert 5. *Invincible*'s Harriers seemed to get the lion's share of the night CAP and deck alerts which seemed odd to me given that *Hermes* had by far the largest Air Group and most pilots.

By last light the weather had improved slightly and *Hermes* was in a position 120 nautical miles east of Lively Island. Special Forces insertions were back on, with a launch time set for midnight. Pete, 'Doc' and I were stood down as it was a single aircraft task to extract two SBS teams from Nigel and 'Wiggy's' sector. Colin Tattersall was stood down and his place taken by Chief Petty Officer Aircrewman Wally Hammond. Bill decided that Bob Grundy and 'Stumpy' should fly a second aircraft as a training sortie because neither pilot had flown on NVG for several days. At midnight the two aircraft departed *Hermes*, and disappeared into darkness and decreasing visibility. The aircraft had not been airborne long before they became separated in fog. Constrained by the fog, Bob and 'Stumpy' returned to *Hermes*. Nigel and 'Wiggy' pressed ahead with their sortie, encountering a mix of dense fog interspersed with clear areas of brilliant moonlight. The navigation features were obscured by fog resulting in a great deal of 'hot' planning and several route changes. After two hours of high workload flying, some of it at walking pace, and equally high workload navigation, including flying close by Mount Brisbane, which unbeknown to the crew at the time had an Argentinean OP on it, Nigel manoeuvred his aircraft to the pick-up point for the first SBS team. On landing the crew was surprised to find only two marines of the original four-man team. As a result of an encounter with an Argentinean patrol, the SBS team had become split, with two of the marines unaccounted for. With the two men safely in the aircraft, Nigel then flew to the second location where he took the team of four by surprise, still lying in their sleeping bags. With six SBS personnel recovered, Nigel started the long journey back to *Hermes*, the fog necessitating several navigation changes en route. Finally, after nearly four hours, thirty minutes of exhausting flying, the aircraft landed on *Hermes*. With just one hour, thirty minutes remaining until dawn, the ship wasted no time in making best possible speed to return to the relative safety of the remaining ships of the Task Force, many miles further to the north-east. But as we headed north-east a question remained: where were the two missing SBS marines?

Later in the morning the weather had worsened with *Hermes* engulfed by thick fog on an almost mirror-calm sea, which ruled out flying for a while. With three nights without flying, I was in danger of mutating into a normal diurnal human being. I was longing for the return of good weather so that once again I could resume my nocturnal activities over the islands, but I was going to have to be patient a while longer. Later in the morning the weather improved enough for the Harriers to resume their CAP programme. The air temperature was only just above freezing so visits to 03 Deck to have a look at what was going on were becoming an infrequent activity, however, I decided to venture out because, quite frankly, I had nothing else to do. I arrived on 03 Deck just in time to see a Harrier emerging from the cloud at a height of about 100 feet. I watched as the pilot skilfully brought the aircraft to a hover alongside the ship, slid to the right and landed amidships. After the aircraft had taxied to its spot and shut down I watched as the pilot, Dave Morgan, walked slowly back towards the Island. I caught his eye and waved. Dave's response was to wipe his brow with a gesture of great relief and then smile broadly. I sensed that he was mightily relieved to be back on deck after what must have been a very hairy approach through the low cloud.

As I was eating lunch in the wardroom, a nasty rumour started to spread rapidly that two Harriers from *Invincible* were overdue, assumed lost. As the afternoon wore on, details started to emerge about the lost aircraft. They had been on two separate CAP missions to the west and south-west of the carriers at medium level and above the tops of the clouds. *Invincible* directed the northern of the CAPs, flown by Lieutenant Al Curtis, to investigate a surface radar contact towards the west by descending into the cloud, and it was never seen again. At about the same time, one of the two Harriers on the other CAP, about 10 miles further to the south, flown by John Eyton-Jones, also descended into the cloud and was never seen again. The two Harriers were on converging headings, one heading west and the other north-west. It was reasonable to assume that, given that their focus was on attempting to locate the surface contact, they were neither in radar nor visual contact with each other and collided in mid-air. What a tragic loss, I thought. To die fighting for one's country is an understandable sacrifice that many were prepared to make, but to die as a result of an accident when chasing shadows, was a lamentable waste.

Later that night I returned to my cabin on 5 Deck to write a letter to Lorraine.

As I did so, I reflected on events of the past six days, from the euphoria of the golden fingers of dawn of the first two days, through its metamorphosis into the despondent mood, sense of loss and dark tempest of the last two days. Two Harriers lost through an accident, one shot down because it did not have a RWR fitted, and one ship lost because of a combination of unfortunate circumstances, none of which were engineered by the enemy. It seemed to me that we were doing the enemy's job for them!

Saturday, 7 May was a particularly tiring day for me. I was programmed to fly an HDS sortie with Bill. The weather was the worst yet for flying. The Task Force was sitting on the eastern edge of the TEZ in dense fog, conditions in which the Harriers were unable to fly. If we had been participating in an exercise in peacetime, helicopters would also have been grounded, but this was war. In these appalling weather conditions, ASW helicopter operations on the screen continued unabated and I would be able to fly the HDS sortie. The weather forecast was for the fog to persist into the hours of darkness, therefore, helicopter insertion of Special Forces was off the menu for tonight. Bill and I were programmed to fly from mid-morning until the task was completed. The HDS task ordinarily involves flying around as many ships of the Task Force as necessary, picking up and dropping of documents, small items of stores and moving people between ships for command meetings, etc. Bill and I set off on what was to prove an HDS sortie of epic proportions. The Sea King IV is not fitted with radar, so navigation in fog is achieved by a combination of TANS, dead reckoning and SCAs.

At 1100hrs we were airborne with me at the controls and Bill concentrating on the navigation. As we disappeared into the fog, it occurred to me that at this very moment the ships of the amphibious force were departing Ascension on their way to the TEZ.

'I bet that they're not hacking their way through dense fog,' I remarked to Bill.

'They'll get their fair share and start earning their pay in due course,' he said with a wry smile. Flying over the sea in dense fog for protracted periods is quite unnerving. In aircraft equipped with radar it is possible to locate solid objects which may be lying in the aircraft's path, but without radar, one is effectively flying blind. Such flying, at very low level, requires considerable concentration and is extremely tiring. An hour later we made radio contact with our first ship, a RFA which was in company with other RFAs. I manoeuvred the aircraft for a SCA and at half a mile astern of the ship I picked up the wake. At 100 metres, the RFA suddenly loomed large out of the fog, a welcome sight indeed.

An hour later we were back amongst the ships of the Task Force and had business with three of them. I was impressed with the performance of TANS. There had been no opportunity to update TANS over a fixed point in over two hours, therefore a fair degree of drift was anticipated but, as it turned out, we were able to rejoin the force without the need for radar vectoring, other than to find the individual ships in turn. There then followed another two hours of flying around the ships of the Task Force before our HDS task was completed. It was four hours after first launching that I was to land the aircraft back on *Hermes* feeling totally drained. I was certainly ready for a caffeine infusion right away. The fog precluded the Special Forces extractions planned for the night. After a tiring day I was ready for an early night, but first a couple of beers were called for. Horror of all horrors, the ship was running out of beer! A lager and a 'horse's neck' later, I was in bed in the quiet comfort of the Captain's day cabin, and was asleep within five minutes.

CHAPTER 7

HMS *Yarmouth* – 'These Things Happen in War'

Experience is simply the name we give our mistakes.

Oscar Wilde

Dawn on 8 May arrived with little change in the weather, until a 'sucker's gap' arrived in the vicinity of HMS *Hermes* at around mid-morning. A 'sucker's gap' is what aviators call a brief improvement in weather conditions, usually fog and/or low cloud, considered sufficient to allow aircraft to fly. Why suckers? Simple: having launched the aircraft through the gap in the weather, it quickly closes behind, in effect trapping the aircraft above the cloud or fog and unable to make a safe recovery to the deck or ground. Through this gap the ship launched a Harrier on CAP to the west of the Task Force. I thought no more of it until after about an hour or so the weather deteriorated – the 'suckers-gap' had closed, as they invariably did, and the ship was once again smothered in dense fog with visibility no more than half the length of the flight deck. The ship had a Harrier to recover in these conditions and having decided that it would be too good an event to miss, I made my way rapidly to 03 Deck. When I arrived I was horrified to discover that I was in the fog and that there was little of the ship visible above the flight deck. It was going to be interesting and I wondered who the unlucky sod was who had to find his way back. I did not have long to wait to find out.

Unable to see anything from 03 Deck, I made my way to the briefing room to collect my flying helmet and went out onto the flight deck. I strolled along the starboard side of the deck, slowly pacing forwards and backwards, but with my focus very much towards the port side and rear of the ship in the expectation of seeing a Harrier in due course appear out of the fog, as if by magic, and land without incident. When wearing a flying helmet it is not possible to hear much, so you can imagine my shock when, as I was walking forward towards the bow along the starboard deck edge, I was stunned by the sight of a Harrier appearing out of the fog, to the starboard side of the bows, below the height of the ski-jump and pointing diagonally towards the port side of the ship. The aircraft then manoeuvred slowly to the port side of the ship, turned left through about 270° and came to a hover heading forward at deck height abeam the forward lift. Power was then applied and the aircraft climbed slowly above the height of the deck, moved to the right and landed rather heavily. Hmm, that was rather unconventional, who is that mad sod? I wondered. I made my way to the Island and saw that it was Dave Morgan. Appearing both exasperated and relieved he muttered something about effing ship and effing weather and stormed off to see 'Wings.'

An interesting morning, I thought, as I made my way to the wardroom for lunch. In my misplaced naivety, I assumed that no more aircraft would be flying for the rest of the day – how wrong I was to be. For it was just a few hours later when having tea, late in the afternoon, that I received the call to see Bill to be briefed for a sortie – what on earth can they want me for, I wondered, as I made my way to the briefing room, where I met up with Bill.

'The weather has improved. You're going flying. Take 'Wiggy' with you. You're off to find *Sheffield*.' I assumed that he meant the burnt-out hulk of a warship and not the city in Yorkshire.

'As soon as you're ready go to the ops room and see Captain Peter Woodhead, the Admiral's General Warfare Officer. He'll brief you.' After a few moments collecting my thoughts and my flying kit, I proceeded to the operations room with 'Wiggy' for a briefing. On entering the ops room I saw Peter Woodhead sitting at his workstation pondering a chart.

'Ah, the "Junglies",' he exclaimed. 'I have a task for you to take Captain Salt and his MEO back to *Sheffield*, or more precisely to *Yarmouth*, so that they can assess the extent of damage to *Sheffield*.' He went on to explain that *Yarmouth* had taken *Sheffield* in tow and was making towards South Georgia. Our task was to rendezvous with *Yarmouth*, winch 'Sam' Salt and his MEO onto her deck, and then return immediately to *Hermes*. It was only two hours before nightfall so I enquired as to whether or not we would require NVG.

'They won't be required,' was his response. 'The ship's not too far away, so you should be able to find her easily in daylight and make it back before it gets dark.'

Armed with *Yarmouth*'s last-known position and her intended course and speed, I made my way to the line office to sign for the aircraft, and then on to the flight deck. My passengers were waiting at the aircraft, dressed in their red-coloured, 'once-only', survival suits and lifejackets. 'Doc' gave our passengers a safety brief on the aircraft and all was set for what should have been a relatively simple task. Ten minutes later 'Wiggy' was fixing our position in TANS, I lifted the aircraft into the hover and transitioned into forward flight before turning onto a heading towards the south-west. The sea was relatively calm and visibility had improved to about 3kms – not, I was hoping, a 'suckers-gap'. My plan was simple: to fly to *Yarmouth*'s last-known position and then fly along her intended course until intercepting; as Peter Woodhead had briefed, it should have been a piece of cake. Flight time to *Yarmouth*'s last-reported position was approximately thirty minutes. I flew the aircraft at 50 feet because as we were moving towards the islands we were coming within range of the Argentine AN/TPS 43 surveillance radar believed to be at Stanley airfield. The radar had a range of over 250 nautical miles, but given the radar inter-visibility trace that we had, I knew that by remaining at 50 feet the aircraft would be well below the line-of-sight sweep of the radar beam.

Having overflown the last-reported position of *Yarmouth* and *Sheffield*, I turned the aircraft onto a south-easterly heading, and flew along *Yarmouth*'s intended course. As we moved further away from the islands I was able to climb the aircraft progressively to 3,000 feet to aid our search. Without the benefit of radar, with visibility no better than 5kms and in failing light, we were, to all intents and purposes, flying blind. Captain Salt was of the opinion that the two ships could not be very far from the last-reported position because, with *Sheffield* under tow, *Yarmouth* would have been making slow progress, assuming of course that the last-reported position was correct. I therefore continued the search along the reported MLA for several minutes but without sighting the ships. I called *Yarmouth* on many occasions, but received no reply. After forty-five minutes and in failing light, Captain Salt decided that we must have missed sighting the ships and passed them, so I made a 180° turn and flew on the reciprocal heading back to the start point and a few miles beyond, just in case the original reported position of the ships had been inaccurate, but to no avail.

It was now almost dark and without the benefit of NVG or a radar vector from *Yarmouth*, it was going to be impossible to locate the ships in darkness. The addition of either NVG or a radar would have made a decisive difference to the outcome of our task, because visibility permitting, it was possible to see the ships at night at distances of around 50 miles. Captain Salt agreed that it was pointless trying any further, so I decided to return my frustrated passengers to *Hermes*. By the time I was in a position to call the ship for a SCA, it was dark and visibility was reducing rapidly with the fog of earlier in the day making an unwelcome return. Having landed back on *Hermes* nearly three hours later, I apologized to my two passengers for failing to have delivered them to *Yarmouth*. They were both most gracious saying that it was not my fault and that the Admiral's staff should have known from the outset that a radar-equipped Sea King was essential for such a task. The Sea King IV was not then, and to this day is still not equipped for surface search tasks. I reported back to Peter Woodhead my failure to complete the task. I also pointed out that I had made several attempts to contact *Yarmouth* by radio, but without success.

At this point he said, 'Well, they would not respond to radio calls because the ship was maintaining radio silence.'

'You could have told me,' was my frustrated reply. To which he replied that these things happen in war and that I should put it down to experience. Most helpful, I thought. Had I known that *Yarmouth* was remaining 'tight-lipped' then I would have insisted on taking NVG with me and would probably have completed the task. I decided, thereafter, that with my life on the line every time that I got airborne from *Hermes*, to treat briefings by the command, including those delivered by aviators, with a healthy degree of scepticism. I made a check list of standard questions to ask after a briefing by anyone other than Bill. Today had been extremely frustrating due to the double-whammy of fog, both real and metaphoric, it had also been my introduction to the 'fog of war'. Fortunately for all concerned, no one was hurt and no damage was done. But the events of the day made it abundantly clear to me that the omission of a simple but germane piece of information had the potential for fatal consequences.

CHAPTER 8

The Narwal Incident

Sunday, 9 May was my birthday, but more importantly, was a rude awakening for the Argentine forces on Stanley Airfield. Throughout the night, HMS *Alacrity* pounded enemy positions on and around the airfield from her gun-line position to the east of Port Stanley. Over ninety shells were fired, having the effect of keeping the enemy awake and serving to reinforce Admiral Woodward's intention of trying to convince the Argentine commanders that Port Stanley was our main area of interest for an amphibious landing. Whether or not it was a convincing strategy was neither here nor there from my personal perspective – what was important to me was that the bombardment drew attention away from the Special Forces activities further to the west, and our now well-established ingress and egress routes.

Dawn broke to reveal a dramatic improvement in the weather. The fog had been whipped up by the strengthening breeze into a low cloud base under which visibility was around 10kms. *Alacrity* had returned to the Task Force from her gun-line, and HMS *Coventry* and HMS *Broadsword* were on their way to a position from which they could impose an air blockade of Stanley Airfield. The Harrier squadrons had received approval for daylight high-altitude bombing raids against Stanley Airfield. These raids would not be without risk. Although conducted from a height of 18,000 feet and, therefore, outside the range of the Roland missile system known to be on the airfield, the Harriers would be flying within range of the radar-laid 35mm Oerlikon guns also in the vicinity of the airfield. It was at approximately 0800hrs that I watched the Harrier pilots manning their aircraft, armed with 1,000lb bombs, in preparation for a raid against the airfield. Within fifteen minutes the two Harriers, flown by Dave Morgan and Gordie Batt, were airborne and on their way towards Port Stanley. As I watched them disappear into the distance, climbing as they quickly opened up a distance from the ship, I lost interest in them and went back into the ship and down to the briefing room.

It was at approximately 0945hrs that Bill burst into the briefing room.

'Get your kit together,' he said rather excitedly. It was unusual for Bill to show great excitement, so I guessed that we had an unusual task lined up. 'We're flying a SBS team to capture an Argentine trawler that has been acting as a spy ship, called the *Narwal*. Dave Morgan and Gordie Batt have attacked her with cannon and bombs and she's dead in the water.' At this point Bill's excitement was becoming infectious and I was champing at the bit to get to grips with the task.

'Where is the *Narwal*?' I asked.

At this point Dave Morgan, who had just entered the briefing room and heard my question replied, 'I'll show you exactly where on the chart.'

'I've been given a lat and long by the Admiral's staff,' Bill responded.

Dave interjected, 'Well that's exactly where she'll be because after what we did to her she won't be going anywhere in a hurry.' From the tone of his voice I sensed that Dave had mixed feelings about the whole event, but I did not have time to go into the whys and wherefores.

'I'll be Captain, you'll be doing the flying and we'll take Corporal Love as aircrewman,' said Bill, 'We'll be accompanied by Nigel, Petty Officer Burnett and Leading Aircrewman Imrie in a second aircraft.'

With that we made our preparations for the sortie. While Bill and I were getting into our flying kit, Dave explained the sequence of events which had led to his and Gordie's attack on *Narwal*.

On reaching Stanley Airfield at approximately 0840hrs, the two Harrier pilots discovered that there was low cloud over the area. Captain Lyn Middleton's orders had been unambiguous: if the target was obscured by cloud or poor visibility the raid was to be aborted. The two Harriers were then taken under the tactical control of *Coventry*, operating some 90 miles to the east, and were directed to a CAP station to the east of Port Stanley. It was whilst the two aircraft were moving to their station that Dave's radar detected a small surface contact to the south of his position. *Coventry* confirmed that there were no Task Force units in the area, so the two Harriers descended through the cloud to investigate the contact. The cloud base was at 600 feet as the aircraft levelled out and looked for the surface contact. Not knowing what type of ship they were investigating, the two Harriers approached cautiously, flying a straight-in attack profile. As Dave made visual contact it was clear that the contact was not a warship but a small trawler. As he manoeuvred his aircraft to fly just a few feet over the trawler, he could see that it was flying a large Argentine flag. Dave climbed his Harrier to report his findings to *Coventry* whilst Gordie flew low and close to the trawler's stern, enabling him to identify the trawler as the *Narwal*, a ship of 1,395 tons displacement, quite large by trawler standards. The order from *Coventry* was short, clear and unambiguous: 'Engage'. Dave relayed the instruction from *Coventry* to Gordie and both Harriers manoeuvred for an attack. Gordie was the first to respond with a burst of cannon fire across the trawler's bows. The *Narwal*'s Captain ignored this internationally recognized signal to heave to and continued moving the ship to the west, towards the safety of Port Stanley. The two Harriers now set themselves up for a bombing run. The 1,000lb bombs had been armed for a high-altitude attack on the airfield, so both pilots realized that they would have to release their bombs from a relatively long distance away from the *Narwal* for the arming fins on the tail of the bombs to run for the full eight seconds required for arming. Dave was the first to make his attack. Running in from the trawler's stern he released his bomb in a standard toss-bombing attack profile. Having released his bomb, Dave manoeuvred the aircraft to observe the flight of the bomb, only to see that it missed the target and splashed harmlessly into the sea just a few feet in front of the ship without exploding, indicating that it had not had sufficient time in flight to arm itself. Dave then decided to strafe the trawler with cannon fire and observed several shells impact the trawler, but still the *Narwal* ploughed on slowly but surely to the west. At this point Gordie lined his aircraft up for an attack run with cannon fire, hitting the trawler several times.

Having still failed to stop the ship, the two Harriers positioned for an attack from ahead of the target. Both Harriers strafed the bows with cannon fire and Gordie dropped his 1,000lb bomb, hitting the forecastle but without exploding. At this point *Narwal* turned to starboard and stopped. The attack had been successful, but at what cost to human life? It would be a few hours before the answer to that question was revealed.

The *Narwal* was in a position about 50 miles to the south-east of Port Stanley. In order to fly a SBS team to the trawler, winch all survivors on board the helicopter and recover the SBS, the two Sea Kings would be constrained to a fuel load of just over 4,000lb, giving a maximum endurance of four hours on task. During this time the helicopters would have to transit to and from the *Narwal* and loiter in the vicinity of the ship long enough for the SBS to be roped down onto the trawler, secure the incident, assess the situation and winch all persons back into the helicopter – no mean feat. It would have been too high a risk to move *Hermes* far enough to the west to execute the task, so it was decided to cross-deck the helicopters and SBS to *Invincible* and mount the operation from there. We launched from *Hermes* at 1100hrs with a team from 2 SBS under the command of Lieutenant 'R' and flew the short distance to *Invincible*. Having landed and shut down, the crews and SBS team made our way to the aircrew briefing room to plan the mission in detail. It was clear from the outset that the two Sea King IVs, without the benefit of radar, would have difficulty in locating the *Narwal*, therefore it was decided that the two Sea Kings IVs would be accompanied by an ASW Sea King of 820 Squadron. During the planning process, *Invincible* moved to a position further to the west to close the gap with the *Narwal*, thereby shortening the flying transit time between our operating base and the trawler. *Invincible* also provided top cover for the mission with a Harrier flown by Sharkey Ward.

An hour later the three Sea Kings launched from *Invincible* and flew in company heading to the south-west and the *Narwal*'s last-reported position. During the flight, Bill used the RWR every few minutes to sweep an arc ahead of the aircraft in the direction of East Falkland for any indication of Argentine radar detection.

The trawler's last-reported position was within easy range of the Argentine AN/TPS 43 radar on Stanley Airfield. It was therefore entirely possible for our aircraft to be detected if we flew at too high an altitude, and for an Argentinean response against us, possibly by Pucara aircraft known to be based on Stanley Airfield. Even though we had Harrier top cover, we were taking no chances. I had suffered from the 'fog of war' just a couple of days earlier so was not about to leave myself wide open to yet another cock-up! Against such a formidable aircraft, Sea Kings would stand no chance and we therefore maintained our RWR vigil throughout the sortie.

After an hour's flight the *Narwal* appeared as a small dot on the horizon. Fifteen minutes later we were close enough to make out details of the helpless trawler, dead in the water, facing north and wallowing quite low in an increasing swell. There was also no sign of life on deck. There was a sea-boat lying off the vessel's stern and what appeared to be badly shot-up life-rafts alongside both sides of the trawler. Bill and I looked at each other in total disbelief at the sight of the life-rafts – we assumed that they had been hit during the strafing earlier in the day whilst still on board and, God forbid, not when they were in the water.

As I manoeuvred the aircraft slowly towards the stern of the trawler, the other two Sea Kings stood off in the hover to the right of the vessel's bow whilst one of the SBS marines kept the ship covered with a machine gun from the cabin door. In my aircraft one of the SBS marines also covered the stern of the trawler with the GPMG mounted in the cabin door. As I closed with the trawler, there remained little sign of life other than a couple of heads popping up from under the cover of the sea-boat, clearly anxious to see what the noise was all about. The vessel showed signs of the earlier attack by the two Harriers. The bridge house was peppered with holes, some small, some large, indicating that rounds had struck the ship from astern and some from the bow. Apart from that, the trawler appeared intact, but low in the water, as if heavily laden.

As soon as I had brought the helicopter to a steady hover over the stern of the trawler, in a tight space above and between the mainmast and aft trawl equipment, 'Doc' immediately lowered a rope from the cabin which was attached to the winch, and the first of the SBS marines, led by Lieutenant 'R', descended rapidly onto the deck. Within a few seconds all of the marines were on the deck of the trawler and I manoeuvred the helicopter to a position a couple of hundred yards astern whilst 'Doc' hauled in the rope and the SBS team made their way quickly into the vessel.

After thirty minutes searching the boat, Lieutenant 'R' called on the radio, 'Can you send down a body bag. There's one body to be recovered.' On receiving the request I flew the aircraft back over the stern and 'Doc' winched down a body bag. An hour after arriving at the *Narwal*, Lieutenant 'R' called on the radio to say that he had recovered important Argentinean military documents, that the vessel was holed at the waterline and was slowly sinking, and that he was ready to recover the crew of fourteen and one body. On hearing this report, Bill decided that the second Sea King should be loaded first, followed by our aircraft. With Nigel's aircraft loaded, it headed back to *Invincible* accompanied by the ASW Sea King. A few minutes later, I flew our aircraft back over the stern of the trawler and started winching first two SBS marines back into the cabin to provide an armed presence in the cabin, before winching up the balance of the trawler's crew and the remaining SBS marines. I glanced back and to my left straight into the eyes of one of the Argentinean crewmen sitting in the seat second from the front of the aircraft on the port side. He managed a very nervous smile. It was clear to me that he had been in fear for his life, first from the threat of drowning and more recently from the menacing sight of heavily armed SBS marines. It was just as well that he had no idea that within thirty minutes he would once again be in fear for his life, were it not for his ignorance of the developing situation. Finally, nearly three hours after leaving *Invincible*, we were ready to depart the stricken vessel and, with one final look over the slowly sinking trawler, we departed the scene and set heading for 'Mother'. During the planning on *Invincible*, the ship's operations team had briefed that *Invincible* would be maintaining a MLA of 190° and 10kts. Unbeknown to us, the ship had altered course not long after our launch and was moving towards the south-east, thereby opening the gap between herself and *Narwal* and, more importantly, us. Throughout the mission, Bill and I had been keeping a careful watch on our fuel level and had calculated that departing *Narwal* when we did, we should arrive back on board *Invincible* with thirty minutes of fuel in hand. We were oblivious to the crisis which was about to engulf us until after we had been flying towards *Invincible* for about thirty minutes. I decided to call the ship on UHF and make the operations team aware of our progress and ETA. After several unsuccessful attempts, I made a call on HF. UHF radio frequencies are characteristically high quality and are used routinely for ship-to-air and air-to-air communications, but are relatively short range. HF radio frequencies, on the other hand, offer relatively poor-quality communications, but have greatly increased range. At my second attempt of calling I made contact with the ship's operations room. The message that we received as we made our way back to *Invincible* was as shocking as it was unwelcome:

'I know who you are and where you are, but you are not where you think you are in relation to "Mother's" position. We are a further fifty miles beyond where you think we are.'

'Bugger,' I said to Bill, 'we're not going to make it back.' After some quick arithmetic, Bill calculated that we would be ditching the aircraft about 25 miles short of the carrier. It was time to share the news with 'Mother'.

'I have news for you then,' I said rather caustically. 'We have insufficient fuel to make it back and will be ditching the aircraft with twenty persons on board approximately twenty-five miles from your current position.'

'Roger, I'll get back to you in a couple of minutes,' came the very matter-of-fact response. Throughout this exchange of radio messages, the SBS and *Narwal's* crew were kept in ignorance of the unfolding situation as there seemed to be little point in worrying them unnecessarily at this time.

Two minutes later the radio crackled back into life: 'We have turned *Glasgow* towards you at best possible speed. She will appear directly ahead of you on the horizon. That is the best that we can do.' The radio operator went on to give HMS *Glasgow*'s position; more quick arithmetic followed. *Glasgow*'s position was such that, even if steaming towards us at 30kts, we would still not have enough fuel to make it to her. Time for some more quick arithmetic. The Sea King's optimum speed for best range is 100 knots. At this speed the twin-matched engine torques would normally be approximately 45 per cent, with each engine using about 500lb of fuel an hour. In theory, if one engine were to be shut down and the aircraft flown at the same speed, its torque would increase to 90 per cent to compensate for the loss of the other engine. However, the efficiency of engines varies with some consuming less fuel than others. On this aircraft the starboard engine, or number two engine as it is commonly called, was more efficient than the number one engine. The die was cast. We would shut down the number one engine and reduce our height to skimming the tops of the waves, thereby gaining some benefit from what is known as 'ground effect'.

Bill and I now went through the procedure for shutting down an engine in flight, with an eagle-eyed 'Doc' in the back anxiously scrutinizing our every move.

We were now flying on just the one engine and had descended to fly just above the wave tops. It was at this point that the fuel warning lights on the central warning panel started to flash intermittently, indicating that we would soon be flying on fumes.

But the Gods were smiling on us that day. As I settled the aircraft at 100 knots and hardly any feet, the torque of number two engine settled at around 75 per cent. We were saving 15 per cent fuel compared to running two engines which, when combined with a stiff following breeze, gained us over 20 miles range – this may not appear very far, but when it is the difference between swimming and staying dry, living or dying, it is all the difference in the world. Now feeling a little more comfortable with our situation, Bill and I shared our predicament with Lieutenant 'R' who was plugged into the aircraft's intercom system in the back of the aircraft and aware that all was not as it should be, given the recent exchanges between the crew and the shutting down of one engine.

As we closed the distance with *Glasgow*, with the fuel warning lights on the central warning panel now lit permanently, I ran through in my mind over and over again the aircraft ditching drill. It was obvious that if we were all to have a reasonable chance of survival then it would be necessary to make a powered ditching having first brought the aircraft to a hover and invited all in the cabin to jump out of the back into a, by now, very rough sea. The aircraft carried a ten-man life-raft, not enough for all in the cabin, but it would at least be a chance for some.

Twenty minutes later we saw a dot on the distant horizon. As we closed I could make out that it was *Glasgow;* never a more welcome sight. The ship had to make only a small turn to starboard, to a more westerly heading, to achieve a flying course. We continued flying on just the one engine as I manoeuvred the aircraft in a long sweeping turn to port to a position about half a mile astern of the ship. As we were on our final approach, Bill restarted the number one engine, again following the flip-cards to the letter to ensure no mistakes. With now just barely fumes in the fuel tanks, the engine started, and as Bill matched the engine torques, I brought the aircraft to a low hover over the flight deck. The Sea King is too big to fit on the deck of a Type 42, but I just managed to get the starboard undercarriage in the middle of the deck, with the port undercarriage resting on the port-deck edge and the tail wheel resting on the aft-deck edge; the rotor disc was about 3 feet clear of the hangar. With the deck moving around violently in a heavy sea, the aircraft was unstable. *Glasgow*'s deck crew moved at lightning speed to get the fuel hose plugged in for a pressure refuel. With the hose securely plugged in I lifted the aircraft into a low hover for the remainder of refuelling. An offer from the ship to check the oil and wash the windscreen was politely declined, although the humour certainly served to break the tension in the cockpit.

With the aircraft refuelled to a comfortable margin, I landed back on the flight deck and the fuel hose was quickly withdrawn. With a quick wave of his flags the FDO signalled for me to lift into the hover and depart to port. As I transitioned the aircraft away from *Glasgow* it was with a feeling of immense relief. The trawler crew had remained in total ignorance of our emergency throughout the flight and must have assumed that the refuel was part of the overall plan – ignorance is bliss! I am grateful to this day to Captain Paul Hoddinott for coming to our assistance and risking his ship in the process.

Twenty minutes later, as the aircraft was approaching *Invincible,* the UHF radio boomed back into life: 'Welcome back to Mother.' I was lost for words. The ship's crew appeared amazed at the sight of the heavily armed SBS marines escorting their charges across the flight deck towards the Island. It was the first opportunity that I had had to see them in any detail. They were mostly older men, some barely able to walk because of the effects of alcohol, one much younger man and one in a body bag being carried by four marines. The trawler crew were accommodated in one of the sailors' mess decks, given clean clothes and treated in accordance with the Articles of the Geneva Convention. The wounded men were treated in the ship's sick bay and all of them were given access to the ship's chapel and padre. On realizing the age of some of the fishermen, some of *Invincible*'s crew donated tobacco and other gifts to make their stay more comfortable. The following day, the fisherman who had lost his life was buried at sea in accordance with internationally accepted protocol. I found out the next day that the younger man was an Argentine naval officer who had been put in command of the trawler when it had been pressed into service as a spy ship.

Having completed our task, I flew the aircraft to *Hermes*, just a few minutes away, landed on after a total of four hours, fifteen minutes of flying and made my way to the briefing room. Whilst I was enjoying a long overdue cup of coffee and a sausage sarnie, Bill went to see the Admiral's staff to be debriefed and make them aware, in no uncertain terms, of our displeasure at having been left in the lurch by *Invincible*: more fog of war. A few years later I was interested to read in Admiral Woodward's book, *One Hundred Days*, his short account of the *Narwal* incident and his succinct comment: 'the near loss (for lack of fuel) of a Sea King Mk 4'. In the overall scheme of events, such a short comment is probably all the incident merits. However, had the aircraft ditched with twenty souls on board, the death toll could have been on a par with that of HMS *Sheffield*. Later that night I heard on the ship's ubiquitous grapevine that *Sheffield* had sunk whilst being towed by *Yarmouth* towards South Georgia. The news made me feel easier in my mind about having been unable to return Captain Salt to *Sheffield* via *Yarmouth* the previous day.

Because Nigel and I had flown a demanding sortie in the afternoon, the composition of aircrew was changed for the SBS extraction sortie planned for later that night. Nigel's place was taken by Pete. As the night wore on, the fog, low cloud and rough sea of the previous few days returned, resulting in Pete having to abort his sortie whilst halfway to landfall. The two missing marines would have to wait at least another night before they could be recovered. As I settled in to my sleeping bag it was with very vivid images of the previous week foremost in my mind. The horrific sight of *Sheffield* dead in the water, with sailors in fear for their lives scrambling over the sides of the helpless burning ship to the relative safety of HMS *Yarmouth* and HMS *Arrow*. The shattered *Narwal*, with her bullet-riddled lifeboats alongside – nothing for anyone to feel proud about. The mixed look of relief and fear in the eyes of the Argentinean fisherman who had been sitting no more than 6 feet away from me just a few hours earlier, as I flew him and his fellow crew mates to the safety of captivity. The realization that human life can so easily perish, not just as a result of enemy action, but also through a lack of situational awareness by our own people. It seemed that success or failure, life or death, were so very finely balanced and, on occasion, determined more by luck and eleventh-hour quick thinking, than through sound operational planning, judgement or military capability.

Tuesday, 10 May saw no respite in the weather. I had become used to walking around the ship in mountainous seas, trying to retain a dignified bearing, but failing miserably. One second I would feel almost weightless as I was left suspended in mid-air when the stern suddenly dropped 60 feet in the trough of an enormous wave, the next second the feeling of positive 'G' as my knees buckled when the stern leapt 60 feet into the air. Some people pay good money for that sort of experience on a fairground ride, but at least those rides are over in a few minutes, or seconds in some cases; this was relentless for hour after hour, day after day. I longed to fly, just to get away from it, but alas, that respite was to be denied me for another two days; two more days of spilt drinks, poor appetite and close encounters with bulkheads and ladders as I moved cautiously around the ship.

During the day the Admiral's staff increasingly turned their attention to matters closer to the impending landing operations: Argentine forces on Pebble Island and mines. Pebble Island occupied a strategic position to the north-west of Falkland Sound. From their airstrip on the island, Argentine aircraft would be only a few minutes flying time from the amphibious ships and troops that would be in the vicinity of San Carlos in less than two weeks. How best to deal with the threat now taxed the planners for many hours. Of the several options under consideration, a raid by Special Forces was slowly gaining the most credibility, but time for planning and rehearsals was short and insufficient to allow the usual protracted period of reconnaissance, detailed planning and rehearsals which were the characteristic hallmark of Special Forces operations. However, undeterred, the Special Forces planning team, under the leadership of Major 'E', set about their military estimate and formulation of a concept of operations. The plan called for an eight-man SAS reconnaissance team to be inserted, preferably overnight on 10/11 May. However, the weather conspired to delay insertion until overnight on 11/12 May.

Meanwhile, in HMS *Alacrity,* Commander Chris Craig had received some very unwelcome news. Admiral Woodward had ordered that his ship circumnavigate East Falkland under the cover of darkness, ostensibly to make lots of noise and fire plenty of starshells, in order to perpetuate the programme of harassing the enemy. The ship's real mission was to check the area of Falkland Sound for mines. How would they know if they had found a mine? Simple, the ship would hit one and be seriously damaged or sunk: another example of the expendability of escorts and the soul-searching decisions that are the bread and butter of senior military commanders. Later that night came the acid test. Commander Chris Craig steered *Alacrity* into Falkland Sound and fired starshell in the direction of Fox Bay, the destination of one of my flights just seven days earlier. A few miles to the north, *Alacrity's* radar detected a surface contact which, on investigation, turned out to be an Argentine naval logistics ship full of aviation fuel, perhaps bound for Fox Bay, perhaps bound for Pebble Island. In any event, her journey was cut short as three 4.5-inch shells from *Alacrity* hit the ship, igniting the fuel in an immense fireball. The disruption of the enemy's supply line had not been a mission for the night, but was a most welcome bonus. *Alacrity* continued her journey without further incident, eventually making her pre-planned rendezvous with HMS *Arrow* to the east of Cape Dolphin in the early hours.

For a few days after this incident I was left pondering whether the decision to harass the Argentine positions to the west of Falkland Sound was such a good idea.

After all, the aim all along had been to draw attention to our phoney interest in Port Stanley and potential amphibious landing sites in the surrounding area, whilst masking our real interest in landing sites to the east of Falkland Sound. Why, therefore, draw attention to the area of our intended landing site and, from a purely parochial perspective, the preferred ingress and egress routes for the Special Forces operations. On reflection I concluded that to show no overt interest in Falkland Sound would probably have served to convince the Argentine command of our real interest in the area, plus it was self-evident that Admiral Woodward had to be sure that there were no mines in the area. Had *Alacrity* attempted to sneak through Falkland Sound without drawing attention to her presence and subsequently hit a mine then I suspect that the game would have been up.

As I was soundly asleep in *Hermes*, my new life-saving friend HMS *Glasgow*, in company with HMS *Brilliant*, spent some time firing 4.5-inch shells from a gun-line to the east of Port Stanley into a known Argentine position at Moody Brook, the military barracks which, until 2 April, had been occupied by the Royal Marines of Naval Party 8901. How strange it must have felt to the sailors on the two ships to be bombarding a former Royal Marine barracks.

The morning of 11 May dawned with the escorts back with the Task Force, having ploughed through atrocious seas to be in position before dawn. The real highlight of the day was the delivery of mail. The word delivery does not do justice to the enormous effort required to move huge quantities of mail from the UK to ships of the Task Force. All mail addressed to BFPO Ships is handled through Mill Hill, London, from where it is transported by a combination of road, air and sea to its final destination. The ships of the Task Force were the furthest BFPO address from the United Kingdom at the time, requiring a huge effort to establish and sustain the attendant logistics support. Receiving mail is, therefore, a major event, with a single letter, bearing either good news or bad, having the potential to either lift or destroy morale. When writing home, I was always careful not to reveal to Lorraine, family or friends, my true feelings about events because I felt it important not to give anyone back home grounds to worry any more than they were already. When reading letters from home I was, therefore, always looking for any tell-tale signs of anxiety because I knew that Lorraine, in particular, would be careful to try and conceal any worries. The tone of our letters was, therefore, really quite matter of fact, conveying news, but hiding feelings as best as possible other than our love for each other – not an easy thing to do.

The good news was that today I received five letters, all from Lorraine. Sensibly each was dated so that I could open and read them in the sequence in which they had been written. A letter, after several days without receiving one, is something to be savoured. I was in no hurry to open and read them all, rather I wanted to spread out this pleasure throughout the day. As I was sitting in the wardroom reading letter number one, I glanced at the scene before me. The compartment was almost full with officers sitting where they could find space, all reading their treasured missives from home. Many were sitting on the floor because all of the furniture which was not fixed to the ship had been upended and tied to the stanchions which were spread evenly through the centre of the wardroom, supporting the weight of the deck-head – or ceiling to the uninitiated. There was, therefore, competition for the few remaining fixed seats around the edge of the compartment. Rank conveys no privileges in such circumstances – it was first come first served. Balancing a cup of coffee and reading a letter whilst trying not to roll around the deck in 60-foot waves is quite a challenge and not without its amusements. On more than one occasion chuckles would be heard at the sight of yet another officer losing what little dignity he had left. A few days earlier, the large mirror which adorned the bulkhead behind the bar had been covered with plywood for the remainder of the war. This was attracting the attention of the graffiti artists amongst the officers and stewards who were never slow to adorn the wardroom's new-found attraction with their latest offerings; some were amusing and apt, some not so. It somehow felt surreal to be sitting in a metal box, dressed for whatever emergency may befall the ship, being tossed around on a violent ocean, with Argentine aircraft hell-bent on sinking the ship, whilst reading a letter reporting news from 8,000 miles away about my son's toothache and how nice the garden was looking.

Having read letter number one, I decided that it was time to stretch my legs and risk making a fool of myself as I attempted to walk around the ship to 03 Deck whilst the sea was endeavouring to deliver me to King Neptune. As if the rough sea wasn't bad enough, the Navy compounded matters by keeping the ship in 'Condition Zulu', with every hatch and watertight door closed. Prior to the attack on HMS *Sheffield* the ship had spent most of the time in 'Condition Yankee' – kidney hatches open, moving to 'Condition Zulu' only when at Action Stations. In 'Condition Zulu', with all hatches tightly shut, movement around the ship became difficult, probably not unlike being in prison. It was done for our own good, of course, as the last thing that anyone wanted was a repeat of HMS *Sheffield* with smoke and fire spreading rapidly throughout the ship. I am reminded of an occasion just a few years later during an official visit to one of HM warships by the then Minister of State for the Armed Forces – to remain nameless to spare his blushes. The ship in question was taking part in an exercise in UK waters and was at 'Condition Zulu'. On attempting to open and negotiate a kidney hatch, it became apparent that the gentleman in question was of too large a girth to fit through. To his obvious embarrassment and the sailors' amusement, the whole hatch had to be opened to accommodate his large frame: there is no place at sea for anyone of a portly disposition.

On days such as these, when flying was out of the question, one's mind turned to amusement and, on occasion, frivolity. Even when at war a chap needs to let off a little steam. The possibility of a chemical attack on the Task Force had been discounted so all of those unwitting but obedient folk who had shaved off their beards a few weeks earlier had started to grow them again; just as well in some cases. They were joined by others intent on wanting to see what sort of a beard they could manage to grow and what they would look like. We 'Junglies' managed to resist the temptation, instead amusing ourselves with some PT on the quarterdeck and the occasional game of 'Uckers' – 'Ludo' for adults. Being a Royal Marine I was doubly determined not to succumb to the trend for excessive facial hair because Royal Marines are not allowed beards, although I see that they are commonplace in 2007 on both Royal Marines and soldiers serving in Afghanistan – how standards have slipped!

CHAPTER 9

Operation Sutton Continues

As day turned into night during 11 May, the weather deteriorated with winds of increasing strength, poor visibility and a building sea. Bill briefed that the insertion of the eight-man SAS reconnaissance team to West Falkland, postponed from the previous night, was on for tonight and that Nigel, 'Wiggy' and Colin Tattersall would be flying the mission. It had been four days since the full moon, so, in theory, ambient light levels should have been very good for NVG flight. However, the sky was generally overcast, so from the outset Nigel realized that the sortie was going to be a real test of the crew's flying and navigation skills. The moon would be at its zenith at approximately 0045hrs local time, but light levels for three or four hours either side were predicted to be good. Launch time could, therefore, be set for 2200hrs to ensure that the aircraft was back on board in plenty of time for *Hermes* to move back to the east under cover of darkness.

At 2130hrs, the crew manned the aircraft in preparation for launch. The team of eight SAS had four 2-man Klepper canoes with them. The combination of eight soldiers and all their kit made for a heavy load and together with the fuel needed for a four-hour round trip, the aircraft would be close to maximum all-up mass on launch. It was 2200hrs as 'Flyco' delivered the customary navigation data. It was time to launch. As the aircraft disappeared into the darkness, I envied them their sortie. My desire of the last two days to be airborne and away from the roller-coaster existence on the ship was going to have to wait another day. Aircrew usually manage to cope and retain the contents of their stomachs when flying in severe turbulence, but how would the SAS cope, I wondered. Added to the turbulence was the poor level of ambient light due to the totally overcast sky. Nigel and his crew could only hope that the weather conditions would be better closer to the islands.

The aircraft had launched from a position 120 nautical miles to the north-east of Port Stanley and flew on a south-westerly heading to make an initial landfall at Cape Dolphin, before flying very low across the north of Falkland Sound to achieve their second landfall and drop-off point close to Mare Rock Peninsula, the most north-easterly point of West Falkland. For the first hour of flight the light conditions were too poor for NVG flight, so Nigel flew the aircraft on instruments whilst 'Wiggy' and Colin maintained as good a lookout as possible with their goggles, in the inky blackness. Nigel needed to be as rested to ensure that he was fresh for the piloting once the aircraft made landfall. After an hour of flight, weather conditions improved. The clouds became broken with approximately half cover and the wind abated slightly; NVG flight became a reality again. Thirty minutes later the foaming sea became visible against the backdrop of the rocky coastline to the east of Cape Dolphin – so far so good.

After just over one hour, thirty minutes since launching from *Hermes*, the aircraft was making landfall at Cape Dolphin. With its position in TANS updated, Nigel descended the aircraft to fly at wave-top height as the aircraft flew south-west across the top of Falkland Sound. The destination was visible as soon as the aircraft departed Cape Dolphin and Nigel was cautiously slowing the aircraft to land at Mare Rock Peninsula within ten minutes. With the aircraft on the ground close to the coast, the SAS team surveyed the scene before them. The plan had assumed that they would launch their canoes across the rocky shoreline, make their way around the Mare Rock headland and set up an OP facing Pebble Island looking directly across the fast-running and tidal Tamar Straight. Assuming that there were no Argentine forces in sight, the team would paddle across to Pebble Island. From their arrival point on the island they would still have to cover about 10 miles on foot to their objective – Pebble Island settlement's airstrip – across a moonscape which afforded no natural cover except for creases of dead ground.

That was the plan; the reality turned out somewhat differently. The heavy surf crashing ashore at Mare Rock made it impossible to launch the canoes from that point. Having surveyed the scene for five minutes, the SAS team commander decided that it would be necessary to find an alternative launch point. The team then climbed back into the aircraft and Nigel flew them to their alternate landing site due south of Round Hill, a few miles closer to the team's objective, Pebble Island. Having dropped of the SAS team to the south of a small ridge, about 10 miles closer to their objective, the aircraft departed the area and set heading back to 'Mother'. The SAS team now had a bit of a task on their hands. They had to move to an OP position north of the ridge and, in so doing, carry their personal kit and canoes. The extended distance necessitated a couple of very tiring round trips. Once there, the team settled down to watch Pebble Island throughout the remainder of the day. At last light on 12 May, the fog was to return, the canoes were launched into the swirling icy waters and made the crossing to Pebble Island, somewhat later than ideal in the overall plan.

Having left the SAS to the mercy of the deteriorating weather, the aircraft slowly closed the distance to *Hermes*, once again Nigel had to rely on conventional instrument flying to complete the sortie. Finally, three hours, forty minutes after launch, Nigel was landing the aircraft back on deck, clearly feeling the strain of an arduous sortie. He was too tired even for his usual post-sortie treat of a bacon sarnie and mug of coffee as he went straight off to bed. Having seen Nigel safely home, I too was ready for bed. As I was settling down for the night at just before 0300hrs, I could not help but think about the eight SAS who were struggling with the elements on the headland just to the south of Pebble Island. I did not know then, but purely by chance, I would be picking them up in just over three days.

Dawn on Wednesday, 12 May was a fiery red with plenty of sunshine and broken cloud – not a mariner's favourite start to a day. The old adage 'red sky at night sailor's delight, red sky in the morning sailor's take warning' was to prove apposite as the day progressed. The first day of reasonable weather for some time was to herald the Harriers returning to CAP sorties to the west of the Task Force and high-altitude bombing attacks against targets on Stanley Airfield. Unusually during daylight, two of the escorts, *Glasgow* and *Brilliant*, were on a gun-line fairly close to Port Stanley. Their mission was to continue the bombardment of Argentine positions around the airfield and attempt to shoot down the Argentine C130 transport that was reported by a SAS OP to be landing regularly at Stanley and resupplying the garrison. The two escorts were clearly visible from Argentine positions ashore. Their ability to bombard targets with relative impunity must have been akin to a red rag to a bull as we rubbed their noses in it; it was merely a matter of time, therefore, before the Argentine Air Force were to strike at such a tempting and infuriating target.

Shortly after midday the Argentine Air Force launched a determined attack against the two escorts with two waves of A4 Skyhawks. By launching their attack from the west at low level, the pilots used the cover afforded by the land mass to remain below radar cover as long as possible. *Brilliant* was first to spot the four aircraft on radar, approximately 18 miles to the west and still over the land, just three minutes away from their targets, and passed the information to *Glasgow*. When at 15 miles, *Glasgow* attempted to engage the Skyhawks with her Sea Dart system, but the system failed for a combination of technical and computer reasons. At this point *Glasgow*'s Captain had no option but to engage with her 4.5-inch gun. With the Skyhawks now just 5 miles away, *Brilliant*'s Sea Wolf system was the last line of defence. Tracking the targets and locked on, *Brilliant*'s Sea Wolf was all that stood between a successful engagement and potential destruction of both ships. With the Skyhawks at 3 miles, Sea Wolf was fired. The first two missiles hit the lead and second aircraft, sending them whirling to destruction. In his attempt to vacate the area, the pilot of the third Skyhawk accidentally flew his aircraft into the sea. The fourth aircraft released its bombs which were observed to splash harmlessly into the sea, straddling *Glasgow* to port and starboard.

After a brief respite, *Brilliant* detected a second wave of four more fighter aircraft and again alerted *Glasgow*. The crew of *Glasgow* were still working frantically to fix the Sea Dart problem after the previous attack and were presented with no option but to engage once again with the 4.5-inch gun and machine guns. On this occasion, however, the Sea Wolf of *Brilliant* malfunctioned and was not, therefore, able to save the day. With the aircraft bearing down on the ships, the captains of *Glasgow* and *Brilliant* ordered their crews to engage with all guns. The Skyhawks penetrated the defensive net and released their bombs. Two bounced off the water and over *Brilliant*, missing the ship by only a few feet; but *Glagow* was not so fortunate. One bomb hit the ship just above the waterline on the starboard side, passing through the ship and out of the other side without exploding. The good news was that no member of either crew was killed or injured; the bad news was that *Glasgow* was taking in water and sustained significant damage to a number of her systems, including electrical and machinery. Meanwhile, undeterred by the attack, the engineers worked on the gun and Sea Dart system and within thirty minutes had both systems ready once again for action. There was not long to wait. Forty-five minutes after the second attack, *Brilliant* detected yet another wave of fighter aircraft approaching as before, low level, from the west. However, after a few minutes the Skyhawks were seen to be circling and after a few more minutes they headed back to the mainland. Perhaps the pilots were deterred from pressing home their attack on learning the outcome of the first attack and on discovering that the pilot of one of the Skyhawks from the second attack had been wounded by small-arms fire from *Glasgow* – whilst overflying Goose Green airstrip after the attack, he had been shot down by his own side.

Their mission completed, the two ships moved to the east to a position about 50 miles or so west of the Task Force from where *Glasgow* was to effect repairs. A close shave, certainly, but news of the endeavours of the two escorts had a galvanizing effect on me and many others in *Hermes*. It was the sort of news that gladdened the heart, to learn that both ships had survived a determined and highly professional attack, one damaged, but still very much at the centre of things. Four Skyhawks had been destroyed, one way or another, and both ships were ready to get stuck in again – very Churchillian and in the finest traditions of the Royal Navy. I felt immensely proud. The internal damage to *Glasgow* proved to be seriously role limiting, with her engines restricted to a speed of just 6kts. She was not to remain with the Task Force for more than another two weeks before making her way slowly back to the UK for essential repairs.

More bad news for the Task Force was the loss of an ASW Sea King. The aircraft had been operating on the ASW screen when it suffered a single engine failure resulting in the aircraft ditching into a fairly rough sea. Fortunately for all concerned, another ASW Sea King operating nearby was on the scene quickly, winching the crew to safety. Only thirteen days into hostilities and the war was starting to exact its toll on Task Force assets: one destroyer lost, one seriously damaged, three Harriers and two Sea Kings lost, not to mention the loss of life. What, I wondered, would our losses be in another thirteen days?

With the return of dense fog at last light, the Special Forces insertion and extraction sorties planned for overnight were close to being postponed, but at the last minute the weather improved slightly and the sorties were given the go-ahead. Some of the teams that had been inserted almost two weeks earlier had completed their tasks and were ready for extraction; other teams, with longer-term missions, were desperate for resupply. It was frustrating that something as simple as fog had the potential to prevented us from performing either task. Years later, the development of thermal imaging and infra-red night-viewing systems would render fog benign and genuine all-weather, round-the-clock helicopter operations would become the norm, but in 1982, fog had the ability to render NVG utterly useless. Technological advances still had a long way to go.

Two operational sorties were planned for that night. Pete, 'Doc' and I were to resupply SAS teams near Port Stanley, and Bob Horton and Paul were to insert a SAS team close to Goose Green. Bob Grundy and 'Stumpy' were authorized to fly in company with Bob Horton and Paul in an attempt to salvage the aborted training sortie of a week earlier. At 2200hrs the three aircraft departed *Hermes* and set heading toward Cape Dolphin. After a one-hour, fifteen-minute flight we made landfall at Cape Dolphin and the three aircraft went their separate ways. Our sortie was uneventful and we returned to the ship without incident having delivered a supply of replacement bergens, crammed full of food and batteries, to the SAS teams 20 miles west of Port Stanley. It was not until debriefing that I learnt that Bob Grundy and 'Stumpy' had exceeded the scope of their authorization by flying over an area of East Falkland close to where Bob Horton and Paul were flying, with the result that they encountered each other unexpectedly and came close to engaging one another with their GPMGs.

Meanwhile 250 miles to the west, the SAS team that Nigel, 'Wiggy' and Colin had inserted the previous night had still not made the crossing by canoe to Pebble Island because of adverse weather. It would be another twenty-four hours before the eight men were to make the perilous crossing to Pebble Island under cover of darkness during the early hours of 13 May. Once established on the island, one patrol remained with the canoes as a base, whilst the other four-man team marched through the night until reaching the airstrip. As night turned into day, the team was able to make out the unmistakable shape of eleven aircraft approximately 2kms from their position. There was no need to get any closer to obtain the information that was needed on aircraft and building dispositions. Armed with this information, the imperative for the team was to remain undetected and return to the base from where the information could be communicated to *Hermes*. The ground all around the SAS position was flat, with no natural cover, which presented the team with a dichotomy: to attempt to walk away during daylight would have been suicidal, to wait until the cover of darkness would build in an even longer delay in getting the information back to the SAS planning team in *Hermes*. The four men abandoned their bergens and slowly slithered away from their position for several hundred metres until descending into dead ground. The remainder of the route to base was exposed leaving the team no option but to lay up with what little kit they had until last light. Under cover of darkness the team completed their journey to base, arriving at the coast and rejoining the other four-man team in the early hours of 14 May. The information that the team had gathered was passed by radio to *Hermes*; detailed planning for Operation Prelim could now commence.

CHAPTER 10

Pebble Island

Success is a science; if you have the conditions, you get the result.

Oscar Wilde

Thursday, 13 May dawned with the Task Force immersed in dense fog yet again. On the assumption that the weather forecast for the night was accurate, with the fog expected to disperse during the day, planning for Operation Prelim got under way, with insertion planned for overnight 13/14 May, despite the absence of a report from the SAS reconnaissance team. Any further delay could have caused difficulties with other operations planned prior to the landings, so it was hoped that reconnaissance information would be received during the day. The plan called for *Hermes*, escorted by *Broadsword* and *Glamorgan*, to detach from the main Task Force at approximately 1500hrs and move to a position just 80 miles to the north-east of Pebble Island by 2000hrs. To ensure that the ships were back with the Task Force by first light, they would need to leave the launch position by no later than 0300hrs thus allowing a total of seven hours to complete the insertion, raid and extraction – a tall order, but feasible.

During the day the SAS Direct Action force of D Squadron made their preparations. Along with the other pilots, I set about planning in particular a detailed map study of Pebble Island. There were also other factors to be taken into account.

The raid would involve fifty-eight men, and also some equipment to be carried, requiring three Sea Kings for insertion. The extraction would require four Sea Kings because the original reconnaissance party of eight men were also to be recovered, making a total of sixty-six troops. The engineers were kept busy throughout the day with last-minute checks of the aircraft. There was also an urgent requirement for stores to be moved between some of the ships, therefore fog or no fog, I was programmed to fly. Late morning, I launched into the dense fog with 'Doc' and set off on a 'Vertrep' sortie. Although under positive radar control throughout, the ships appeared alarmingly big and menacing when they suddenly became visible in just 20 metres visibility. One hour, fifteen minutes and five SCAs later, having lost about 5lb in weight through sweat, I regained sight of *Hermes* and was mightily relieved to be landing back on board.

At 1500hrs, *Hermes*, *Broadsword* and *Glamorgan* started the transit towards Pebble Island. Our plan was simple enough. As soon as *Hermes* was in her launch position, approximately 75 miles north-east of Pebble Island, *Glamorgan* would move inshore to a gun-line from where she could bombard targets on Pebble Island by way of a diversion with both 4.5-inch guns and Sea Slug missiles. As the ships closed the distance with the target area, I could sense the excitement and tension building amongst the aircrew – this was to be our first major Direct Action task of the war, not counting *Narwal*. The excitement was to be short-lived. After nearly three hours transit towards Pebble Island, the mission had to be postponed because the SAS reconnaissance team had yet to report their findings. The excitement of the last three hours was now replaced by feelings of anti-climax, disappointment and, to an extent, nervous relief.

The entertainment in the wardroom that evening was scant compensation for the missed opportunity and my deflated elation of earlier in the evening. It was a film night, a regular feature of wardroom life in peacetime, but a rare treat in war. The wardroom dining room was cleared of the usual tables and in their place were rows of seats facing the small screen suspended from the ceiling. The film show started with the usual Tom and Jerry cartoon, always popular with the officers, and was followed by the feature film *Gallipoli*, a surprising choice for a ship at war. I was left wondering if the film would prove to be portentous; it was most certainly no morale booster! During the course of the film I observed several officers, who had clearly formed the same opinion as myself, leaving the film show, which was hardly surprising. I do not know to this day who chose the film for showing that evening, but it was either the result of poor judgement or exceedingly bad taste.

There were two significant improvements early in the morning of 14 May – the fog cleared and the SAS reconnaissance report was received from the team on Pebble Island. Detailed planning for the raid could now continue in earnest. Before my aircraft could be ready for the coming night's raid, it needed a Check Test Flight (CTF) following rectification of a snag. Mid-morning I launched from *Hermes* with Richie Burnett to check the performance of one of the engines. All was well and, without further ado, I landed back on board after just fifteen minutes flight, with a fully serviceable aircraft. I assumed that I was stood down for the remainder of the day pending the night's long flying programme: how wrong can one be. Within fifteen minutes of landing, I was authorized for an HDS sortie with 'Doc'.

HDS sorties are a routine feature of naval operations. Today's task would be no different, with one exception. Having carried out the pre-flight walk around the aircraft, I was about to climb on board through the cabin main door when

I saw Bertie Penfold sitting in the seat to the right, just inside the door. Bertie explained how he was feeling about his first air-to-air engagement with the Mirage of the week before and the profound impact that it had had on him, so he was returning to the UK. He was clearly distressed and, understandably, neither he nor I wished to prolong the conversation. I was relieved that there had been a resolution of his situation and wished him well. It was a sad occasion for his squadron to lose such an able and popular pilot, and for Bertie to have been suffering with a tortured mind for so long.

Armed with a plot of where ships were expected to be in relation to each other, we set off in search of the first one in our HDS programme – the RFA which would be taking Bertie towards Ascension. A number of what became known as 'motorway stations' were established at sea to bridge the long gap between the TEZ and Ascension. At these stations, ships could transfer personnel and stores between each other in a long relay. These stations were established at latitudes 20° south and 40° south. The RFA on which we dropped Bertie would take him north to the station at 40° south where he would transfer to another RFA making its way to the next station north until, finally, after several days at sea moving between ships, he would reach Ascension and a flight back to UK. The traffic between stations became very much two way, but on occasions urgent stores would be delivered to the Task Force directly from Ascension by parachute into the sea and be picked up by one of the Sea Kings.

Twenty minutes after launch I was approaching the RFA. Having rendezvoused with the ship, we bid Bertie a fond farewell and headed for the next ship in the programme. After a total of two hours, thirty minutes flying, the HDS programme was complete and I landed back on *Hermes* just as the weather was once again deteriorating, with particularly strong winds. Having signed the aircraft in, I made my way to the briefing room to start planning for the Pebble Island raid.

It was at 1500hrs that *Hermes* detached from the remainder of the Task Force, accompanied by *Broadsword* and *Glamorgan*, and started the long passage towards Pebble Island. By now weather conditions were atrocious with a southerly gale and mountainous seas; progress was slow. We had another consideration: the range of the Sea Kings. The aircraft were going to be operating at close to maximum all-up mass and, with the strong headwind, we would struggle to achieve the 160-mile round trip if launching from the position originally selected 75 miles north-east of the island. Admiral Woodward therefore ordered that *Hermes* close to a position just 40 miles from Pebble Island, a courageous decision given that in such appalling weather the Harriers could not fly to provide top cover, and the two escorts would be unlikely to be able to protect *Hermes* against a concerted attack by the Argentine Air Force.

As launch time approached, another problem became apparent. One of the four Sea Kings was on deck, with the other three in the hangar. When Sea Kings are not required for flight, their rotor blades are folded, thereby facilitating movement around the deck and enabling the helicopters to be parked close together. The blades are spread after the number one engine is started which brings on line the aircraft's electrical and hydraulic systems. However, in strong wind conditions it is not possible to either spread or fold the rotor blades because there is a high risk that the wind could get under or on top of a rotor blade either lifting it high, or forcing it down uncontrollably, resulting in serious damage to the rotor blade and/or aircraft, and possibly injuring the aircraft maintainers who are required to handle the blades during folding and spreading.

With less than an hour remaining before the time set for launch, and with three aircraft still in the hangar, there was a sudden and dramatic lull in the wind. The crew of the lead Sea King – Nigel, 'Wiggy' and Colin – quickly set about manning their aircraft and managed to get the rotor blades spread and engaged. By this time my aircraft had been moved from the hangar to the flight deck and was positioned behind the second Sea King, with the last aircraft quickly moved into position line astern. Bob Horton, Paul and Richie leapt in the second aircraft and got the number one engine started in record time, but, just as they were about to spread the rotor blades, the gale-force winds returned and they had to abandon their attempt at spreading the blades. If the mission was to be salvaged then drastic measures were called for. As quickly as possible the three Sea Kings were moved back onto the lift and returned to the hangar. In turn, each of the aircraft was moved back onto the lift. We now had no choice but to break nearly every rule in the book: the number one engine of each aircraft was started whilst still in the hangar and the rotor blades spread. Next the aircraft were raised to the flight deck on the lift, one at a time, and manoeuvred forward onto their spots. By now the lead aircraft had been rotors running for nearly an hour and needed a refuel. Finally, nearly one hour, thirty minutes later than planned, the three Sea Kings, carrying fifty-eight troops, were ready for launch, with the fourth aircraft in reserve.

As the minutes of delay passed the hour mark, the level of anxiety within the SAS Direct Action group started to mount. There would not be enough time to complete the mission as planned, the plan had to be revised at the eleventh hour. The result was that only one of the two objectives, the destruction of the aircraft, could be achieved. The lives of the Argentineans manning the small garrison would, for now, be spared. The final plan was much simpler requiring just one assault group to attack the airfield, with a second group in reserve and a third group to cover the approaches from the Helicopter Landing Site (HLS) to and from the airfield. The eight-man reconnaissance team, inserted three nights earlier, would secure the HLS and provide protection for Captain Chris Brown RA (the NGFSO) and the SAS mortar team.

At 2230hrs the three Sea Kings finally lifted from *Hermes* and disappeared into the darkness carrying fifty-five SAS soldiers, Chris Brown and two gunners. The night was very dark, with broken cloud cover and no moon for another five hours; we were certainly flying at the absolute minimum level of ambient light. We settled into our now very familiar three-aircraft formation at five rotor spans and 60 feet above the surface. With a headwind approaching nearly 70kts, progress was slow. Visibility was, on the other hand, very good, with the islands coming into view after only a few minutes. Turbulence at such a low level was severe, again restricting our airspeed. After just over an hour, we were making our final approach to the LZ on Pebble Island.

Awaiting us was the reconnaissance team of eight men who had secured the LZ. The three aircraft landed almost simultaneously, just over 3 miles from the airfield, and the troops disembarked quickly, but being careful to handle their explosive charges and mortar bombs with considerable care. After only one minute on the ground, the three Sea Kings lifted and headed back towards *Hermes*. The return journey with a strong tail wind was over in no time. At one stage I saw 180kts on the Ground Speed Indicator (GSI), a remarkable speed for a Sea King. At 0010hrs, just one hour, forty minutes after launch, the three aircraft landed back on board. For the crews of the other two aircraft, there was little for them to do until required to extract the SAS group six hours later, but for me a busy night lay ahead.

Meanwhile, on Pebble Island, having delivered a final briefing to his team, Captain John Hamilton led his group on the 3-mile march to the airfield. Each man carried with him from *Hermes* two 81mm mortar bombs which were deposited at the mortar base-plate position en route to the target area. It was 0300hrs before the assault group arrived at the airfield. According to the timings in the plan, by now the SAS should have concluded the attack and be on their way back to the LZ; there was little time left to get the job done. Had the team delayed their return, it would have placed *Hermes* at risk because there would have been insufficient time for the ship to move the 200 miles or so back to the relative safety of the Task Force. With little time to get the job done, the assault group started their attack by firing on each aircraft with small arms and 66mm anti-tank missiles. The attack drew little response from the Argentine troops whose positions were being engaged by gunfire from *Glamorgan*.

As it became clear that the Argentine troops had no stomach for a fight, John Hamilton led his team onto the airstrip in close proximity to the aircraft and started the systematic destruction of each of the eleven dispersed aircraft. Using a combination of standard demolition charges and 66mm missiles, each aircraft was rendered unflyable. As the team went about their work, the shells from *Glamorgan* continued to rain down on Argentine positions around the airfield hitting ammunition and fuel dumps which lit the darkness with huge orange balls of flame. Thirty minutes later, with the job done, the SAS assault group broke contact with the Argentine forces and started their withdrawal towards the HLS. The group was clearly silhouetted against the burning aircraft and fuel dump and, as they made their way across the centre of the airstrip, a landmine was exploded in the middle of the group on command from the Argentine lines. The blast hurled one SAS corporal into the air causing him concussion, while another of the group was wounded by shrapnel. The two wounded men were helped towards the LZ escorted by two other soldiers. When on reaching the edge of the airfield they heard Argentine voices shouting nearby, the SAS group opened fire with grenade launchers until screams from the Argentine position indicated that the target had been hit. So far as it is known, these were the only Argentinean casualties of the night. As the operation turned out, the destruction of the aircraft, ammunition and fuel, with minimal bloodshed, appeared as a model of clinical, constrained use of force, though that had not been the original intention.

Recovery of the SAS Direct Action group was planned for 0630hrs. Given the need also to pick up the SAS reconnaissance team, all four Sea Kings would be required for the extraction of the sixty-six men. As I mentioned earlier, I had a particularly busy night. Having returned to *Hermes* after the insertion, the crews of the other Sea Kings were stood down, whereas I had another mission to complete, resupplying one of the SAS OP teams on East Falkland, before rejoining the other Sea Kings to effect the Pebble Island extraction. 'Stumpy' was paired with Bill for the Pebble Island extraction to crew the fourth Sea King.

At 0300hrs, Pete, 'Doc' and I launched from *Hermes* and set off towards the islands carrying four bergens crammed full of food, batteries and other resupply essentials, to be exchanged for four bergens full of waste and expended batteries. Still battling a strong headwind, the flight at 50 feet was extremely uncomfortable and speed was restricted due to the severe turbulence. The moon had risen an hour earlier so the light level had improved to a more acceptable level for flight over land. The earlier sortie to insert the Pebble Island Direct Action group had not required flight over land because the HLS was very close to the coast. My second sortie required flight over several miles of low-lying and pretty featureless terrain so I was grateful for the assistance of moonlight.

After nearly thirty minutes, the familiar coastline east of Cape Dolphin came into view. There was no need to focus too much on navigation at this stage because I could clearly identify our landfall waypoint. Thirty minutes later we were flying overhead Cape Dolphin and Pete updated TANS. I then descended to 20 feet as I flew the aircraft on a similar heading to pass close by Fanning Head 30 minutes later. The Sound had the effect of squeezing the wind into an almost impenetrable buffeting headwind, making progress painfully slow. From this point I flew due south past San Carlos, giving the area as wide a berth as possible, not wishing to compromise the SBS and SAS OP positions in the immediate area. After another twenty minutes, I turned the aircraft east to fly across Lafonia, crossing Choiseul Sound ten minutes later heading north-east towards the RV position 15 miles west of Mount Kent. Bill had agreed with the Special Forces planning team that Morse light signals would be used by the SAS and SBS teams to identify themselves and their exact positions. The Morse signal would change on a task-by-task basis. Tonight as we approached the RV, all eyes in the aircraft were strained searching forward on the ground for the Morse signal . - (Alpha).

Just thirty seconds before reaching the RV, 'Alpha' was seen by all of us, directly ahead of the aircraft at a quarter of a mile. I slowed the aircraft and manoeuvred into wind for the landing. As I did so I said to 'Doc', 'Man the GPMG just in case the SAS team have been captured, their codes compromised and we're about to fly into a trap.'

'I'm already doing it,' was 'Doc's' immediate and excited reply. I brought the aircraft into the hover and descended to land as Pete called out our height. Two shadowy figures arrived at the cabin door and immediately threw four well-stuffed and rather smelly bergens into the cabin; 'Doc's' comments in response are not printable! Four replacement bergens were handed down to the SAS soldiers who quickly melted into the darkness. Thirty seconds after landing, I lifted the aircraft into the hover and transitioned into forward flight, turning immediately south-west and headed back towards Choiseul Sound. For the next 60 miles the wind was still against us, so it was an hour later before we arrived at our waypoint on the west coast of Lafonia and I turned the aircraft north towards Fanning Head.

The sortie had been timed so that on reaching the north end of Falkland Sound, my aircraft would RV with the other three Sea Kings which had launched from *Hermes* at 0415hrs to pick up the SAS from Pebble Island. As the aircraft passed Fanning Head I saw the unmistakable shape of three Sea Kings, dead ahead, at about 5 miles, heading south-west towards the HLS. I had the advantage of a tailwind so was able to manoeuvre the aircraft quickly to join the other three as 'tail-end Charlie'. As I turned my aircraft left towards Pebble Island, with about 5 miles to run to the HLS, my attention was drawn immediately to the bright, flickering, green images of numerous fires, some small, one much larger. I quickly looked under the goggles to see several fires burning bright orange in the vicinity of the airfield. This was the first indication that any of us in the aircraft had that the SAS mission had been successful, the question on all of our minds being: at what cost? I did not have long to wait to find out. Five minutes later three of the four Sea Kings touched down in the same location where five hours earlier we had dropped off the fifty-five SAS soldiers and the NGFSO. The fourth aircraft held off in reserve. Within a few seconds, the SAS appeared from out of the darkness and started to embark in each of the Sea Kings. Two of the men were being assisted, so it was clear that they had been wounded, but all others appeared to be able-bodied, which was the good news that we were looking for. I was expecting to embark twenty-two passengers and then, along with the other two Sea Kings, take off and return to *Hermes*. The two other aircraft were airborne again very quickly with my aircraft having been the last to land, taking the longest to load. 'Doc' had just counted in the eighteenth man when he said, 'Shit, I don't believe it.'

'What's up?' I asked.

'The whole of the reconnaissance team has just turned up and are climbing in – there are eight of them and all of their kit, including four canoes.'

'Bugger,' was my immediate response, adding, 'we'll be above maximum all-up mass for take-off. I'll do some quick sums.' When planning the sortie, Pete and I had calculated the fuel load needed for the extraction from Pebble Island predicated on the total duration of the sortie, which was expected to be four hours, plus the weight of up to sixteen passengers and three crew, plus a small contingency, minus fuel used during the sortie. We had, therefore, fuelled the aircraft to full on departing *Hermes*. At the time of landing on Pebble Island, the aircraft had 3,500lb of fuel remaining of the original 6,000lb which, with the expected number of men to pick up, would have resulted in a take-off mass comfortably below the maximum permitted. However, the surprise addition of eight men and some heavy kit would put the aircraft at over 1,000lb above MAUM on take-off.

Pete did a quick distance, speed, time and fuel calculation for the 40-mile trip back to *Hermes*. The wind had veered slightly to the south-west with the effect of ensuring a good tailwind component, so the flight back to 'Mother' would take twenty-five minutes at the most, and consume just over 600lb of fuel with a heavy aircraft. Allowing for the Minimum Land On Allowance (MLA) of 400lb, but no other contingency, Pete was prepared to jettison 2,500lb of fuel to a revised total of just 1000lb. Having double-checked his figures with me, Pete decided to call Nigel to task the reserve aircraft flown by 'Stumpy' and Bill to pick up the canoes and the large packs. With the possibility of an Argentine counter-attack, the imperative was to get the hell off Pebble Island ASAP. 'Doc' checked that the fuel jettison pipes were clear of the ground. Pete opened the fuel jettison cocks and we watched as the fuel level started to reduce slowly. With the fuel level going down, I applied full power whilst Pete increased the rotor revs to the maximum transient limit permitted, and I pulled full torque to the maximum transient limit permitted. As the fuel level reached 1,200lb, the aircraft slowly clawed its way off the ground and I transitioned into forward flight. Pete closed the fuel cocks as they passed the 1,000lb mark and re-balanced the fuel tanks. With sighs of relief all round, we were on our way back to *Hermes*, with no one the wiser as to our difficulty. The ship was visible through the goggles immediately on heading north-east and was a most welcome sight to three weary aviators after a sortie duration approaching four hours.

Finally, four hours, ten minutes after launch, I landed the aircraft back on *Hermes*, signed in and made my way to the briefing room. I had flown a total of five hours, fifty-five minutes since departing *Hermes* for the first time earlier in the night and was ready for some much-needed sleep. The mood amongst the SAS and aircrew was one of quiet satisfaction rather than jubilation. The job had been done with just two minor casualties amongst the SAS. Having debriefed the sortie, Bill left the briefing room to return a few minutes later to make an announcement that was to have far-reaching ramifications for me, two other aircrew and the Task Force.

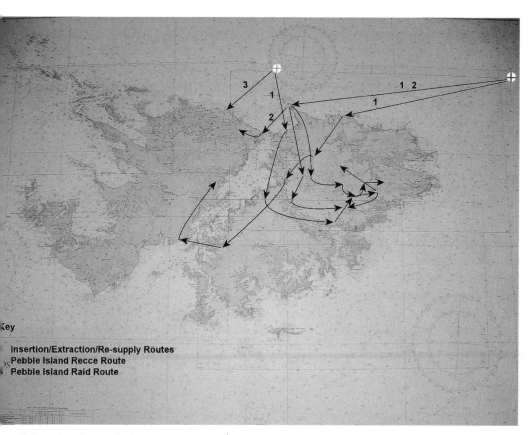

Map 1 - Special Forces Insertion/Extraction and Resupply Routes. © Crown Copyright

Part 3

The Mainland Option

CHAPTER 11

'You're Never Going to Believe This'

The great defence against the air menace is to attack the enemy's aircraft as near as possible to their point of departure.

Winston Churchill

'Y ou're never going to believe this,' exclaimed Bill. 'The Government has approved a plan for an SAS operation on the Argentine mainland to destroy the Super Etendards and Exocet missiles.' Bill's announcement was met with a stunned silence for a few seconds. I did not know how to react; none of us did. The silence was broken by numerous utterances signifying a mixture of disbelief, amazement and incredulity.

'What's it all about, Splot?' I asked.

'I can't say much more at this stage for security reasons,' replied Bill. 'I want you all to go away and rest for the remainder of the day. By 1800hrs I want each of you to let me know whether or not you wish to volunteer for the mission. Oh yes, there's just one more thing, it is a one-way trip – there will be no way that the aircraft will be able to return to the Task Force.'

The long night, together with the unbelievable news, left most of us feeling pretty numb. With no further conversation on the matter, we filed out of the briefing room and went our separate ways. I headed straight for the wardroom for a much-needed breakfast. A decision of such magnitude could not be made in haste or when feeling almost brain dead, so I turned in for a few hours of desperately needed sleep.

It was turning daylight as *Hermes* got underway, heading back towards the relative safety of the Task Force, some 150 miles to the north-east. Later that morning, two Harriers flown by Dave Morgan and Ted Ball conducted a photographic reconnaissance mission over Pebble Island. The results revealed that all eleven aircraft on the airfield had been rendered non-flyable, having been either almost destroyed or severely damaged. Later Admiral Woodward commented, 'In my view, this single operation is easily the best example of a successful all-arms special operation that we are likely to see in a very long while.' For much of the morning and early afternoon, I slept the sleep of the dead, comfortably snug in the Captain's day-cabin, oblivious to all that was going on around me, in particular the preliminary preparations that were in train for the audacious SAS raid in Argentina.

Shortly after dawn, the military commanders in London had received reports from the Task Force of the total success of the SAS Direct Action mission on Pebble Island. Admiral Woodward and commanders at Northwood and Hereford were now busy putting the final touches to a plan for dealing with the remaining Argentine Exocet missiles. The success of the SAS raid did much to convince military planners of the feasibility of mounting a second such operation, only this time against the Exocet missiles and their delivery aircraft, the Super Etendards, at their home base of Rio Grande, on the island of Tierra del Fuego, some 400 miles or so to the west of the Falkland Islands. The recent success against the targets on Pebble Island now gave the idea fresh impetus and momentum. In fact, the War Cabinet had already given tentative approval to what became known as 'the mainland option', having taken advice from Sir Michael Havers, the Attorney-General, that such an operation would be legal under international law.

After the attack on *Sheffield*, the mainland option was increasingly viewed as the only feasible method of preventing the deployment of further Exocet missiles against the Task Force, and the Joint Intelligence Committee had requested the SAS to draw up the necessary plans. The detailed planning for a raid against Rio Grande had started with the SAS team at Hereford over two weeks earlier. The option of inserting the preliminary reconnaissance force by Sea King, mounted from the Task Force, had its genesis in an idea thought of by Captain Lyn Middleton, although coincidentally the SAS planning team at Hereford had arrived at the same conclusion having discounted the parachute and submarine insertion options.

Leaving aside for one moment the obvious hurdles to be jumped to achieve the necessary political approval for such an operation, there were significant practical considerations. Before a raid could be authorized it was essential to establish, beyond any doubt, that the aircraft and missiles were at Rio Grande. Although not known at the time of hostilities, after the war it was revealed that in order to conceal aircraft losses from their pilots, the Argentine Air Force pilots based at Rio Gallegos were ordered to recover to Rio Grande after missions. There was, therefore, every possibility that a reciprocal arrangement applied to the Super Etendards. A small force would be required to reconnoitre the base in order to confirm the presence of the aircraft and missiles before a Direct Action mission could be authorized. During the previous few days, exchanges of signals and secure conversations by satellite took place between the Task

Force, Fleet Headquarters at Northwood, the MoD, Director SAS (DSAS) and the commanders of the Amphibious Task Group. Various options to execute the preliminary reconnaissance and the raid were discussed and batted backwards and forwards between the various commanders. Finally, it was decided that a single Sea King IV from the Task Force would insert the reconnaissance force of nine men.

Early in the afternoon I managed to crawl out of bed having enjoyed more sleep than I had achieved for days. The decision as to whether or not I should volunteer for the one-way mission did not prevent me from sleeping soundly – I was far too tired after the previous night's epic flight of nearly six hours to have any concerns: a supermodel could have walked naked into my cabin – perhaps I should say the Captain's cabin – and I would not have batted an eyelid.

After a late lunch in the ACRB, I went onto 03 Deck to see what was happening in the big wide world of daylight. I needed as clear a head as possible if I was to arrive at a sensible decision as to whether or not I should volunteer for the Argentina operation. The weather had improved enormously: the gale of the previous night was replaced by a gentle breeze and the sea was calm under sunny skies; the clean South Atlantic air was refreshing. There were four hours before I had to give Bill my answer and I needed the relative calm and private space afforded by 03 Deck, away from everyone, to gather my thoughts. At first I tried to arrive at a decision dispassionately by excluding any thoughts of Lorraine, my children and my parents, instead focusing on the military imperatives.

I went through in my mind a military estimate, or what in 1982 was known as an appreciation. Admiral Woodward considered the task to be vital to the survival of the capital ships of the Task Force and ultimate victory; that judgement was clear and above reproach. There were two courses open to me: to volunteer or not to volunteer. There had to be a volunteer crew, but why should I be a member? With the exception of three of the pilots, each of the remaining six of us had the requisite flying and navigational skills. The pilots who must be exempt from the operation were Bill, because of his command function, Bob Grundy, because of the trauma that he sustained when ditching three weeks earlier and Paul because of his relative inexperience as a pilot. The remaining six of us had a similar number of flying hours and operational experience. As soon as the flying task was completed, remaining undetected and survival would become the imperatives, and I was the only one of the six who was a marine, had trained with the SAS and had the skills to operate and survive behind enemy lines: these skills were my métier. I owed it to the others to make this unique set of skills available for the common good. Finally, although I had tried to remain dispassionate and entirely objective, I allowed emotion to play a part in my decision. Each of us was married and most had young children; emotionally the books were pretty evenly balanced. I had made my decision: I would volunteer.

Whilst I was leaning on the guardrail, overlooking the comings and goings on on the flight deck and staring far out to sea, I was unaware that a few miles to the north-east, the SAS reconnaissance team was jumping from a C130 into the sea after a marathon 28-hour flight from the UK. The team was quickly picked up by ASW Sea Kings and deposited on RFA *Fort Austin*. It was to come as a surprise to discover, some hours later, that the leader of the team that was to be delivered to Argentina was an old friend whom I had last seen two years earlier when we attended the same military training course.

Shortly before the 1800hrs deadline, I made my way to Bill's cabin and informed him of my decision.

'Thanks Dick,' was Bill's response, adding, 'I'll let you know the decision later.' With that there was nothing further to be said and I went to the wardroom for dinner wondering who else had volunteered. As I sat eating my meal, I could not help but glance up and down the table at the other pilots, wondering which of them had volunteered and which had not, and what had influenced their decisions. I was never to find out.

The night was young and there was a sortie programmed for overnight yet to be planned. Some of the SAS and SBS teams had been operating on the islands for almost three weeks and were either in need of extraction, having completed their tasks, or resupply. Tonight there would be a three-aircraft formation to East Falkland. The moon was now in its last quarter and was not set to rise until 0245hrs. The conditions at sea remained calm and after sunset the skies cleared, creating reasonable light levels for the first part of the sortie and, following moonrise, even better conditions. Launch was therefore set for 2300hrs. Whilst we were making our preparations, we were not to know that *Fort Austin* had rejoined the Task Force and the SAS team, which had been parachuted into the sea during the afternoon, had been transferred to *Hermes*, dripping wet and very tired after their ordeal.

By 2230hrs the aircraft were ranged on their spots and Pete, 'Doc' and I made our way to the aircraft. On cue, 'Flyco' delivered the navigation data and the three aircraft launched into the darkness, 140 miles north-east of Port Stanley. Transit time to landfall would be just under one hour, thirty minutes, so we settled into our well-established formation at 50 feet and enjoyed the much-improved weather conditions. Gone were the near-impenetrable buffeting headwind, turbulence and mountainous seas of the previous night. In their place was an almost eerily flat calm sea, offering little by way of definition to the goggles. Was this the lull before yet another storm, I wondered, as we slowly closed the distance to East Falkland. We had become used to really bad weather and the calm conditions seemed somehow incongruous, but I was grateful for the smooth flight.

One hour, twenty minutes later we made landfall at Cape Dolphin and the formation split as the three aircraft separated and headed towards their destinations. In my aircraft we had two tasks to complete. Pete descended the aircraft to 20 feet as we flew over what, by now, was very familiar terrain towards the RV 10 miles west of Fitzroy. As we approached the RV the expected Morse light signal of - - . (Golf) was seen with about a quarter of a mile to run. Pete manoeuvred the aircraft into what little wind there was and I talked him down for the landing. With the wheels firmly on the ground, two SAS soldiers made their way quickly to the cabin door and threw in two very full-looking bergens in return for which 'Doc' handed down two replacements crammed full of food and batteries. One minute later, Pete lifted the aircraft into the hover and transitioned into forward flight, turning north-west towards a position near to Teal Inlet. The next task was expected to be a little tricky.

Several days earlier, a SBS team of four, moving under cover of darkness towards a site chosen for an OP, had heard a group of Argentine soldiers moving in the area. In the fog and confusion the team became split with two of them, both corporals, losing contact with the team leader and subsequently assumed to be missing. Despite the best endeavours of the team leader searching for them via a series of emergency RVs, the two men remained unaccounted for over several days.

Having been extracted by helicopter, the team leader and another three marines were reinserted to the area several days later to continue the search for the missing men. After searching the emergency RVs for a second time, the two corporals were found. Our second task of the night was to fly to the RV and pick up all six men. However, there had been difficulties with communications between the team and *Hermes*, so it was not known whether or not the team leader had received the message confirming their extraction and the Morse light signal to be used. We approached the RV with more caution than had become the norm with 'Doc' manning the GPMG. As we neared the RV the Morse light signal of - . - . (Charlie) was seen – the message from *Hermes* had been received indicating that all was well. The aircraft having landed, the six marines clambered into the back of the cabin, two of them certainly looking bedraggled and grateful to have been found. The six were all smiles as the aircraft lifted into the hover and transitioned north-west towards Foul Bay and the long flight back to *Hermes*.

As we made our way towards 'Mother', I took control from Pete so that he could have a rest after the intense concentration of flying around East Falkland for an hour at just 20 feet. The journey was uneventful, but, as we slowly closed the distance to the ship, the weather started to deteriorate. The familiar fog of recent days had made an unwelcome return and for the last forty-five minutes of the flight the goggles were of no use. I reverted to instrument flying, only managing to regain visual flight as we neared the ship. Finally, after exactly four hours of flying, I landed on *Hermes* for what was to be the last time during the war.

Having signed the aircraft in, I made my way to the briefing room for the usual post-sortie debrief. No one had much to say, the tasks had all been completed with several, by now, hungry SAS and SBS teams resupplied and two missing marines recovered: all in all a most satisfying night's work. The question on everyone's mind was, who's going to Argentina? We would all have to wait until later in the day to find out. The priority now was for sleep.

It was late morning when I awoke, refreshed after a good night's sleep and ready for anything that the day was to throw at me. I had lunch in the wardroom before making my way to the briefing room. After a few minutes, Bill entered the room.

'You're it, Dick,' said Bill, short and very much to the point. Is this how one finds out that one has been chosen to fly a one-way mission, I wondered? I decided it must be – there was certainly no point in ceremony; there was a job to be done and someone had to do it. 'Who do you want for your crew,' asked Bill.

'Who can I have?'

'It doesn't work that way. You tell me who you want and I'll tell you whether or not that person is available.' It was clear that I was not to discover who had and who had not volunteered; and rightly so. I had no hesitation in asking whether or not 'Wiggy' was available to be my co-pilot and navigator – he was undoubtedly the best operator of the TANS system in our team and accurate navigation would clearly be of the utmost importance to the successful outcome of this task.

'You've got him,' replied Bill. 'Who do you want as the aircrewman?' For all of the NVG sorties thus far, 'Doc' Love had been my aircrewman. We had worked well together and I could see no reason in needing to change.

'"Doc" Love,' was my immediate reply.

'Not available,' replied Bill. Hmm, this is going to be difficult, I thought. The task called for a competent aircrewman, but I knew from the outset that Bill would be reluctant to break up the remaining NVG crews if he could possibly avoid it.

'How about Pete Imrie?' asked Bill. Pete had flown a number of the NVG sorties, but not as many as any of the other aircrewmen. I was confident that he possessed the skills needed for the job. If Pete was a volunteer then he would be ideal.

'OK.'

'You've got him.' So, in the space of less than five minutes, the crew had been chosen. In reality, the selection process had taken place over a somewhat longer period of time. Bill had given the matter a great deal of thought over the previous few days and had arrived at the ideal crew composition long before he and I had our five-minute chat. What I was not aware of until back in England some weeks later was the rearguard action that had been fought by the Royal Marines in an attempt to persuade Admiral Woodward not to sacrifice a Sea King IV but, instead, to substitute an ASW Sea King II for the mission. I can understand the reluctance of the Royal Marines to lose yet another valuable support helicopter. With the amphibious landings at San Carlos scheduled for 21 May, the amphibious force needed as many support helicopters as possible. The Sea King lost on 23 April had reduced the number of commando Sea Kings to thirteen; my departure from the Task Force would reduce this to twelve. Tragically, on 19 May, another Sea King was to ditch at night with the loss of twenty-one lives, including my former aircrewman, 'Doc' Love, leaving just eleven Sea King IVs and two squadrons of Wessex Vs to support two brigades. In the Brigade Commander's position, I would have been making similar protests. However, the dwindling number of helicopters was not the determining factor. The ASW Sea Kings were not NVG compatible and in the short time available, conversion of an aircraft was not practicable.

Planning could now start in detail. Bill and I made our way to the wardroom annex which was being used by the Special Forces planning cell. On entering the compartment the SAS team leader had his back to me. On turning round I was surprised to see the face of my old friend Captain 'A'.

I greeted him saying, 'Hello Andy, I understand that I'm flying you to Argentina.'

Andy's previously anxious expression changed to one of smiling recognition.

'Hello Dick,' he replied, 'it's good to see a friendly face.' Andy and I continued to exchange pleasantries and he told me about his soaking having parachuted into the sea the previous afternoon. Andy, Major 'E' and I started to talk about the mission whilst Bill left to find 'Wiggy' and Pete Imrie.

Andy had brought with him from the UK satellite photographs covering Tierra del Fuego and the area of Chile from the border with Argentina to some distance inland of Punta Arenas. The imagery was contemporaneous, at a scale of 1:50,000 and of excellent quality, kindly provided by the USA. The same cannot be said of the available mapping. In planning this mission, the SAS had scoured the UK for large- and small-scale maps of the areas of interest, but unfortunately mapping was scarce. Having looked high and low, the team had to make do with black and white photocopies of maps produced in 1939 which were unearthed in the geographic archives of Cambridge University. Armed with satellite photographs and maps of Tierra del Fuego and Chile, I headed back to the briefing room to start a study of them.

The plan called for the operation to be mounted from *Invincible*, launching at approximately midnight local time, the following day, Monday, 17 May. The chosen Sea King, crew and SAS team would cross-deck from *Hermes* during the Monday afternoon and make our final preparations. Cognisant of the forecast for fog over Tierra del Fuego in forty-eight hours, Admiral Woodward had been keen to mount the operation twenty-four hours earlier. However, with the SAS team recently arrived from UK after a long and tiring flight, and with their clothing and equipment soaked during their dunking in the sea, a 24-hour delay was agreed, albeit reluctantly on the part of Admiral Woodward, who was later to record in his diary: 'I had no alternative but to agree, I hope with adequate good grace. I ordered *Hermes* to be brought about and to return to the main group. As the carrier made her turn, I felt somehow the success of the project was making an about turn with us.' His misgivings were to prove well founded.

Seated in the briefing room and pouring over the maps and photographs, my concentration was broken after a few minutes as the door opened and in walked Bill, accompanied by 'Wiggy' and Pete, both bearing broad grins, which I sensed concealed a level of apprehension. We started to talk about the operation when some of the Harrier pilots entered the room. Needing to conduct our planning in total secrecy, I quickly gathered up maps and photographs and we abandoned the briefing room to the 'jet jockeys' and adjourned to my cabin on 5 Deck. Safely away from prying eyes, we carried on with our study of the maps and photographs. Whereas the photographs presented an excellent level of detail, even a cursory examination of the maps was enough for the three of us to appreciate their limited value. We would be unable to take the photographs with us because of the sensitivity of their origin, so we busied ourselves with tracing paper, copied all relevant detail from the photographs and started the painstakingly slow process of transposing it onto the maps. The outcome was impressive by any standard, resulting in maps that gave all the information necessary for accurate navigation at a scale of 1:50,000.

At the time of planning the sortie to take the SAS team into Argentina, the Sea King crew were aware that the team that we were inserting were preliminary to a larger operation but, for reasons of operational security, we were not privy to the detail attendant to the bigger picture. It would be several weeks before I was to learn the extent of the complete operation. However, in compiling this definitive and detailed account, events are described within the context of the bigger picture to ensure a holistic chronology that is contiguous and complete.

The plan, codenamed Operation Mikado, called for the majority of a SAS squadron to be loaded into two C130 aircraft which would be 'crash-landed' onto the runway at Rio Grande. The objective for B Squadron was to locate and destroy the five Super Etendard aircraft believed to be based on the airfield and to destroy the three remaining Exocet missiles. With their mission accomplished, the Squadron was to withdraw under cover of darkness and move to neutral Chile either in the C130s, if they survived the raid, or on foot, some 50 miles to the west, if the C130s had been rendered non-flyable. The planners assessed that by approaching the airbase from the west at low level, the C130s could remain below the cover of the Argentine AN/TPS 43 radar at Rio Grande, until as close as 30 miles. Once the C130s were detected, the Argentine forces would have a maximum six minutes warning time of the raid – assessed as barely sufficient for an effective response. As soon as the C130s had come to a stop, three of B Squadron's troops would locate and destroy the Super Etendards and

Exocets, whilst the fourth troop would attack the officers' mess, killing as many Argentine officers as possible.

For such a high-risk, ultimately high-profile and politically sensitive operation to receive final approval, accurate intelligence was an essential pre-requisite. To this end, as a preliminary operation, a team of volunteers under the command of Captain 'A' of 6 Troop would be inserted into Argentina to conduct a close-target reconnaissance. Their mission would be to confirm the presence of the Super Etendards and Exocet missiles, and to assess the strength and readiness of the Argentine defence forces. If the team identified an opportunity to destroy the aircraft without further assistance then they were to do so and would be equipped with this option in mind. If not, then the main assault force would be deployed in the C130s. A number of options for the deployment of the reconnaissance team were considered by the planning cell at Hereford, to include insertion by either parachute or submarine. Both were discounted early in the planning process: the parachute option could not be achieved without the delivery aircraft being detected by radar, thereby eliminating the elements of surprise and concealment; and the submarine option was impractical due to the shallow water off of the coast of Tierra del Fuego and the lack of availability of a conventional-powered submarine in the required timeframe. This left deployment by helicopter as the only practical option for insertion, as proposed by Captain Lyn Middleton, some days earlier.

Meanwhile, back in the UK, the assault group of B Squadron spent a week training, attacking RAF airfields in Wales and Scotland at night to simulate the Rio Grande raid. During each exercise, the defending RAF personnel reported the point at which the approaching aircraft had been detected on radar – the results were disappointing, with detection somewhat further from the airfield than expected on most occasions. However, undaunted, the planning cell continued with preparations for the raid, to include the procurement of specialist weapons and equipment. But the plan was not without its detractors; many in the Regiment, including some senior officers, had misgivings about the efficacy of the mission – in the minds of some there were too many uncertainties and too many things that could go wrong. Operation Mikado became nicknamed Operation 'Certain Death' by most of the rank and file. Nevertheless, preparations continued unabated and, whilst Captain 'A' and his team were unceremoniously delivered to *Hermes*, approval for their clandestine insertion into Argentina was given by the War Cabinet.

For the remainder of the afternoon and early evening I continued with route study and aircraft preparations whilst Captain 'A' and his team were cleaning their weapons and drying their clothing and equipment following their unceremonious dunking. *Hermes* would not be able to move far enough to the west to mount the operation the following night, so that task was delegated to *Invincible*. The following afternoon the aircraft, crew and nine Special Forces (eight SAS and one SBS) would cross-deck, but in the meantime there were other considerations. I had been mulling over in my mind for some hours whether or not it would be possible to save the aircraft by converting a one-way mission into a return journey. I decided to share my thoughts with Bill and 'Radar'. The Sea King IV can be refuelled only from the outside of the cabin. The two refuelling points, one for pressure and one for gravity, are aft of the cabin door and cannot be reached from inside the aircraft. I asked 'Radar' whether it was possible to devise a temporary refuelling rig so that the aircraft could be refuelled from inside the cabin. After careful thought he said that such an arrangement would be possible. With a full fuel load the Sea King has an endurance of just over six hours. With a launch position immediately due south of the islands, the aircraft had sufficient range and endurance to reach Argentina, drop off at the required location and return to sea to a position approximately halfway between the Argentine coast and West Falkland. I wanted to explore the technical feasibility of refuelling the aircraft, under the cover of darkness, just to the west of that point, from a submarine or escort. I reasoned that during the hours of darkness, a submarine could surface and RV with a helicopter that could transfer by winch a number of 45-gallon drums of fuel. Twenty-four hours or so later, I could RV with the submarine, winch the drums into my aircraft and Pete would be able to refuel the aircraft through the temporary rig from inside the cabin. Technically all of this was feasible – the question was would my suggestion meet with approval? I did not have long to find out. After a few minutes Bill returned to explain that my suggestion was not an option – it was considered too high a risk to both a submarine or escort.

Early in the evening I went to my cabin to pack all of my personal belongings; I would not be needing them again in a hurry. As I did so my thoughts turned to my wife and children back in Somerset, and my parents in Essex. What would they make of all this? I wondered. I knew that my mother would be worried out of her mind, while my father would feel immensely proud – he was dying from cancer so I reasoned that it was good that he should have positive feelings with not many months left to live. I sensed that Lorraine would have mixed feelings, but it was important to me to know that she understood the importance of what I was about to do. It was fifty/fifty whether or not I and my friends would survive to tell the story, so I decided to write letters for both my parents and Lorraine and leave them with Bill – in the event of my death I knew that he would ensure their safe delivery. The letter to Lorraine is reproduced below:

HMS Hermes at Sea

16 May 1982

Dearest Darling – the Task Group is in a tight spot and I have volunteered for a mission into Argentina which is of necessity one-way and high risk. In the short time that is left before I travel on this last journey, I am taking advantage of a lull in the weather and enemy action to write letters preparatory to my possible death. The first is to you, the love of my life, who is constantly in my thoughts, day and night. If anything happens to me I should like you to know how much you have meant to me during our time together and that happy memories are with me as I leave. Please take what comfort you can from my feelings. I shall leave the world all the stronger for my emotional bond to you and the boys. I am uncertain as to what exactly lies ahead over the coming hours and perhaps days. But I am well prepared for whatever fate throws my way. I am not alone in the venture on which I am about to depart and will have close friends with me to the end. We are all apprehensive, but fairly confident that we'll come through a very tough test of our resolve. With each passing day now the weather deteriorates, the ship often assumes the characteristics of a fairground ride – it will be good to be airborne just to get away from the relentless motion.

I am in good spirits and have been so since leaving England seven weeks ago. It has been rewarding to see so many friends and colleagues rising to the challenge whilst maintaining a good sense of humour. There have been a few casualties, you will be aware of those from the news, but there have also been a few cases of psychological stress – this war fighting is proving too much for some, I pity them. For my part I feel strongly that the Government's decision to go to war was the right one. It is a just war; a war for the liberation of British people from a fascist tyranny.

I am sure that you will deal with the whole thing with your usual gritty determination and common sense. The boys will be your comfort and strength. I had looked forward to us raising them together, but I am comforted to know that they are safe with you. You should comfort yourself by knowing that mine will have been the very best example of sacrifice.

Don't torture yourself over undying loyalty to me. If the right man comes along you should seize the opportunity to be happy and get on with your life to the full. I hope I shall be a good memory – certainly my death is nothing for you to be worried or embarrassed about and I like to think that the boys will have a good start in life and fine role models to be proud of.

We have been together now for long enough for you to know how I have loved you, you know my thoughts must have constantly dwelt on you and you must know that quite the worst aspect of this situation is the thought that I shall not see you again – the inevitable must be faced. I know you felt that this deployment would be dangerous – I am content that I have done my bit.

I am anxious for you and the boys' future – encourage the boys to be interested in the things that really matter in life, doing one's duty, being loyal to one's conscience above all else, loyal to one's family and friends and loyal to the truth. Sadly the society in which we live today does not foster these qualities. I know you will face the future stoically – your picture and the boys are always with me. What a tale you will be able to tell one day.

Please be good to my parents. Dad is not long for this world; stay close to them. Put on a strong face for everyone to see – only don't be too proud to accept help for the boys' sake – they ought to have fine careers and make something of themselves. I haven't time to write to any of our friends – tell them I thought much of them and valued their friendship.

God bless you my own darling. I shall try and write more later if I get the opportunity before I depart tomorrow.

I have written a letter to my parents which I have enclosed with this, my last letter to you. Please take it with you when you go to see them.

Your loving husband.

Kit packed and letter written, I sat in my cabin for a few minutes reflecting on the past few weeks since leaving England: the successes and the tragedies; the fine examples of spirit and courage that I had witnessed; the ever-present humour, sometimes black, but always well intentioned; the sound of Rod Stewart's 'Sailing' as the Task Force left Portsmouth; the 'Crossing-the-Line' ceremony; those early pioneering NVG sorties; the mammoth 'Vertrep' programme when at Ascension; the loss of 'Ben' Casey; the sinking of the *Belgrano* and *Sheffield*; the Pebble Island raid; *Narwal*; the large number of Special Forces teams inserted and supported. Some of these events seemed very distant; how time had flown.

After dinner I made my way to the wardroom for a beer where I met with 'Wiggy'. After several minutes we were joined by Major Cedric Delves, the OC of D Squadron. Later to be promoted to Lieutenant General, Cedric was interested to know how we felt about our one-way trip to Argentina.

'I can't speak for "Wiggy", but I feel good about it,' I said. 'Wiggy' was of the same outlook. From his general demeanour, Cedric gave the impression of being in the camp of the SAS sceptics. We talked at some length about the task before I decided that I needed to be alone with my thoughts for a while, so I adjourned to the briefing room via my cabin to collect maps and satellite photographs. The briefing room was empty of aircrew, so I set about spreading out the maps and photographs, and studied them for several minutes running over in my mind every mile of the journey. Reminded of the proverb 'There's many a slip twixt the cup and the lip', I found myself asking what could go wrong. Had I identified every possible eventuality? What was to be done in the event of something unexpected occurring? My deliberations were interrupted by Dave Morgan entering the room. He came over and glanced at the odd-looking photocopied maps. I gathered them together quickly but unhurriedly so as not to arouse too much interest on Dave's part.

'Going somewhere nice then?' Dave enquired.

I thought it best not to reply directly to his question, but instead gave him a rather withering look saying, 'This is one of the few places where a chap can find some peace and quiet to do a little studying. If I do find somewhere nice to visit I'll be sure to let you know.'

During the course of the afternoon and evening, Bill and 'Radar' had been considering which of the aircraft would be best suited for the one-way flight. Clearly the aircraft had to be up to the job, but when setting out with the express intention of destroying one of Her Majesty's aircraft, such a decision could not be taken lightly.

After careful consideration, ZA 290 ('Victor Charlie'), the aircraft that I had been flying for all of the NVG sorties, was chosen. Modifications were to be made the next day following arrival on *Invincible*. All equipment not required for the task would be removed, including the winch, load-lifting equipment, sound proofing, flotation gear, FOD deflector and a small number of ancillary items.

There was nothing more to be done by way of preparation until the following day, so I decided to have an early night. There would be no opportunity for sleep the next day prior to mounting the operation, so one last night of quality sleep was essential. As it turned out it was to be my last night of decent sleep for many days. I returned to my cabin to write the letter to my parents, a copy of which is shown below:

HMS Hermes at sea

16 May 1982

Dearest Mum and Dad,

You are reading this letter because I will never again have the joy of seeing you and being in your company. At the time of writing, the Task Force is in a tight spot which calls for a mission to be flown into Argentina. The flight is of necessity one-way and therefore high risk. The outcome of the mission is unlikely to be revealed for many years, but for my part, I did not live to fight another day. That's war I guess: I have done my duty.

By the very nature of what I have to do, the end would have come quickly. I would not have been alone, but in the company of close friends and colleagues to the end. I have been in good spirits throughout my time with the Task Force. It was rewarding to see so many friends and colleagues rising to the challenge whilst maintaining a good sense of humour. There have been a few casualties, you will be aware of those from the news, but there have also been a few cases of psychological stress – war fighting proved too much for some, I pitied them. For my part I felt strongly that the government's decision to go to war was the right one. It was a just war; a war for liberation of British people from fascist tyranny.

Please take what comfort you can from my feelings and from each other. I shall leave the world fresh from attachments other than my emotional bond to you, Lorraine and the children, and in good health and spirit.

Your loving and dutiful son

Monday, 17 May was Argentina Navy Day. To mark the event, many on *Hermes* believed that the Argentine Navy would launch another Exocet attack on the Task Force. The weather for the Super Etendards was ideal: broken cloud and excellent visibility. There were indications during the day that the Etendards were looking for us, but ultimately an attack never materialized. All of this now seemed somewhat distant to me as my thoughts on what I had to do became more focused and crystallized with each passing moment. I awoke unusually early, either because I had enjoyed an early night and had recharged my batteries, or because of nervous expectation at my forthcoming task; I did not know which. No matter, I had things to do and an early start was called for. After eating a hearty breakfast – it was to be my last for many days, I made my way to 03 Deck for a breath of fresh air and to be alone with my thoughts for the last time. Was I doing the right thing? I kept asking myself. Each time the answer was the same: yes. The planning for the task was complete; final admin matters had been attended to. All that was required now was to cross-deck to *Invincible* and kill yet more time waiting for darkness and the moment of launch. I felt something of how a condemned man must feel in the hours before his execution; the minutes seemed like hours. With little to do, my thoughts turned increasingly to family – how would Lorraine cope if I were never to see her again? Was I being selfish in volunteering for this mission, or was it more selfish not to? I had to clear these doubts from my mind, so I left 03 Deck and made my way to the briefing room.

'Wiggy' and Pete were already in the room when I arrived. The previous day I had asked the ship's Principal Medical Officer (PMO) for a supply of diamorphine.

Where we were going there would be no medical attention available. If any one of us became seriously injured, it would be at least eight days before we could seek help from the Chilean authorities, so we needed to be self-sufficient with effective pain control available to us. After a few minutes, the PMO entered the room carrying our supply of diamorphine, in all handing me a container of fifty ampoules. I straight away handed two each to 'Wiggy' and Pete. Each of us attached two ampoules to the cord which carried our ID discs around our necks so that they would be immediately available if required. I placed the container with the remaining forty-four ampoules in my Bergen and not long afterwards we were joined in the briefing room by 'Wings' and Captain Lyn Middleton. The Captain briefed me as to exactly what I was to do and, as importantly, what not to do. He also asked that I send him a postcard if possible, to let him know that we were alive and well . . . somewhere. Having wished us good luck, the Captain and 'Wings' left the briefing room, to be replaced by Nigel and Pete Rainey, both offering sound advice on aspects of the task. After Nigel and Pete had left the room, I handed Bill my last letters home.

'God willing, they will never be read,' said Bill with great sincerity and some emotion.

'Amen to that,' I replied.

Following an early lunch, it was time to bid farewell to *Hermes* for the last time and fly the short distance to *Invincible*. I loaded my bergen and navigation bag into the aircraft, but for this last departure from *Hermes* I would not be flying the aircraft. Instead, the three of us, together with the Special Forces team, 'Radar' and a small group of maintainers, were flown as passengers in two Sea Kings. The purpose of the second aircraft was twofold: a spare in the event that 'Victor Charlie' became unserviceable and, following our launch from *Invincible*, to return 'Radar' and his team of maintainers to *Hermes*. I sat back to 'take in' all that was going on around me. As the aircraft lifted from its spot and transitioned away from *Hermes*, I realized with some trepidation that I was leaving for the last time the ship that had been my home for the last seven weeks.

CHAPTER 12

HMS *Invincible*

It felt strange to be landing on HMS *Invincible* as a passenger on that sunny Monday afternoon. As a pilot I had never been a good passenger and today was no exception, so I was relieved to be out of the back of the aircraft and onto the deck. I watched as *Invincible*'s aircraft handlers manoeuvred 'Victor Charlie' into 'the green', aft of the Island. It had been decided not to fold the rotor blades, but rather to leave them spread. With recent memories of the Pebble Island operation and the ninety-minute delay caused by the strong winds, we could not afford the risk of a recurrence. The spare aircraft, rotors folded, was moved to a position just aft, so as to be immediately available in the event of any problem with my aircraft. Compared to the ageing, rusting and war-torn *Hermes*, *Invincible* showed little sign of distress. The ship appeared remarkably fresh, so much so that I was left wondering if she had been participating in the same war. My observation was in no way critical of *Invincible*, but served to draw a distinction between the appearance of two carriers at the opposite ends of their respective lives.

Having been embarked in *Invincible* and HMS *Illustrious* in the past when they had been configured in the LPH role, operating in support of amphibious exercises, I was familiar with the ship's layout. With the exception of 'Radar' and his team, the rest of the group quickly found our way to the aircrew briefing room. Meanwhile 'Radar' and the maintainers set about establishing themselves in the Line Office before busying themselves carrying out the modifications to 'Victor Charlie' in preparation for our mission. The briefing room was larger than the one that I had become accustomed to in *Hermes*, but then *Hermes* had two aircrew briefing rooms and *Invincible* only the one. 'Wiggy', Pete and I found ourselves an area towards the back of the room, and continued our planning and deliberations. Captain 'A' and his team occupied an area right at the front of the room. We were far enough apart so as not to disturb each other, but close enough to be able to hear each others' discussions.

The briefing room was shared by the embarked Harrier Group, 801 Squadron and the 'Pingers', 820 Squadron. The Sea King aircrew duty officer that day was Prince Andrew. We had served together at RNAS Culdrose during 1980 when 'H', as he liked to be known, was attending the basic helicopter course with 705 Squadron and I was attending the Sea King conversion course with 706 Squadron. 'H' entered the room after we had been there only a few minutes. As soon as he saw me he smiled in recognition and explained to us all that he was the duty officer and would endeavour to do all that he could to facilitate our short stay; we had only to let him know what our needs were and he would make the necessary arrangements. His offer of assistance was tested on several occasions during the afternoon and evening and the goods were delivered without fuss as promised. However, on more than one occasion 'Radar' invited him to leave the briefing room during periods when we were discussing aspects of the operation – the 'need to know' principle applied to even the second in line to the throne (at that time)! Every time that 'H' left the room rather disgruntled, 'Radar's' chances of a Knighthood diminished!

It was not long before we were joined by *Invincible*'s Captain, Jeremy Black, and 'Wings', 'Dusty' Milner. I knew 'Dusty' from my time at Yeovilton. During my SAS course at Hereford the previous year, 'Dusty' had been the 'friendly face' who was to tell me that the interrogation phase of my training was over. Having completed his time at Yeovilton, he was appointed to *Invincible* as Commander Air. His was the second friendly face that I was to recognize on board and seeing him again was most welcome. The Captain introduced himself, not that he needed any introduction, and spent a long time sitting alongside me talking about aspects of the operation. His presence was reassuring. I was immediately struck by his warmth and ability to put me and others totally at ease. I felt flattered that he was prepared to devote so much of his valuable time to such a junior officer. I was, of course, cognisant of the importance of my mission and realized that Jeremy Black would, therefore, take an interest, but I felt that the care that he took over providing reassuring counsel, his relaxed approach and ability to communicate on equal terms, were indicators of the outstanding quality of his inspirational leadership. Over the hours that we talked, I began to appreciate that underneath the façade of easy professionalism, there also lurked a mischievous sense of humour. On a number of occasions this came to the fore and was always appropriate to the moment. Some years later I was to meet again the then Admiral Sir Jeremy Black when he was the Commander-in-Chief Naval Home Command and Second Sea Lord. He was understandably keen to find out the outcome of my mission. Despite the restrictions placed upon me by the rigours of the 'thirty-year' secrecy rule, I had no hesitation in presenting him with a full account of the operation. With the exception of the late Lord Lewin, two members of the Special Operations Group (SOG) and the two MoD officials who formally debriefed me, I had not, at the time of writing this book, shared this knowledge with another soul.

Early in the evening, the Captain left the room and 'Wiggy', Pete and I decided that it was time for dinner. After eating a large meal, sufficient to sustain me for more than a day, I returned to the briefing room to complete final preparations for the operation. In the meantime, 'Radar' and his team had finished the modifications to 'Victor Charlie' and were putting the final touches to the paperwork. Not long after the arrival of Captain 'A' and his team on *Hermes*, they had been weighed, along with their equipment, to establish the total weight to be carried in the aircraft. *Invincible* was in the process of moving to a launch position as far west as the Captain dare in order to reduce to a minimum the distance to be flown to the Argentine coast, thereby leaving as much fuel as possible for use whilst flying over Argentina and, to a lesser extent, Chile. Nevertheless, full fuel would be required for the mission. The combination of full fuel and a heavy payload would put the aircraft well above MAUM on launch. A Sea King had never been flown at this weight before and I had no way of knowing how the aircraft would handle whilst so heavy; I needed guidance. To this end, the previous day Bill sought advice from the Flight Test Centre at AAEE Boscombe Down, in Wiltshire, via satellite telephone. The advice from the test pilots was to take off into the maximum strength headwind possible, avoiding wind from the starboard quarter – tail rotor control issues, use the maximum transient rotor revs and torque as necessary, keep the airspeed to below 75kts initially and keep the angle of bank to below 20° for the first two hours of flight, after which time the aircraft would be at MAUM. In order to shed unnecessary weight and save from destruction as much of the aircraft as possible, equipment not needed for the mission had by now been removed, including the winch, flotation gear, SACRU, load beam, sound proofing, life raft, GPMG mounts, FOD deflector, fire extinguishers, most troop seats and some of the avionics – in all a saving in aircraft weight of 800lb. Some accounts of the mission which have been published, including that written by Nigel West, state that the aircraft was fitted with additional 'long-range' fuel tanks. This was not the case.

I was amused and also bemused to learn that, although I was required to sign for the aircraft in the MoD Form 700, a standard prerequisite to flying a military aircraft, no one was prepared to give me a written authorization for the sortie. The explanation offered for this unique situation was that authorization for a flight from a ship is intrinsic in the Captain's approval for launch. This was and remains the case, but the purpose of the Squadron's written authorization is a written record of the exact scope of the sortie, any restrictions and the aircraft Captain's acknowledgement. The anomaly to this day is that 846 Squadron has no written record of the authorization for my sortie. I imagine that had there been one then it would, of necessity, have been classified Top Secret. I have, however, reproduced opposite a facsimile of the MoD Form 700 page.

As the evening progressed, Captain 'A' presented me with Argentinean, Chilean and USA foreign currency to cater for the unexpected. As I was counting the tens of thousands of pesos and dollars, it occurred to me that a small quantity of sterling would be a prudent addition to my stash of cash. By this time, Jeremy Black had rejoined us and made a phone call requesting the ship's Supply Officer to join us in the briefing room. After a few minutes, a

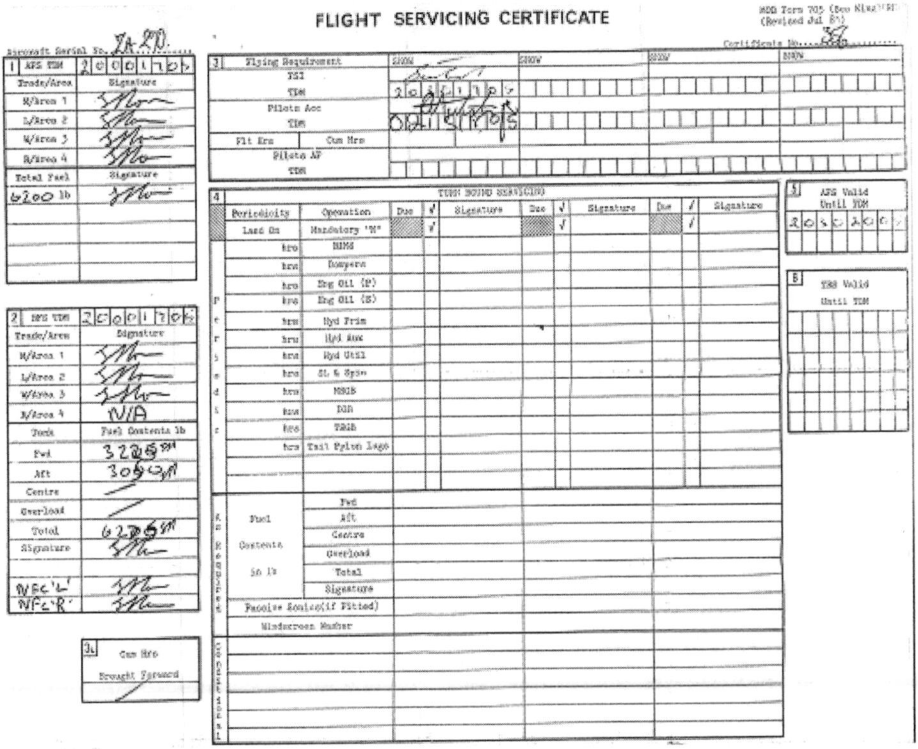

Figure 1: ZA 290 Flight Servicing Certificate.

rather bemused Commander entered the room, curious as to why on earth a 'Pusser' should be needed in an aircrew briefing room. Jeremy Black explained that we three aircrew needed some sterling to tide us over for a few days. After careful thought we decided on £40 each. This does not sound much, but allowing for compound inflation, today it would be the equivalent of just over £100. After several minutes, the Supply Officer returned bearing the money. Whereas the foreign currency was unaccountable, the sterling, on the other hand, had to be signed for; I was quite taken aback. I needed some sterling to cater for operational contingencies, not to fund a piss-up in London! In fact, as it turned out the money was needed to pay for certain necessities, as will become apparent in a later chapter.

I also mentioned to Jeremy Black that my Spanish was rather rusty and that I would be most grateful if a Spanish phrase book or English/Spanish dictionary could be found on the ship. The Captain made another phone call, the ship's Education Officer duly appeared in the room a few minutes later and was invited to scour the ship for the aforementioned books. Imagine our amazement when a few minutes later we heard throughout the ship the pipe: '*Anyone with a Spanish phrase book or dictionary please bring it to the education officer.*' Jeremy Black and I looked at each other in total disbelief and horror.

'Bang goes the secrecy,' muttered a clearly rattled Captain. Several minutes passed before a sheepish-looking Education Officer entered the room bearing gifts of two Spanish phrase books, kindly donated by members of the ship's company. I never found out to this day who gave the books, but if they ever read this account then I would like to say to them, thank you – they did come in handy.

In all, 'Wiggy', Pete and I spent the best part of ten hours on *Invincible*, a good part of it in the briefing room, with the occasional outing to the wardroom or flight deck to see how 'Radar' and the maintainers were getting on with their task. It was during the periods spent in the briefing room that I became privy to some of the discussions within the Special Forces team. It was clear that there was disagreement amongst them as to the actions to be taken in certain circumstances; at one stage Captain 'A' stormed out of the room following an altercation with a fellow team member. The SAS and SBS have a clear rank structure like all elements of the Armed Forces, however, the teams try to plan their missions through consensus rather than from slavish deference to authoritarian leadership. As time went on it became apparent that there was some unease within the team about aspects of the mission. The team comprised an officer and eight assorted other ranks, including three experienced NCOs, one of them a Royal Marine from the SBS. In all, a talent-packed group. Captain 'A' was a rather unconventional SAS officer, who was popular with his men. His second-in-command was a Scottish SNCO, a seasoned SAS veteran who was battle hardened, tenacious and resolute. Having heard a number of disagreements from within the team which caused me concern, I felt that before departure I had to share my observations with the Captain as to their apparent disquiet. As I left the briefing room to walk to the flight deck, I could not help but think that the operation was destined to get off to an inauspicious start.

CHAPTER **13**

A One-way Trip to Argentina

aunch was set for midnight local time from a position close to Beuchene Island, approximately 30 miles due south of East Falkland. With an hour to go, I walked around the aircraft conducting a pre-flight inspection, paying the utmost attention to every detail required by the check list. The Special Forces team climbed into the aircraft and 'Wiggy' and I went through the start checks. Pete ensured that the passengers were as comfortable as possible and that all of their heavy kit was secure for take-off. I gave myself plenty of time just in case the aircraft developed a critical snag on start-up, leaving me no option but to use the spare aircraft. With both engines running and all systems on line, I engaged the rotors. So far so good; no snags. We had some time in hand before arrival at the launch position and the aircraft remained on deck for several minutes, during which time we were burning precious fuel. The Sea King has both pressure and gravity refuel capabilities. It is not possible to fill the tanks completely using the normal pressure refuelling system; gravity refuel is not permitted on board ships because of the risk of spontaneous fuel ignition – rather akin to smoking or using a mobile phone whilst filling a car with petrol in a service station. However, on this occasion the Captain made an exception and 'Radar' ensured that the fuel tanks were full to the brim immediately prior to take-off. With just a few seconds remaining, I took off my expensive 'Gucci' shoulder holster and handed it to 'Radar' for safe-keeping, saying, 'I'll be wanting this back.'

'I'll keep it safe,' he replied. 'Keep yourselves safe.'

At 0015hrs, 'Flyco' delivered the navigation data and 'Wiggy' fixed our launch position in TANS. The ship was steaming directly into wind at approximately 30kts, creating a relative wind of dead ahead at more than 60kts. As 'Wiggy' increased the rotor revs to the maximum transient limit, I cautiously applied power. With a near hurricane-force wind rushing through the rotors, the very heavy aircraft with a mass of 23,350lb, lifted effortlessly into a low hover and transitioned quickly into forward flight. Using no more than an average amount of twin-matched torques, the Sea King transitioned across the edge of the flight deck and away from the ship heading 265° into the dark, moonless night. Operation Plum Duff was under way.

Immediately following the aircraft's departure, *Invincible* and her escorts, *Brilliant* and *Coventry*, were turned around to head initially east then north-east to rejoin the Task Force over 300 miles away. The ships would need every minute of the remaining seven hours of darkness and more to close with the Task Force. Nevertheless, *Invincible* took time out from her long transit to draw attention away from our westward flight by launching two Harriers in the early hours of the morning to drop Lepus flares over Port Stanley. This distraction was followed at dawn by a raid on Stanley Airfield by three Harriers dropping six 1,000lb bombs.

Meanwhile, now steadily closing the distance to the Argentine mainland, the Sea King continued on its thus far uneventful journey. Once well clear of West Falkland, there was no danger of being detected by Argentine radar based on the Islands, so for the first two hours I flew the aircraft at a height of 200 feet instead of the by now customary 50 feet. The additional height would create a small cushion of extra time for manoeuvre in the event of an emergency requiring the aircraft to ditch. The flotation kit had been removed from the aircraft to save weight and ensure that in the event of ditching en route the aircraft would sink without trace. The early stage of the journey was flown into a strong but slowly reducing headwind, which restricted our ground speed initially to approximately 40kts. With passage of time the wind decreased and backed with our ground speed increasing to nearer 100kts. Total flight time to the Argentine coast would, therefore, take approximately four hours. Throughout the flight, 'Wiggy' made regular sweeps with the Omega RWR to establish that we were remaining undetected by Argentine radar. The radar inter-visibility traces that were available to us took account of all known Argentine land-based radar systems, but could not, of course, cater for ship-borne systems. The Task Force had no way of knowing the whereabouts of the Argentine Navy, so we remained alert to the possibility of Argentine warships being in the sea areas off the Argentine coast. My orders were that the aircraft was to retain radio and electronic silence throughout the mission – with one exception. If we encountered the Argentina carrier, ARA *Veinteccinco de Mayo*, then we were to break radio silence and transmit the ship's position using the long-range HF radio. It would have been a really long shot getting a message through over such a long distance, but we were to try. As it transpired we did not make contact with Argentinean ships of any kind, nor they us, throughout our journey.

As the wind decreased and backed, the visibility also steadily decreased. With 100 miles to fly to reach the Argentine coast, the visibility had reduced to less than 5 miles and I had reduced height to 50 feet. As each few minutes passed, the visibility decreased by a few hundred metres. When reaching a position just over 50 miles to the east of our intended landfall on the southern tip of Bahia San Sebastian (San Sebastian Bay), 'Wiggy' and I became aware of an eerie green glow, low in the sky, directly ahead of the aircraft. I looked under the goggles to see a long orange light on a constant relative bearing, which appeared to be flickering. Initially unable to make out its form I continued flying on the same heading, but slowed the aircraft to 60kts. When approximately 4 miles away I realized to my horror that the light was a long flame, a flare burning from the end of a tower on an exploratory oil or gas platform; we had stumbled across an Argentine off-shore gas or oilfield. I decided to give the platform a wide berth and turned north to fly a circuitous route aiming to make a revised landfall to the north of San Sebastian Bay.

I was later to discover that we had flown into the southern part of the Argentine Carina gas field which, in 1982, had just started exploratory drilling. In turning north I had unwittingly flown further into the gas field, but fortunately encountered no other platforms. At the time I was furious that the planning team had potentially jeopardized the mission through their failure to identify Argentina's off-shore tapestry – after all it was not as if such activity was either covert or even low profile. Quite the opposite, as I was to discover some weeks later when trawling through newspaper articles written at the time of the Falklands War. An article featuring the Carena gas field was published in the *Sunday Telegraph* on 11 April 1982 under the headline: 'The Lure of Oil in Troubled Waters'. In mitigation, the planners would argue that the available satellite imagery of the area, kindly supplied by the USA just days earlier, did not extend seaward beyond coastal waters, and intelligence and research sources were rather thin on the ground at the time. I guess that this was yet another example of the 'fog of war', but, nonetheless, it was a planning/intelligence failing that I could have done without when having to cope with the real fog that was slowly enveloping the aircraft.

CHAPTER 14

Fog, Now What?

If a man will begin with certainties, he shall end in doubts; but if he will be content to begin with doubts he shall end in certainties.

Sir Francis Bacon

The detour to the north was to add approximately twenty minutes to the flight and consume valuable fuel. It was at 0430hrs when we finally caught sight of the Argentine coast, two hours after the moon had risen over Rio Grande. The moon was in the final vestiges of its last quarter, providing very little additional ambient light. I flew the aircraft due west to intercept the Argentine coast at the northern tip of San Sebastian Bay. The waves breaking on the long sandbar which extended south into the mouth of the bay provided much needed contrast in what were becoming increasingly difficult flying conditions. The visibility was no greater than a mile as, on arrival at the coast, I turned the aircraft south to fly the 18 miles to our pre-planned landfall on the southern tip of the bay and for which the coordinates were already programmed into TANS. We had covered a distance of 320 nautical miles thus far and used 4,000lb of fuel, nearly 500lb of it through circumnavigating the gas field. With another 200 miles to be flown and with just over 2,000lb of fuel remaining, I remarked to 'Wiggy' that it was going to be tight. As we flew closer to the southern shoreline I could just make out the waves breaking on the sandy beach at the southern end of the mouth of the bay, which was our landfall waypoint. 'Wiggy' and I were taken aback by the poor visibility. Neither of the met officers in *Hermes* or *Invincible* had made any mention of fog during their weather forecasts for our mission.

As we flew overhead the waypoint, 'Wiggy' fixed our position in TANS as I turned onto a heading of 180° towards our next waypoint, reducing height to 20 feet and slowing the aircraft once again to 60kts. The terrain was low lying and covered predominantly in short grass and clumps of the marsh grass indicative of boggy ground. As we flew south, the visibility and light level deteriorated rapidly with each passing mile. I had no option but to slow the aircraft still further until reaching a stage of flying at no faster than a hover-taxi. I knew that it would not be long before I would run out of external visual references by which to fly the aircraft. The surface of the ground to either side of the aircraft was the same: featureless and devoid of contrast. Climbing the aircraft to fly above the layer of fog and in an improved level of ambient light would have exposed us to detection by the AN/TPS 43 radar known to be at Rio Grande and was, therefore, not an option. Fast running out of ideas and options I landed the aircraft in the certain knowledge that it would be my last opportunity to make a safe landing whilst remaining in full control of the aircraft. The planned drop-off location for the Special Forces team was a point close to an isolated estancia, 12 miles to the north-west of Rio Grande airbase. In the increasingly adverse weather and light conditions, we had managed to fly to a point 7 miles short of our intended destination, in the vicinity of Seccion Miranda. Captain 'A' had been listening and talking to us via the aircraft intercom system throughout the flight. As we landed he came to the front of the aircraft so that 'Wiggy' could point out to him our exact location on the map from the coordinates in TANS. After a few moments Captain 'A' announced that he was aborting the mission because he did not have confidence that the aircraft was exactly where 'Wiggy' and I said it was. Despite our best endeavours to persuade him to the contrary, he would not accept the grid reference of the aircraft's landing point and asked to be flown into Chile. Whilst 'Wiggy' and I remonstrated with Captain 'A', three of the team had already disembarked from the aircraft and were standing on Argentine soil beside the cabin door. At this point Captain 'A' shouted to the three men on the ground,

'I'm sorry, it's Chile after all.'

The response from one of the team on the ground was as memorable as it was apposite, 'Chile, it's fucking freezing!'

Ten years later, Admiral Sandy Woodward was to write an outline account of the planning of the operation in his book, *One Hundred Days*. I was surprised by his comment, 'In my opinion it would be damned nearly impossible to get the helicopter down at all, never mind with any geographical accuracy, in the kind of weather the forecasters were giving for the Rio Grande coastal area tomorrow night.' I do not know to this day why, if the Admiral was cognisant of the appalling weather forecast for our mission, I had not also been informed?

It would be another fourteen years before a supposedly 'definitive' account of the operation was published. In 1996, the author Nigel West was invited by the SAS to their headquarters in Hereford, to be briefed on Operation Mikado, to include the conduct of the preliminary operation, Plum Duff. On 18 February 1996, the *Sunday Times* published an article by Nigel West under the headline: 'Who Dares Wins – Operation Mikado: The Last Secret of The Falklands War'. One year later, Nigel West's book, *The Secret War For The Falklands*, was published. In both publications, the account of the preliminary operation, Plum

Duff, misrepresents events in Argentina. The *Sunday Times* article stated: 'As the helicopter approached the target area, 20km north of Rio Grande, the Omega radar warning receiver in the cockpit began to "ping", alerting the pilot to a lock-on by hostile radar. Then the co-pilot reported seeing a flare, some distance away. After a quick consultation with Captain 'A' it was agreed the mission should continue, but as they landed a second flare was seen, much closer, arching into the night sky. The patrol was already scrambling out of the side door when Captain 'A', after an agonizing few moments, decided the mission had been compromised. The whole scheme depended on surprise, and his principal task was to avoid discovery.' The account in my book accurately describes events on the night, as formally recorded in official MoD records. The Omega radar warning receiver did not detect Argentine radar until the aircraft was established in a climb to clear the mountain range, after the decision had already been made by Captain 'A' to abort the mission. There were no flares seen on the Argentine mainland at any time. The only 'flare' seen during the operation was the flame from the gas exploration platform, 50 miles off of the Argentine coast. Miguel Pita's (the base commander at Rio Grande) account of events that night also confirms that no flares were fired. One can only speculate as to why the SAS-briefed accounts published in the *Sunday Times* and reproduced in Nigel West's book misrepresented actual events and it is not appropriate for me to hypothesize. I'll leave it to others to draw their own conclusions.

CHAPTER 15

Chile? It's F****** Freezing!

With the mission having been aborted by Captain 'A', the priority was to leave the area as quickly as possible and fly to Chile. During planning of the operation, three potential locations for landing and destroying the aircraft had been chosen from a study of the maps and satellite imagery of Tierra del Fuego and mainland Chile. The location finally chosen would be dictated by a combination of fuel available at the time and a final confirmatory reconnaissance of each location as necessary. The worst-case option assumed little fuel remaining after crossing the border – a small but prominent beach on the southern shore of Bahia Inutil (Useless Bay). The bay was so named by British geographers in the late nineteenth century because it was assessed as unusable as a port. It is a large expanse of water orientated east-west to the eastern side of the Straits of Magellan and less than thirty minutes flying time from the planned landing site in Argentina.

'Wiggy' selected the waypoint in TANS, and I lifted the aircraft into a hover and transitioned forward onto a heading of 290°. Lying directly in our path was a mountain range named Sierra de Carmen Silva (The Mountain Range of Carmen Whistles). In the fog it was impossible to maintain NOE flight, I therefore had no option but to climb the aircraft to altitude to safely negotiate the mountains. Reaching over 3,000 feet in height, the mountains formed an obstacle orientated roughly north-south extending to the coastal regions north and south of Tierra del Fuego. Given our low fuel level and the fog, there was no way of circumnavigating the mountains. In climbing the aircraft I realized that we would be exposed to the Argentine AN/TPS 43 radar just a few miles away at Rio Grande, but it was a risk that had to be taken. 'Wiggy' orientated the RWR towards Rio Grande when, just 200 feet into our climb, the Omega burst into life, confirming that the aircraft had been detected by a radar system. The question was what type and where?

After just a few seconds we were able to identify positively the unmistakable signature of an AN/TPS 43 surveillance radar. The bearing of the signal confirmed the location as Rio Grande. The radar has a range of 300 miles, so we were certain we would remain illuminated until able to descend below the crest of the mountain range. The aircraft had been detected, the Argentineans at Rio Grande knew therefore that there was a slow-moving aircraft flying on an opening vector from the area of the airbase. I continued to climb the aircraft as we slowly closed the distance to the mountain range. As we climbed above 1,000 feet the aircraft emerged from the fog into a deep layer of broken stratus cloud. In the breaks in the cloud I could see the moon for the first time, low in the sky. Visibility above the fog was poor. After three minutes I had achieved an altitude of 3,000 feet and levelled the aircraft. The Omega was wired into the intercom system, therefore throughout the climb we could hear the relentless buzz of the radar. Every ten seconds there was a pulse of sound reminding us, as if we needed any reminding, that the Argentineans were watching our every move.

What next I wondered? Would an Argentine fire-control radar lock onto the aircraft? For such an eventuality we had Chaff and Pete kept a supply in his hands ready for deployment, just in case. We asked ourselves if there was anyone on the ground at Rio Grande watching the radar screen? By now the aircraft was over 20 miles away from the airbase so out of range of radar-controlled artillery and the Roland SAM system we knew to be there. The Argentinean's only night-capable fighter was the Mirage III, based at Rio Gallegos. By the time that operations at Rio Grande could respond to our presence and task an interception from Rio Gallegos, we would be out of Argentine airspace and over the border into Chile. I reasoned that, even though the aircraft was clearly visible on a radar screen, our presence was most likely to be assessed as mysterious, but not posing an immediate threat.

Research that I conducted in Argentina in 1997 was most revealing. The base defence commander at Rio Grande in 1982 was Brigadier Miguel Pita, in command of a force of over 2,600 marines. The Argentine account of events indicated that an attack on the airbase was anticipated days before our arrival in the area. During the early hours of 18 May, Brigadier Pita claimed that a slow-flying aircraft, assumed to be a helicopter, was detected by radar approaching Rio Grande from the direction of Chile. Radar detection was lost for a few minutes before contact was re-established as the slow-flying aircraft was monitored heading back in the direction of Chile. The Argentine military command assumed that a party of Special Forces had been infiltrated from Chile and that their target was presumed to be the airbase at Rio Grande. Two elements of the Argentine account do not withstand closer scrutiny. Firstly, our approach to Rio Grande had been from the north, from San Sebastian; Chile is to the west. Secondly, we were aware of the Argentine AN/TPS 43 surveillance radar at Rio Grande. The radar's propagation properties were well documented. The propagation profile was replicated on the intervisibility trace produced by RSRE Malvern. It would have been impossible for the helicopter to be detected when being flown at no higher than 20 feet, at a distance no closer than 19 miles from the radar. I was flying the aircraft below detection height throughout the infiltration phase of the operation. Had the aircraft been detected during infiltration, the fully serviceable Omega RWR in the cockpit would have indicated as much, but it remained silent until I climbed the aircraft through 200 feet as we were heading west to Chile. If the Argentine radar did detect a slow-moving aircraft inbound towards Rio Grande that night from the direction of Chile, it was not 'Victor Charlie'.

Level at 3,000 feet and heading 290°, I was aiming initially for a point in the middle of Bahia Inutil from where I could start the last stages of a descent. With fog and low stratus to the east of the mountains, I assumed that there would be similar conditions to the west. Letting down over the land through low cloud and fog would have been reckless and dangerous, so descent over the sea was the lowest-risk option. After ten minutes steady progress westward, I could see the tops of the mountains dead ahead. At our current height the aircraft would comfortably clear the mountain tops after which I could start a steady descent towards the centre of the bay. My inputs to the flying controls and 'Wiggy's' operation of the TANS were accompanied by the rhythmic pulses of the Omega, reminding us of the ever-present danger posed by the Argentine radar. Fifteen minutes into the flight we were in Chilean airspace and the aircraft would shortly be cresting the summit of the mountain range. Just five more minutes and I could start the descent – how I longed to be screened from the ever-present buzz of the radar. The tension in the aircraft was characterized by our near silence. Each of us had a job to do, but none of us was minded to talk any more than necessary. Our long transit from *Invincible* to the Argentine coast had been quite a chatty affair, but now our silence was punctuated by essential dialogue only – instructions for a change of heading or altitude. All the time we were close to being mesmerized by the radar pulses loud and clear in our headsets.

CHAPTER 16

Arrival at Useless Bay

Clear of the mountain range, I steered the aircraft towards the middle of the bay and started a slow descent. To the west of the mountains the cloud layer was thinner and more broken, and the wind lighter. As the aircraft dropped below the crest of the mountain range, the Omega fell silent; the relentless rhythmic pulses of the Argentine radar had stopped, like a heartbeat finally extinguished. As the aircraft descended, the wind decreased and the visibility improved. At 800 feet we broke out of the bottom of the stratus layer and the surface of the bay came into view; thankfully there was no fog. It was at this point that 'Wiggy' and I handed our 9mm pistols and sub-machine guns to Pete and invited him to drop them from the aircraft into the deep water of the bay below. On seeing this, some of the SAS prepared to throw out their weapons, but were stopped by Captain 'A' in the nick of time. The plan all along had been for the aircrew to fly into neutral Chile on completion of the mission in Argentina. The planning team had considered it inadvisable for the aircrew to enter Chilean territory carrying firearms, hence their wanton destruction. Turning south-west towards the southern shore, I continued the descent to 50 feet. On reaching the shoreline I turned the aircraft west and flew towards our worst-case option landing site, a low-lying spit of land jutting out prominently into the water, 10 miles east of the mouth of the bay. Approaching the landing site, 'Wiggy' made a fuel calculation – we had sufficient to fly the 50 miles to our second-best option landing site. As I manoeuvred the aircraft for landing into a very light easterly wind, I asked Captain 'A' what his intentions were. With the aircraft firmly on Chilean soil, pointing back in the direction of Argentina, Captain 'A' studied his map. I pointed out to him on the map the first- and second-preference landing sites, both on the Chilean mainland to the south of Punta Arenas. After due consideration he decided that his team would leave the aircraft at this point because it was the only option of the three landing sites which afforded direct land access to Argentina if required. It was of note that Captain 'A' did not question the accuracy of our navigation once the aircraft was on Chilean soil – gone were any doubts! I explained to Captain 'A' that it was my intention to fly west to the option-two landing site and, fuel permitting, further to option one. Captain 'A' offered 'Wiggy', Pete and me the opportunity to remain with his team. Furthermore, he also offered to destroy the aircraft where it was. I thanked him for his offer, but declined. I had my orders which were to achieve the best-case landing site if at all possible and I could see no advantage and several potential disadvantages to remaining with his team. Captain 'A' handed me two explosive demolition charges should they be required with quick instructions as to their use. I decided to accept the charges because I had no way of knowing exactly what lay ahead.

With Captain 'A' and his team set down safely on Chilean soil, 'Wiggy' selected the TANS waypoint for landing site two. I lifted the aircraft into a hover and transitioned into forward flight heading initially east before turning onto a heading of 290° towards the Peninsula de Brunswick, the southernmost area of the Chilean mainland. As I turned the aircraft west I caught sight of Captain 'A' and his team moving slowly to the east in the direction of Argentina – the last time that I or any of the aircrew were to see him or his team again. With each passing mile the visibility improved and the wind decreased. After just a couple of minutes in the air I could clearly make out the island of Dawson in the middle of the Straits of Magellan, 20 miles ahead. Our heading took us just to the north of the island and out into the middle of the Straits. On passing the island the visibility improved and I could see to the distant horizon the land mass of mainland Chile. The wind died away to nothing and the surface of the Straits was mirror calm. As I was marvelling at the excellent flying conditions my thoughts drifted to the contrast in weather conditions on either side of the mountain range which we had crossed fifteen minutes earlier. I remarked to 'Wiggy' that had we been in Argentina a day earlier or later, the weather conditions would have been ideal and our Argentine destination not compromised by fog. As it was, even in the dense fog, we had managed to fly as close as 7 miles from the planned drop-off point. Admiral Woodward's concerns about the weather conditions and the delay in mounting the operation had been borne out by the events of the night.

With the second-best option landing site only five minutes away, 'Wiggy' made another fuel calculation – we had just enough to reach our first-option landing site, although we would be flying on fumes when we arrived there. With no need to overfly the waypoint and to save a little more fuel, I turned the aircraft north towards our final waypoint, a small beach at Agua Fresca, approximately 11 miles south of Punta Arenas. In 1982, the stretch of coast for several miles south of Punta Arenas was largely uninhabited but for one or two isolated estancias. To avoid alerting anyone to our presence, I flew the aircraft at 20 feet and at half a mile parallel to the coast as we made our way north. There was not a breath of wind and the sea was flat calm, reflecting what little moonlight there was like an enormous, dark mirror. Without the advantage of the 'radalt hold', it would have been impossible to fly accurately at such a low height given the total absence of surface definition or contrast for visual reference. After another ten minutes the option-one landing site came into view, I slowed the aircraft and manoeuvred to land for the second time on Chilean soil, six hours after launching from *Invincible*.

CHAPTER 17

The Beach South of Punta Arenas

Courage is being scared to death – but saddling up anyway.

John Wayne

The landing site that had been chosen as the best-case option was a small beach approximately 11 miles south of the large provincial capital town of Punta Arenas. Our orders were to remain undetected if at all possible, but to avoid capture in any event for a minimum of eight days following our arrival on Chilean soil, after which time we were to make contact with the British Embassy in Santiago, for which I had a phone number. Our eventual exfiltration would have been considerably more difficult from Chile had the aircraft's fuel state dictated a final landing in a position to the east of the Straits of Magellan, on the island of Tierra del Fuego, hence the selection of two alternate landing sites to the south of Punta Arenas. As I made the final approach to landing, I could see that the beach had a marked slope down towards the sea, small dunes to the west and a minor road running approximately north-south a few metres inland of the dunes.

Having landed, 'Wiggy' and Pete set about preparing the aircraft to consign it to its watery grave and to history. The plan agreed with the Special Forces planning team was to ditch the aircraft in deep water. To this end, 'Wiggy' and Pete used a combination of a small hand axe and a heavy survival knife to make holes in the aircraft fuselage at positions which would be below the waterline when the aircraft was ditched. 'Radar' had briefed Pete as to the best positions to make holes. After five minutes of frantic activity and with our kit on the beach, 'Wiggy' and Pete attached a short length of strong thin line to the aircraft's tail-wheel. Attached to the line, a short distance from the tail-wheel, was a 'Jablex' float, to which was bound the hand axe using 'Gaffa' tape. A 'Jablex' float has an eye at each end. To the other eye a long length of line was attached. With all preparations made, I lifted the aircraft into a low hover and flew slowly out to sea. As I did so, the fuel low-level warning lights started to flash on the Central Warning Panel (CWP). The effect of this was to temporarily and intermittently blind me each time the lights flashed because they appeared with the intensity of searchlights when amplified by the NVG. In spite of this difficulty I managed to fly the aircraft to a position approximately a quarter of a mile off the beach at which point I landed the Sea King on the water. My intention had been to turn the Sea King over by moving the cyclic from side to side, thereby inducing a roll whilst the rotor was still turning. Having escaped from the sinking helicopter I would then swim away. In the event of the helicopter not sinking I would use the axe to make further holes in the upturned aircraft to encourage it to sink. All being well, I would then make my way back to the beach in my survival dinghy by following the length of line. However, the flat-calm sea conditions had not been anticipated and the Sea King, which has a boat-shaped hull to facilitate water landings, remained stubbornly upright and stable on the surface with no hint of it either rocking from side to side or sinking of its own volition. I decided that the only course of action was to fly the helicopter back to the beach to have more and larger holes made in the bottom of the fuselage. I also needed to locate and pull the circuit breakers in the control panel which would deactivate the fuel low-level warning lights. The control panel in question is located high in the roof of the Sea King, between the two pilots' seats, and is difficult to reach. As I was about to take off from the water, the last words to me by Captain Lyn Middleton, before I departed HMS *Hermes*, were resounding loud and clear: 'Having dropped the SAS, take no unnecessary risks and don't do anything foolhardy.' I reasoned that what I was attempting to do was both a necessary and calculated risk to ensure operational secrecy and was not unduly foolhardy. But that is for others to judge.

When flying back to the beach the fuel low-level warning lights came on constantly indicating that the fuel level was dangerously low. This was not an issue given that I was on the point of destroying the aircraft and there were still a few minutes of fuel remaining. More to the point was that I was now blinded, not intermittently, but permanently. Unable to see properly where I was going, I carried on flying slowly towards the beach as best I could. My arrival was unexpected and, as I manoeuvred the aircraft to line up with the length of the beach, I saw the shadowy figures of 'Wiggy' and Pete running for cover behind the sand dunes. Now blinded and without external visual references the aircraft made a hard landing on the sloping beach resulting in the port undercarriage collapsing and the main rotor blades making contact with the sand dunes to my left. With the helicopter about to shake itself to pieces, I closed the fuel cut-off levers which had the effect of stopping both engines and I quickly applied the rotor brake. With the Sea King perched precariously half on its left side, I evacuated the aircraft.

As I stood on the beach, surveying the near wreckage of the aircraft, I glanced at my watch. It was a little after 0615hrs and it would be dawn in another hour.

We had much to do and not much time in which to do it. I considered it essential to burn the seriously damaged Sea King to destroy the nature of the mission. Amongst our kit there were 2 gallons of petrol as fuel for our small cooker and I had the two explosive devices given to me by Captain 'A' forty-five minutes earlier. Before setting fire to the aircraft, 'Wiggy' and I destroyed the NVG as ordered so as not to leave any hint of our operating methods. The goggles were smashed into small pieces using boulders on the beach and the pieces thrown into the sea. With all of our kit placed behind the dunes, I re-entered the Sea King and switched the battery master switch on so that I could drain what little fuel remained in the tanks to form a small pool under the aircraft. I next poured one gallon of the petrol over the inside of the aircraft from the cockpit to the main door and threw into the cabin the two explosive devices set for a delayed explosion. Finally, I ignited and threw a night distress flare into the aircraft cabin and a second flare underneath the aircraft into the small pool of fuel. In a flash the aircraft was burning fiercely. Within one minute much of the main cabin had been consumed by fire and the main rotor gearbox was on the ground. After two minutes the charges exploded. With the aircraft ablaze, 'Wiggy', Pete and I grabbed our bergens, crossed the minor road and made our way into the hills to the west.

Map 2: Operation Plum Duff Insertion Route. © Crown Copyright

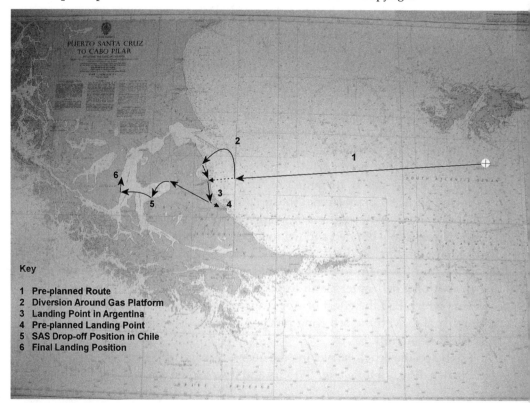

Key

1 Pre-planned Route
2 Diversion Around Gas Platform
3 Landing Point in Argentina
4 Pre-planned Landing Point
5 SAS Drop-off Position in Chile
6 Final Landing Position

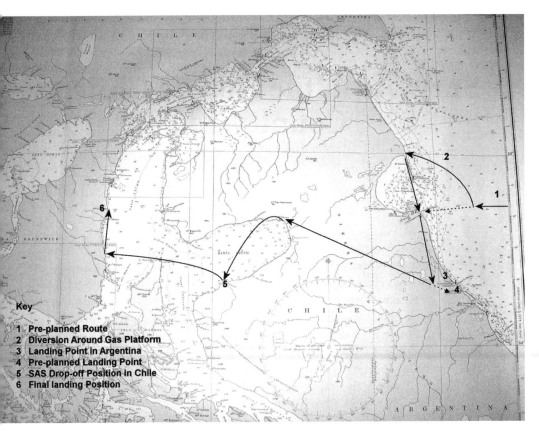

Key

1 Pre-planned Route
2 Diversion Around Gas Platform
3 Landing Point in Argentina
4 Pre-planned Landing Point
5 SAS Drop-off Position in Chile
6 Final landing Position

Map 3: Route Flown in Argentina & Chile. © Crown Copyright

CHAPTER 18

Survival in the Hostile Chilean Countryside

I was keen that we should travel as far as possible under the cover of what little darkness remained. With less than a quarter moon, it was a dark night. Having walked just a few paces into the gently sloping countryside, I struck an object lying across my path and fell arse over tit. I picked myself up, cursed and kicked the object which lay in my path. It was a large fallen tree. I advised 'Wiggy' and Pete who were a short distance behind me and carried on. Four or five more paces and I was arse over tit again, and so it was for the remaining hour – every few paces we were confronted by yet another fallen tree. I picked up a length of wood and tapped the ground in front of me like a blind man feeling his way forward with a 'white stick'.

'Wiggy' and Pete followed suit. At least now we could make progress without tripping over every few paces. As the first vestiges of dawn made an appearance on the distant horizon over Argentina, I could start to make out the lie of the land before us. The route ahead was a scene of devastation. Fallen and felled trees covered the entire area from the minor road, westward for several miles. There was another 10 miles or so of this savage, desolate and challenging terrain to be negotiated until we would reach our destination: a small wooded hill overlooking Punta Arenas from the south-west.

With the level of light improving, I decided to call a halt to our painful progress. We could not afford to be seen under any circumstances, so movement in daylight was out of the question. Although we had managed to cover only a quarter of a mile in an hour, we were a comfortable distance from the beach. There was no difficulty finding somewhere suitable to lie low as the fallen trees provided ideal cover. Looking back towards the beach I could see no evidence of fire, and reasoned that the aircraft must have burned itself out. The wreckage of the Sea King was screened from the small road by the sand dunes and the slope of the beach. I assessed that it would be a day or two before the burnt-out remains of the aircraft were discovered – ample time to make our getaway.

Sunrise on 18 May was spectacular, with the eastern sky a fiery red. A gentle breeze picked up with the rising sun. It felt cool, but not unduly cold. 'Wiggy', Pete and I discovered that if we sat bolt upright, the top part of our bodies would be visible above the fallen trees. This of course was unacceptable so for the remainder of the day we had to assume a semi-inclined position whilst eating and drinking, and lay flat on our backs whilst sleeping. We were wearing DPM arctic windproof jackets and trousers, so our camouflage was not out of place amongst the fallen trees. We made two small, low-to-the-ground shelters, using ponchos. Having been awake for over twenty-four hours, each of us was ready for sleep, but we needed to remain alert to any potential dangers, so I decided to take the first watch whilst 'Wiggy' and Pete slept. With some cold food and a cold drink of water inside me, I turned my attention to the task ahead: moving to our objective whilst remaining undetected for eight days. Movement towards our objective near Punta Arenas could take place only in darkness. The fallen trees and increasing height of the terrain dictated that the going would be extremely slow; fortunately the days were short and the nights long. I estimated that half a mile an hour might be achievable, but there was no imperative to force the pace. Movement would not start until an hour after dark, to be completed no later than an hour before dawn. With thirteen hours of useable darkness, the arithmetic suggested that we should be able to reach our objective in two nights: time would tell.

Meanwhile, 50 miles to the south-east across the Straits of Magellan, Captain 'A' and his team had moved away from the landing site to the cover of scrub and were preparing to lie low for the remainder of the hours of daylight. Their first priority was to get under cover to remain undetected, which was easily achieved given the dense scrub along the southern shore of Bahia Inutil. Their second priority was to send a 'mission aborted' signal to SAS headquarters at Hereford via secure satellite communications and to await further orders.

As the morning wore on, I surveyed the area around us from the cover of the trees. The ground was undulating, rising to the west to a height of around 1,500 feet. There was no sign of a way around the myriad of fallen tress – we would just have to soldier on, and grin and bear it. I looked in the direction of the beach from time to time for any sign that our presence had been detected. The road was quiet, with little movement of vehicles, perhaps just two or three an hour and no pedestrians. Our selection of the beach, from nothing more than a study of the map, had been a sound choice. The surface of the Straits, which had previously been mirror calm, was now rippling in the breeze. As I looked across the water towards Tierra del Fuego, I wondered what Captain 'A' and his team were up to.

'Wiggy' and Pete woke early in the afternoon. By now all three of us were hungry. We were too close to the road to risk the smells of cooking wafting towards any locals who might be in the area, so it would have to be a diet of cold food and water or 'limers' until we had moved further inland and north. To save weight, we were carrying arctic rations. Although highly nutritious and packing thousands of calories to sustain us, water was needed to reconstitute the meals, a scarce commodity in the area. We were not carrying much and would soon need a resupply. A cursory glance at the terrain ahead did not look as though it contained possible sources of water. With a stomach full of biscuits and chocolate, washed down with water, I decided to try and snatch a few hours of sleep before nightfall.

As the day progressed, the SAS planning team at Hereford were wrestling with the ramifications of the aborted mission. With the element of surprise lost, John Moss, the OC of B Squadron, reasoned that Operation Mikado should revert to the option of an overland infiltration from Chile, but this suggestion was quickly vetoed. The option of inserting a second reconnaissance team from the Task Force was also discounted. Instead, Brigadier de la Billière, Director SAS (DSAS), gave orders to proceed with the mission without the benefit of reconnaissance. This decision gave rise to dissent from some members of B Squadron, including its OC – there was a general feeling amongst them that, without the benefit of timely and accurate intelligence, the mission was suicidal. One very experienced SNCO went as far as withdrawing from the mission. Because he was now lukewarm to the operation, the OC was removed from his command by DSAS and replaced by the unit's second-in-command, Major Ian Cooke. That afternoon, whilst I was attempting to sleep in the Chilean countryside, the refashioned B Squadron team made final preparations for their departure the following day by coach to RAF Lyneham, and a sixteen-hour flight to Ascension Island.

After four hours of fitful sleep, I awoke late in the afternoon. The day had remained dry and sunny, but cool. With the benefit of another hour or so of diminishing daylight, the three of us had another cold snack and prepared for the short but nonetheless difficult slog that lay ahead. From time to time I looked towards the road and the beach but there was no sign of activity. Indeed, the area was eerily quiet. In the wilderness to the west of the Straits of Magellan, there was no evidence of man-generated noise: no industry, little agriculture, no background drone from traffic; no strong wind blowing through trees or against man-made infrastructure. There was absolutely no source of sound other than the three of us talking in low voices and whispers. Under other circumstances, it would have been a fascinating area to explore and I determined that one day I would return and enjoy the environment at leisure. I had no way of knowing that the opportunity would present itself in just a few weeks time – for the present, the imperative was survival. I looked east over Argentina towards the rapidly disappearing, distant horizon. Another hour and it would be dark. As I surveyed the gathering gloom around me, I became aware that nature's colours were slowly draining from the landscape. The distant land across the water, which throughout the day had been a light green, was now grey. The sea had turned from a rich dark blue, to black. Slowly distant features disappeared. As darkness descended, the light breeze diminished. All was still. Moonrise was not until the early hours of the following morning and I realized, therefore, that the first few hours of movement overland would be especially difficult in the pitch black. With our kit packed, it was time to set off.

With my trusty 'white stick' in hand, I made a few tentative steps forward before encountering the first of the many trees that were to test our resolve over the coming nights. When carrying a reasonably heavy bergen, climbing progressively and clambering over fallen trees every ten paces or so, both one's strength and determination are tested. It was clear that all three of us were finding the going hard and, after half an hour, I called a halt for a short rest and drink of water. We had covered barely 100 metres. My estimate of covering half a mile an hour was consigned to history – a more realistic target would be nearer a mile each night. After ten minutes rest we set off again. And so it was for the next few hours – half an hour's frustrating slog over the world's biggest obstacle course, followed by a short rest. At around 0330hrs the moon rose. Low in the sky and in its last vestiges, it added little extra light. How I wished that we had not destroyed the goggles so soon after our arrival on Chilean soil. For the first few hours the weather remained dry. At first it was a clear night and with no light pollution I could see more stars than I had ever witnessed in my life. These were ideal light conditions for NVG but, alas, without them we were effectively blind. As time wore on the weather changed with light but persistent rain for a couple of hours.

After very nearly ten hours of frustratingly slow and literally painful progress, we came across a small valley offering excellent cover from view. I decided to call a halt to any further movement and remain in this location until the following night. Leaving 'Wiggy' and Pete to erect our small survival tent, I explored the surrounding area, looking for water. I took three water bottles with me and set off into the darkness. I followed the line of the valley and, after about a quarter of a mile, encountered a small stream. Having filled the water bottles, I returned to the bivvy site, arriving as the first hint of dawn appeared on the distant horizon. Looking back towards the beach I estimated that we had walked a pathetic 2 miles. Being well over 2 miles from the beach and approximately half a mile from the road, we were far enough inland to risk heating water and cooking food. I decided, therefore, that as soon as it was light, we would get a hot meal and a drink inside us. As I lay back against a tree stump, using my bergen as a back rest, the three of us marvelled at the amazing sight of the sunrise over Argentina. The red fingers of sky on the distant horizon were replaced by the sun as it made a slow appearance over the mountains to the east. I mentioned to 'Wiggy' and Pete that the last time that I had seen such a vivid red sky at dawn was on the day that *Sheffield* was hit by an Exocet missile. I hoped that this sunrise was not as portentous for either the Task Force or ourselves. The three of us then speculated as to what might be happening with the Task Force. We knew that the leading amphibious ships had rendezvoused with *Hermes* the previous day, but it was frustrating not knowing what was happening right now, 700 miles or so to the east.

The day had got off to a fine start, with full sun and blue sky, and just a hint of Breeze; a bit chilly though. Conversely, the three of us hoped that the Task Force was yet again immersed in fog, thereby limiting the options of attack for the Argentine Air Force. With thoughts of the Task Force foremost in our minds, we set about lighting our cooker to heat water for a brew and to cook our first hot meal for over twenty-four hours. As we ate what to us was a gourmet meal, my thoughts moved to our cover story. To add credibility to the story which had been agreed with Captain Lyn Middleton, I decided that we should keep a survival log. In our ration packs we had a plentiful supply of toilet paper, although not for us the luxury of the 'kind-to-your-arse' soft tissue adored by the British public. No, the Armed Forces are treated to individual sheets of 'Pussers' smooth and shiny – not much use for what it is intended, but excellent as writing paper. After due consideration, we decided that our log should accurately reflect our movements, if you'll pardon the pun, but that the narrative should first reflect the cover story of how we came to end up on Chilean soil. The task of writing the log was handed to Pete. The last job to be done each day before setting off on the night's 'yomp' over the Chilean countryside would be to record the activities of the previous twenty-four hours. I reasoned that, in the event of our capture, the log would be useful collateral to back up our story.

With the combined benefits of being extremely tired, a hot meal inside us and the warming sun, sleep was easier to achieve than the previous day. I decided that again I would take the first watch. Whilst 'Wiggy' and Pete were sleeping, I took stock of our situation and studied the lie of the land for the coming night's 'yomp'. It would be more of the same, but the terrain further north appeared steeper than anything that we had encountered. As the morning wore on I kept a close eye on the area of the beach and the road, but the situation was unchanged – two to three vehicle movements each hour, no pedestrians and no sign of anyone taking an interest in the beach. So far so good. After a light lunch of chocolate and biscuits washed down with a mug of tea, it was my turn for sleep whilst 'Wiggy' and Pete kept watch. Late in the afternoon I awoke from a sound sleep and made preparations for our next move. So far we had been lucky with the weather during the day, with not a hint of rain. As we ate a cooked dinner, Pete started to write the first two days' activities in the survival log. We were careful to concoct a version of events that would be convincing to the Chilean authorities should it prove necessary. The log was therefore an amalgam of fact and fabrication.

With daylight dwindling, we struck camp and set off. After thirty minutes, we arrived at the stream where I had filled the water bottles during the previous night, and took advantage of the cover of darkness to fill our water bottles again before enjoying the luxury of a dhobi (strip wash); the water was near freezing. Feeling refreshed we set off again. Unfortunately, not long into our journey it started to rain, which continued for much of the night. After a couple of miles of tree vaulting, we were confronted by a fast-flowing river running across our path. We were already wet from the rain, so there was no point in stripping off and crossing the river as trained to do by the SAS. Instead we ploughed through it. Not long afterwards we had to scramble up a steep and muddy hill. Having been walking for five hours, soaking wet, muddy, extremely tired and in danger of developing hypothermia, I called a halt for the night. In keeping with the terrain already covered, the area was littered with fallen trees, affording good cover from view. With several hours until dawn, we pitched the survival tent, stripped off our wet clothing and settled into our sleeping bags.

It was two hours after dawn, on 20 May, before I awoke from a sound sleep. I put on dry clothing and left the tent to survey the landscape. Our position was well screened from view, but there was a small settlement alongside the road, approximately 2 miles away, so we would have to be careful to remain out of sight. The first priority was to camouflage the tent using the small branches and twigs laying nearby. The second job of the day was to hang out our wet clothing to dry; the steady breeze would help in that regard. A low-level poncho was erected over the wet clothing as a safeguard in case of further rain. Breakfast was a rare treat of hot rolled oats and apple sauce, washed down with hot chocolate. Well rested and with a full stomach, I again studied the terrain. There was a promising-looking route to the north which appeared to be in dead ground. Leaving 'Wiggy' and Pete at the bivvy site, I set off to the north in search of water and located a stream after approximately 2 miles. Having filled my water bottle I headed back to rejoin my comrades, arriving at midday.

Early in the afternoon we saw a helicopter flying south along the coast towards the area of the beach, which was no longer in view, but it appeared that the helicopter descended in that general area. Our cover was apparently blown.

From now on we could expect Chilean police and military personnel to be searching for us. In mid-afternoon we saw a man on foot walking with a dog from the direction of the high ground to the west of our position, downhill towards the coast. He passed within a few hundred metres of us, fortunately downwind of him and his dog. During the course of the afternoon, the helicopter made several trips north and south along the coast. Late in the afternoon we observed military vehicles carrying engineering equipment and plant moving south from the direction of Punta Arenas to the area of the beach. It was now clear that the wreckage of the Sea King had been discovered.

Whilst I was watching the activities of the Chilean military and contemplating our fate, 4,000 miles away on Ascension Island, B Squadron was sorting out their equipment following their long and tiring flight from RAF Lyneham. Later that day the Squadron was informed that Operation Mikado had been postponed because an Argentine radar picket had been identified off the Argentine coast in the vicinity of Rio Grande, thereby jeopardizing their insertion by C130 Hercules. An approach to the area over the sea, even at low level, was now out of the question; the window of opportunity had closed.

Meanwhile, in the UK, news of the discovery of the Sea King had broken and made the evening news. Lorraine was watching the news intently as she had done on every day since the Task Force had departed Portsmouth. On seeing the news she was convinced that I was one of the crew of the aircraft, although at this stage no names had been released by the MoD. I do not know to this day whether her insight was a case of female intuition or witchcraft; both run in her family.

With an hour to last light, 'Wiggy' and I struck camp, whilst Pete wrote up the survival log. Our clothing had dried in the strong breeze throughout the day; fortunately there had been no rain all day. Having concealed any trace of our presence, we set off on the next leg of our journey. Meanwhile, 50 miles to the east, Captain 'A' and his team remained under cover awaiting further orders. With Argentina to their east and water on all other sides, their options were limited. For now it was a case of wait and see. But for us there were no such constraints and the relentless slog north continued.

After moving one and a half miles, we walked into a dense thicket of gorse bushes amongst the fallen trees which appeared to offer excellent cover from view in all directions. The combination of solid wood and gorse would also provide overhead cover. With the likelihood of Chilean military forces using aircraft to search for us during the hours of daylight, effective overhead cover would be an imperative from now on. With three hours until first light, we pitched our tent, camouflaged our position as best we could in the darkness and slept until daybreak.

21 May started quietly for us, but not for Lorraine back in Crewkerne. At 0730hrs there was a knock on the front door and when she opened it she found herself facing a Royal Marine Captain dressed in uniform who introduced himself as Nick Beyts. The previous day, Nick had completed a tour of duty on the staff of FONAC at Yeovilton and was travelling to the Commando Training Centre at Lympstone to take up a new appointment as the Commandant's personal staff officer. En route he called in to break the news to Lorraine that I was missing in

action, but presumed to be alive; mixed news indeed. He offered timely comfort, reassurance and support at the beginning of what became several very trying and testing days for Lorraine. Nick excelled himself that day, even though he was nursing a hangover from the previous night's 'leaving run' at Yeovilton. Lorraine made him breakfast and filled him up with coffee before sending him on his way. I am eternally grateful to Nick for the sensitive way in which he provided support to Lorraine. We remain close friends to this day.

Meanwhile in Chile, the first priority for the three of us was to improve the camouflage of our bivvy site. By using the plentiful supply of branches that were lying all around us, we constructed a framework overhead our position and covered it with gorse. I defied anyone to see us from any direction, including from the air. After breakfast, I set about cautiously reconnoitring the area immediately around our position. Seventy-five metres to the west I stumbled upon a small stream and during the morning we were able to move between the bivvy site and the stream whilst remaining in dead ground. It felt strangely civilized, but at the same time surreal, to be able to wash and shave whilst endeavouring to remain unseen and at large. After our usual lunch of chocolate, biscuits and a hot 'wet', 'Wiggy' and Pete slept for a while whilst I kept watch.

Early in the afternoon I was alerted by the sound of a horse. At first I could not see it, but realized that it was close by and to the south of our position. Moments later I was alarmed to see a man leading a horse from the area of the high ground behind us, downhill towards the coastal road. I awoke 'Wiggy' who, in turn, nudged Pete, as the man, horse and dog passed within 30 metres of our position.

All three of us remained still and quiet as our unwelcome visitors made their way slowly away to the east, apparently unaware of our presence close by.

'Phew, that was close,' I exclaimed in hushed tones.

'Too bloody close', replied 'Wiggy' and Pete in unison. The three of us were now as alert as junkies high on 'speed' and ready for the possibility of more surprises. We did not have long to wait. About an hour later, a small fixed-wing aircraft flew low level directly overhead our position from the north. It was a Skyvan type, but its passage was too fast to positively identify the aircraft from its markings. It could have been either military of civil registered.

'This place is like Piccadilly Circus at rush hour,' remarked Pete.

With a couple of hours remaining until last light, we cooked a hot meal and returned to the stream to fill our water bottles. Whilst Pete wrote up the survival log, 'Wiggy' and I packed up the tent and our kit in readiness for the mile or so move to the wooded hill. Apart from the excitement of unwanted visitors and snooping aircraft, the day had been good to us. The weather had remained dry, we had eaten well and had full water bottles. The helicopter activity of the previous day had not been repeated and there had been no further sign of military vehicles on the coast road. As the final vestiges of daylight were extinguished, we set off on the final leg of our journey north. The distance to travel was about one mile, but the terrain was difficult being uphill all the way with fallen trees and gorse bushes encountered at every turn. At twenty-minute intervals we stopped for a drink and a short rest. It was hard going. At last, after a six-hour slog, much of it on our hands and knees, we arrived on top of the hill. In the darkness it was not possible to find the optimum location for our bivvy site, so we plumped for a spot roughly in the middle. In daylight it would be possible to adjust our position if necessary, but for now the priorities were shelter and sleep.

CHAPTER 19

The Hill

The morning of 22 May started dry, but it had rained during the night penetrating the tent in a few places. Using two ponchos we constructed a fly sheet over the tent before settling down to enjoy a breakfast of rolled oats and apple flakes, after which I walked around the top of the hill to take stock of our situation. From the north-east side of the hill I could clearly see Punta Arenas a mile or so away. On the southern side of the town, alongside the coast road and extending west into the countryside for some distance, was a large establishment. Surrounded by a high wire fence and razor wire, it had the appearance of being a military base; there was plenty of vehicular activity on the road. Walking around the top of the hill anti-clockwise, I could make out a stream in the bottom of the valley to the north-west, but decided that I would reconnoitre a route from the bivvy site to the stream a little later. Moving to the southern edge I could observe the route that we had walked over the previous five nights. There was no sign of activity in the vicinity of the beach or along the route that we had taken, which convinced me that we had not been tracked. The hill was thickly wooded on the top, while our bivvy location was well sited and could not be observed from the ground in any direction. There was, however, danger of being seen from the air, so we rearranged some of the smaller trees and saplings to form cover over our position.

With the bivvy site well camouflaged, I set off down the hill to the north-west in search of the stream; the route was straightforward, but steep. I returned to collect 'Wiggy' and Pete and the three of us made our way to the stream to fill our water bottles and wash. Arriving back at the bivvy site at midday, we had a snack and tea. Although a reasonable distance away from civilization, we could not risk the strong aroma of coffee being detected and alerting someone to our presence. For the same reason, lighting a fire was out of the question. Leaving those factors to one side, in selecting the hill as our final objective, we had chosen well. We were out of view to any observers on the ground, the hill dominated the surrounding terrain making it impossible for anyone to approach our position unseen, and we were close enough to civilization that, when I judged it appropriate, it would not be too far to walk to find a telephone to make contact with the British authorities.

Over the next two days we settled into a new and novel routine of sleeping at night and remaining awake by day. Pete added to the survival log and demonstrated his skills as a handyman by turning some small logs and thin green twigs into a dining table, making it all very civilized. We sat on our bergens rather than trusting our luck to newly made chairs because we did not want to test Pete's carpentry skills too far, not even with our by now diminishing body weight. With a lot of time on our hands, we turned our attention to brushing up on our rudimentary grasp of Spanish, using the phrase books kindly donated by crew members on *Invincible*. The most useful phrases learned were: 'Excuse me, what is the way to the British Embassy?' 'I don't speak Spanish'; 'I need to speak to someone who speaks English'; 'My name is'; and 'Please connect me to the British Embassy.' We tested each other over and over again until we were word perfect. Having plenty of time on our hands we observed the area of the military establishment in particular and Punta Arenas in general, noting a large number of aircraft movements into and out of the airport, to include military flights by C130 and F5s. It was not until I returned to Chile in November 1982 that I learned the truth of the loan of two C130s from the RAF. My suspicions about the C130s were to be aroused three days later.

It was not long before we turned our attention to food. Having been in survival mode for approaching eight days, we were bored with eating military rations and longed for some real meat. To this end we placed a few rabbit snares along likely routes, but to no avail. Amongst the wood on top of the hill was one prominent dead tree which stood alone in a small clearing. Throughout the three days, we were visited regularly by a large, eagle-sized bird of prey. Although we all so much wanted to eat that bird, it also occurred to us that the bird was probably harbouring similar thoughts about us. During my SAS survival training the previous year, I had become friendly with two officers from the Danish armed forces. They were the only soldiers who managed to trap fresh meat during the course. When asked how they did it they revealed a bow and arrow made using wood and string. This gave me an idea. I selected a suitable-looking piece of wood and fashioned a bow. The nylon cord from my aircrew survival knife doubled as the bowstring. Whilst I was making the bow, 'Wiggy' and Pete fashioned some arrows and made flights using the white plastic aircrew knee boards. The arrows were honed to a sharp point and lightly weighted near their points using mud.

The scene was set. First it was my go – after all, it was my idea to make the bow. We slowly advanced towards the dead tree being careful not to alarm the bird, and when no more than 20 metres away I released my first arrow. It missed the bird by about 3 feet; not bad for a beginner. Unperturbed by my wayward shot, the bird held its position. I released a second arrow, fairing no better.

'Give me the fucking thing,' demanded Pete, clearly exasperated by my poor marksmanship. The arrows were recovered and it was Pete's turn. He took aim and released his arrow. To our collective amazement, it struck the bird which for a few seconds looked at the arrow lodged in its chest in disbelief. Sensing that it was about to fall off of its perch, the three of us rushed forward. On seeing our full frontal assault, the bird managed to get airborne, freeing itself from the arrow as it flew away towards the sea.

'Bugger,' I exclaimed.

'Bollocks,' said 'Wiggy' and Pete in harmony. That was the last we saw of the bird, which I was later to discover was a Sea Eagle, rare and protected in Chile. We had already caused an international incident, so it was just as well that we did not compound our transgression by eating a protected species.

During the last day I turned my attention to how best to make contact with the Air Attaché in the British Embassy in Santiago. I needed access to a telephone, but had no Chilean coins. I reasoned that there would be a public call-box somewhere in Punta Arenas, or even better, we might happen upon the house of an expatriate Brit – there were plenty of them living in Punta Arenas in 1982. Some owned property which was clearly distinguishable as being of British occupancy by being painted in the colours and design of the Union flag – a bit of a give-away. Between our position and a telephone lay the imposing group of buildings which we assumed to be a military establishment with no obvious way around it. We had three options. The first was to cut our way through the perimeter fence of the military facility, make our way through the maze of buildings and firing ranges and emerge on the other side; this option would only be feasible at night. After careful consideration, we discounted it for two reasons: firstly, such behaviour would be inconsistent with that expected of British aircrew who were seeking sanctuary in a neutral country; secondly, we ran the risk of being shot! Option Two was to walk up to the main gate of the military establishment and simply turn ourselves in. This behaviour would be entirely consistent with that expected of a group in our situation. This option was also discounted because it was the last resort. Our orders were to make contact with the British Embassy if possible. Option Three was to brazenly walk straight past the main gate of the military establishment and hope for the best. We noticed during the day that there had been some movement by pedestrians on the coast road in the vicinity of the military establishment, but no such activity at night. We therefore settled on Option Three in broad daylight, but not as a group of three. I reasoned that three British aircrew were assumed to be in the area, therefore we needed to split into a pair, 'Wiggy' and me together, with Pete some distance behind us. The plan was finalized. The penultimate activity that night was to enjoy a small nip of 'Pussers rum' that Pete had been carrying in a hip flask, kindly donated by Terry Short, one of the 846 Squadron aircrewmen. It was a very cold night so 'Wiggy' and I decided to share a sleeping bag. Just as we were settling down for the night, 'Wiggy' was heard to utter the immortal words, 'You feel nothing like my wife.' I, of course, could offer no comment. The final action before settling down was for the last entry to be made in the survival log.

CHAPTER 20

'Are you the Three British Airmen?'

W e were up at the crack of dawn on 25 May; it was a clear sunny morning and there was much to do. After breakfast and a wash and shave, 'Wiggy' and Pete broke camp whilst I dug two large holes in which to bury our bergens, the tent and the rest of our kit, including the fifty ampoules of diamorphine, with a street value of tens of thousands of pounds. We estimated that the road was a mile away and the entrance to the military establishment about half-a-mile beyond the point at which the obvious route from the hill intercepted the road. Our observations of the area over the previous three days indicated that the busiest time on the road was between midday and 1400hrs, which we assumed to be lunchtime for the locals. Notwithstanding the fact that we had only DPM windproof smocks and a rag-bag assortment of trousers to wear, I reasoned that we would appear less conspicuous to a casual observer if we were moving amongst other pedestrians and vehicles. Having had a final tidy of the bivvy site late morning, we left the cover of the wooded hill and set off slowly downhill towards the road.

It was 1300hrs when we intercepted the coast road and 'Wiggy' and I made our way north along the eastern side of the road, away from the military establishment, followed a few minutes later by Pete. As we walked north, we passed a sign indicating that we were about to enter 'Punta Arenas, Republica de Chile'. We were passed by several civilian vehicles travelling in both directions and a few pedestrians walking in the opposite direction. No one appeared to take a blind bit of notice of us. After ten minutes we approached the main gate of the military establishment to discover that it was the regional Carabineros headquarters, barracks and training establishment – a huge facility. Standing in the road was an armed soldier on sentry duty. He paid us no more attention than a casual glance as we passed by. So far so good. 'Wiggy' and I slowed our pace so as not to get too far ahead of Pete. Within a few minutes Pete had also passed the remarkably disinterested soldier and was within a couple of minutes of joining us. After five minutes the three of us had passed the frontage of the Carabineros establishment and were heading for a quiet side street, each of us breathing a sigh of relief. At that precise moment, a car travelling in the opposite direction pulled up just behind us. Out of the car stepped a Carabineros Captain who called to us in Spanish and approached. He introduced himself as Captain Marcos Moya Torres of the Prefectura Carabineros de Chile. He asked us in Spanish if we were the three British airmen, to which we replied that we were sailors from a British merchant ship in the port, whilst trying hard to keep straight faces at this rather 'Allo Allo' moment.

'There are no British merchant ships in the port,' was Captain Torres's reply. 'You are the British airmen.'

The game was up. Captain Torres invited us into his car and we were driven into the Carabineros headquarters, wondering just what lay ahead.

Having parked the car, Captain Torres invited the three of us into his office and promptly made a phone call to his Commanding Officer to report our arrival.

A few moments later, Lieutenant Colonel Haroldo Carrasco Galvez and his Adjutant, Lieutenant Cesar Pradenas Moran, joined us and the two groups were introduced to each other. After some pleasantries, we were offered a glass of Chilean red wine, which was most welcome, in spite of being a little on the chilly side for my liking. A few minutes later we all went outside for some photographs to be taken before returning to Captain Torres's office. Our final act was to make gifts of our military compasses to our hosts as a token of our appreciation for their short-lived but, nevertheless, kind hospitality.

It was an hour or so later before we were driven to another facility to be questioned formally about our presence in Chile. On entering the building it appeared to be redolent of the Villa Grimaldi, one of the interrogation centres allegedly used by Chile's secret police as described by survivors of interrogation.

Seeing the apparatus that was in some of the rooms caused the hairs on the back of my neck to rise. What did they have in store for us? I wondered. The questioning was conducted not by the secret police, whom out of interest I was to meet on a return visit six months later, but by a Commander from the Chilean Navy who was charming and spoke fluent English. When I asked him how he came to have such a good grasp of the English language he explained that he had spent some time in the UK attending training courses with the Royal Navy. I was surprised that the three of us were questioned collectively and not individually. It was clear that the interrogation was therefore a formality. The Commander asked how we came to be in Chile. I delivered the cover story as agreed with Captain Lyn Middleton, namely that we were conducting a patrol off of the Argentine coast in search of Argentine naval vessels, when the aircraft suffered an engine failure. Being a long distance from the Task Force and with the possibility of the second engine failing, I decided to seek refuge in the nearest 'friendly' country. Armed with only sea charts of the area, we had no way of navigating accurately, so we headed west until short of fuel, landed and destroyed the aircraft to prevent it falling into enemy hands in the event that we were in Argentina. I decided that we should lay up for several days until we could be certain that we were in Chile and not Argentina. During the hours of darkness on our first night in Chile, we could see the lights of a large town to the north and decided to make our way across country towards it. After five days we arrived at the hill and kept the town under observation for another three days. Under the cover of darkness, during the penultimate night on the hill, I descended towards the town to reconnoitre the area. On reaching the road I saw the sign for Punta Arenas, thereby confirming our location as Chile.

The Commander appeared to be satisfied with my story, but during the questioning asked me to confirm on three occasions that we had not dropped off any military personnel on Chilean soil. I answered that we had not dropped off any military personnel. He put a hypothesis to me that we had dropped off Special Forces either in Argentina or Chile and had then destroyed the aircraft as part of the plan. I assured him that this was not the case. He seemed to accept my version of events. After an hour or so of questioning, the Commander explained that we would be flown to Santiago that night and then back to the UK. After the formality of the questioning, I asked of news of the Task Force and he proceeded to update us on the major events of recent days. This was our first news for eight days. We learned of the amphibious landings, the loss of the Sea King with twenty-two lives, including 'Doc' Love, the sinking of HMS *Ardent*, the shooting down of two British helicopters, the attacks on RFA *Argonaut*, HMS *Antrim*, RFA Sir *Galahad* and RFA Sir *Lancelot*, the sinking of HMS *Antelope* and HMS *Coventry* and, on this very day, the Exocet attack on SS *Atlantic Conveyor*. It was a lot of news to take in and was our first indication that with the Exocet attacks, Operation Mikado must finally have been aborted.

CHAPTER 21

The Flight to Santiago, Courtesy of the RAF

I t was late afternoon and getting dark by the time our questioning was completed. Lieutenant Colonel Galves's initial telephone call to his superior, reporting our arrival in Punta Arenas, had generated a cascade of subsequent calls up the Carabineros chain of command to the Defence Ministry, President Pinochet and the British Embassy in Santiago. John Heath, the British Ambassador, had been alerted to the presence in Chile of British aircrew following the discovery of the wreckage of the Sea King. During the previous week, exchanges of diplomatic telegrams and signals between Santiago and London had communicated the UK Government's decision that we should be repatriated to the UK as quickly as possible and with the minimum of fuss and public exposure. To this end, it was agreed between the British and Chilean authorities that the three of us were to be flown to Santiago overnight as passengers on a routine military flight and handed over to the British diplomatic staff.

Before we departed, we were handed three quilted civilian jackets which had been purchased for us by the Carabineros. Early that evening we said our final farewells to our very hospitable Chilean hosts and were driven under cover of darkness through Punta Arenas to the airport, some 5 miles or so to the north of the town. On entering the airport, the vehicle was driven to the aircraft dispersal where it stopped and we waited several minutes until the military C130 was ready to embark passengers. Whilst we were sitting in the car killing time, there was a knock on the passenger window and the door opened to reveal a familiar face from my time at Hereford the previous year. I had known Captain 'H' professionally for some years and was surprised to see him in Punta Arenas. The driver got out of the vehicle so that the three of us and Captain 'H' could have a private conversation. I explained the sequence of events in Argentina and on arrival in Chile, explaining in detail the location at which we had dropped off Captain 'A' and his team. Captain 'H' confirmed that Operation Mikado had been cancelled and that he was making every effort to find the missing SAS team. He went on to explain that, following cancellation of the mission, there had been no need for us to remain in hiding and that he had been scouring the countryside south of Punta Arenas for several days, calling out our names and looking for us. Given the relatively small amount of ground that we had covered, I was surprised that we had neither seen nor heard him, and concluded that our approach to survival and evasion had clearly been highly successful. Finally, before boarding the aircraft, Captain 'H' gave me his wife's telephone number in England and I agreed to call her following my arrival in UK to say that I had seen and spoken to him recently, and that he was well and keeping busy.

With the aircraft ready for departure, it was time to board. We bid Captain 'H' and our driver farewell and walked towards the aircraft. I was surprised to see that the C130 was painted in standard UK camouflage livery and bore the lettering 'Fuerza Aera de Chile'. Even with my rudimentary grasp of Spanish, I realized that Aera was a misspelling of 'Aerea'; my curiosity was aroused. We entered the C130 Hercules, took our seats in the back and as the aircraft taxied, I glanced around the cabin. There was a small amount of equipment being moved, but the aircraft was mainly carrying passengers and was fitted with electronic equipment with which I was not familiar. I studied our fellow passengers carefully, all of whom were wearing flight overalls with pilot's wings and flying badges, so I assumed that they were aircrew. A closer look at the badges revealed the aircrew to be F5 pilots. As soon as the aircraft was airborne and established in cruise flight, I spoke to a few of the passengers who were as curious about the three of us as we were about them. It was explained that a squadron of F5s had been deployed to Punta Arenas for the duration of the Falklands War and that every week there was a roulement of pilots between Santiago and Punta Arenas in order to sustain the F5s at a high state of readiness. The pilots went on to explain that there was widespread confidence amongst the Chilean population that the British would emerge victorious. In the likely event of Argentina being defeated, the Chilean authorities were concerned that General Galtierie might order the invasion of the islands in the Beagle Channel. The sovereignty of the islands had long been contested between Argentina and Chile and there was concern in Chile that General Galtierie might attempt to mitigate failure in the Falklands and placate the Argentine people by achieving a small victory elsewhere through seizure of these Islands.

The general appearance of the F5 pilots took the three of us somewhat by surprise. At risk of appearing racist, it came as a shock to identify that the majority of the pilots were of Arian extraction and had surnames such as Muller, von Reinhart, Schmitt and Brandt, to name but four. There were few pilots of Hispanic appearance or name. The markings of the aircraft were also something of a surprise. The external livery of the aircraft was matched by the internal markings, which were RAF, including the aircraft's registration number which was British and from RAF Lyneham.

Flight time to Santiago was five hours. For those unfamiliar with the C130 Hercules, I should explain that the aircraft was designed primarily to transport freight, with a secondary role of carrying paratroops and passengers. The level of noise in the back of a C130 is therefore very high, making prolonged conversation impossible. There was nothing for us to do, therefore, but attempt to sleep for most of the journey.

Meanwhile, in the UK, the MoD had released our three names to the media. Having seen a report on the late evening news, Lorraine anticipated receiving considerable press interest. With two small boys to look after, a distraction that she did not need was to be bombarded with questions by the media. She needed help. To this end Lorraine telephoned our brother-in-law, Ken Lewis, who at the time was a Petty Officer aircrewman serving at the Royal Naval Air Station at Portland, and he offered to spend a day or two with her to 'field' any press enquiries. Late that evening, with the boys being cared for by neighbours, Lorraine drove to Portland and collected Ken, arriving back in Crewkerne during the early hours of 26 May.

CHAPTER 22

Santiago – 'It's a Small World'

After a little over five hours enduring the noisy and uncomfortable conditions in the back of the C130, it was a relief to arrive finally at Santiago Airport in the early hours of Wednesday, 26 May. Although dark, it was possible to make out that the airport was surprisingly small for a country's capital, but with the benefit of a long runway and was located on the south-western outskirts of the city. Having taxied to a halt and the engines stopped, the aircraft ramp was lowered and the F5 pilots disembarked before making their way to a crew bus to complete their journey.

Meanwhile, 'Wiggy', Pete and I remained seated waiting for someone to give us instructions as to what to do next. After a couple of minutes, two cars swept up to the rear of the aircraft, the doors opened and two officials of the Chilean authorities climbed out, boarded the aircraft and invited us to join them in the cars. 'Wiggy' and I climbed into the first car and Pete into the second. Without delay or ceremony the two cars were driven away from the aircraft towards the airport exit. After a couple of minutes we had departed the confines of the airport and were speeding through the unlit and largely deserted back streets of Santiago.

Half an hour later the cars finally came to a stop in a residential area outside a large house, and after a few moments the front door of the house opened to reveal a man and woman standing in the entrance. Whilst 'Wiggy', Pete and I were invited to get out of the cars by the Chilean officials, the man walked over to us and introduced himself as John Cummins, the British Consul. A short conversation in Spanish took place between the Chilean officials and the Consul, during which the three of us were formally handed over from the custody of the Chilean authorities to British jurisdiction. The two officials climbed back into their cars which departed, leaving John and the three of us standing on the pavement watching them as they disappeared into the night.

Without further ado, John led us into the house and introduced his wife, Gillian. He explained that we would be driven to the British Embassy at around 0900hrs from where we would be repatriated to the UK later in the day. He then gave us the fascinating news that President Pinochet had extended an invitation for the three of us to meet him and to spend the night in the Presidential Palace.

The offer had been politely and diplomatically declined on our behalf by the Ambassador. It was undoubtedly a wise decision on two counts: firstly, we looked most unkempt in our rag-bag assortment of scruffy and dirty clothes which we had been wearing for the last eight days, an image that was most definitely not the personification of professional British servicemen; secondly, the plan had been to repatriate us to the UK as quickly as possible with the minimum of public exposure. A night in the Presidential Palace would no doubt have been followed by a high-profile press event, something that we and the British authorities were keen to avoid.

For the next few hours we were able to relax for the first time since being on Chilean soil, safe in the knowledge that we were in British hands. During the early hours of the morning we were offered refreshments and talked about our activities since leaving HMS *Invincible* eight days earlier. John was already aware of the Special Forces operation, but not the fine detail. We had been talking for a couple of hours when he suddenly rose from his seat and walked towards a bureau whilst saying rather knowingly, 'I've just realized exactly who you are.' Returning with a family photograph album, John opened it halfway through and pointed to one of the photographs.

'Isn't this your brother?' he asked expectantly.

'Bugger me, yes. What's he doing in your album?'

'He stayed with us in March when *Endurance* was in Argentina receiving assisted maintenance. He's a family friend'.

'That's amazing – it's a small world!'

At around 0300hrs, John excused himself and retired for what remained of the night, whilst 'Wiggy', Pete and I grabbed what little sleep we could by relaxing in the large comfortable armchairs in the lounge. It was 0730hrs when we were awoken by the tempting smells coming from the kitchen. Fresh coffee and bacon had been off the menu for us for many days so were a rare treat and were consumed with gusto. After breakfast we each had a shower and shave, and made ourselves look as presentable as possible for our arrival at the Embassy and meeting the Ambassador. On the dot of 0900hrs, two cars drew up outside the Consul's home. We thanked Gillian for her kind hospitality, said goodbye and climbed into the cars with John to be driven the short distance to the British Embassy.

Meanwhile in Crewkerne, Ken had a rude awakening at 0730hrs when he answered the first of many telephone calls from the media, the calls from the press coming thick and fast throughout the morning. Ken batted them away with the ease of a professional PR executive. Both the MoD and I owe him a debt of gratitude.

In Chile, 'Wiggy', Pete and I had the full support of the diplomatic and military PR machine supporting us and safeguarding the security aspects of our mission.

On the home front in 1982, there was no such support made available to families who found themselves suddenly thrust into the spotlight without the benefit of training in handling media enquiries, or understanding fully the sensitivities attendant to Special Forces operations. Leaving aside the distress caused by intrusive media interest, on this occasion the MoD failed to appreciate the potential for Lorraine – or indeed the families of 'Wiggy' and Pete – answering questions which could have compromised aspects of the operation. For example, the press might have discovered my past involvement with the SAS and drawn conclusions which could have undermined the security of the mission.

Meanwhile in Chile, on arrival at the Embassy, we were ushered inside and taken to a small reception area where we were offered refreshments. A few moments later we were approached by a member of staff who was introduced by the Consul as Group Captain Sid Edwards, the Air Attaché. We exchanged the usual pleasantries before I went on to answer his questions about aspects of our operation. After half an hour we were joined by the Head of Chancery, Robert Gordon, who broke the news that the Chilean authorities were demanding that we attend a press conference and that I make a statement as to how we came to be on Chilean soil. I considered this to be an undesirable but nonetheless not unexpected development, and agreed to prepare a statement, starting work on it right away with advice from the Air Attaché. After twenty minutes Sid and I we were joined by the Embassy's resident MI6 officer, who introduced himself; I'll call him 'Geoff'. For the next thirty minutes I worked on the press statement, the wording of which was agreed with Sid and 'Geoff'. The statement was short, to the point and reiterated the cover story as agreed with Captain Lyn Middleton. The statement was handed to the Head of Chancery. After reading it he said that it was unacceptable because it was too short and did not contain enough information to satisfy the large press corps which was slowly gathering in the Embassy. At that moment we were joined by John Heath, the Ambassador, and Robert handed the draft statement to him for consideration. Having read it he ruled that it was entirely appropriate and that no further information was to be added. With the direction given, the Head of Chancery departed to have copies of the statement prepared in English and Spanish, and to make final preparations for the press conference. Meanwhile, the Ambassador remained and talked to the three of us about the operation for several more minutes.

As John Heath made his excuses and left, the Consul rejoined us. John explained that for our journey to the UK we were to be issued with new passports and identities. To keep matters simple we decided to keep our Christian names, but before the photographs could be taken, we would need to change into civilian clothes. A group of male staff from the Embassy, chosen for their range of build and height, were paraded before us. It was reminiscent of an identity parade as the three of us walked along the line of a dozen or so young men and chose various items of clothing. Over the next fifteen minutes the men removed the chosen items of clothing as we took off our uniforms and dressed in our new attire. I still have the shirt and tie to this day. As we made our way to the Embassy photographer to have our passport photographs taken, Sid undertook to dispose of our uniforms. My new passport was issued in the name of Richard James, an English tutor at Cambridge University. The Consul's wife, Gillian would be travelling to England with me as my 'honorary' wife. 'Wiggy's' new identity was Alan Shaw, an architect, and Pete's was Peter MacDonald, an engineer; he too was to be accompanied by a female member of the Embassy staff. Dressed in an assortment of poorly matching civilian outfits and armed with new passports, the stage was now set for the press conference.

At 1400hrs 'Wiggy', Pete, the Head of Chancery, the Embassy's Press Officer and I stepped into the small lift to go up to the large room chosen for the press conference. As the lift doors opened, the three of us followed Robert out of the lift. We had barely enough time to exit the lift before the doors half closed, almost trapping 'Wiggy' inside but fortunately they opened again and he was free to join us. As we made our way towards the table and chairs set up for us, I was acutely aware of the large number of representatives of the media gathered in the room and the bright television camera lights. To the sight and sound of flashing cameras and murmurs from the press corps of 'here they are' and 'that's them', we took our seats at the table. Glancing round the room and trying to count the number of press present, I estimated that there were between eighty and a hundred, all of them looking intently at us. I recognized just one face, that of Jon Snow.

For the first time since leaving *Hermes* on 17 May, I realized just how big a story we were. As soon as we were all settled, the Head of Chancery explained that I was going to read out a statement in English which would be followed immediately by him reading a Spanish translation; no other information was given, for good reason. As a hush settled on the room, I received my cue from Robert and read out the following statement:

I realize how interested you must all be in us. I am sure that you will understand that we are all very tired after our recent experience and you will appreciate that our main wish is to get back to our families and our friends as quickly as possible. At this stage I would like to say how correctly and sympathetically we were received and treated by the Chilean authorities and we would like to express our thanks publicly. We have given a full account to the Chilean authorities. I understand that details of our flight have already been released to the press and I hope you will therefore forgive me if I don't repeat it all again. But for the benefit of those of you who may not yet have received the details, briefly, the situation was whilst on sea patrol we experienced an engine failure. Due to adverse weather conditions it was not possible to return to our ship in this condition. We therefore sought refuge in the nearest neutral country. I am afraid that I can add no more.

It would be several more days, following my return to the UK, before I was to see television news recordings of the press conference and the reports by Jon Snow and Brian Barron detailing events in Chile during the days following discovery of the aircraft wreckage. I was amused to learn that 'Wiggy', Pete and I had apparently spoken to a local farmer close to Punta Arenas and had also flagged down a passing helicopter with consummate ease, within which the three of us had been 'spirited' away.

With my statement delivered, the three of us immediately rose from our chairs as briefed earlier and moved towards the lift as the Head of Chancery started to read the Spanish translation of my statement to the melee of press who had surrounded him. The members of the media were in two minds as to what to do next: stay and listen to the Spanish translation or attempt to follow us out of the room. There was a mad scramble as the Spanish-speaking members of the press decided in the main to stay put, and the English speakers pushed their way around the others in an attempt to find out where we were going. In just a few seconds we were back in the lift and on our way to the ground floor. The instant the lift doors opened, we were ushered out of the building and into two cars parked at the side of the Embassy. Without delay, the vehicles, complete with police escort, moved off at breakneck speed, with members of the press scrambling to get in their vehicles and follow in hot pursuit. It was a bright sunny afternoon as the small convoy of vehicles sped through the streets of Santiago towards the airport on the outskirts of the city. Thirty minutes later the vehicles came to a halt outside a building close to the airport. The stay in the 'safe house' was a brief hiatus in the journey whilst arrangements were made to collect our flight tickets, boarding passes, and to complete the immigration formalities in absentia. When the LanChile flight was ready to board, we were driven directly to the aircraft, embarked, took our seats and settled down for the long flight ahead.

Meanwhile, late afternoon at my house in Crewkerne, the media interest was waning, or so Lorraine thought. The phone calls had dried up by mid-afternoon and only one member of the press arrived at the house. He was from a local newspaper and was anxious to get a national scoop. Ken dealt with him politely, but firmly, refusing any comment. With apparent normality restored, Lorraine drove Ken back to Portland that evening. As events the next day were to prove, his return to Portland would be premature.

CHAPTER 23

The Flight to London – What no Interpol?

It was 1640hrs on 26 May when the LanChile flight departed Santiago bound for Madrid, via Rio de Janeiro. The flight time to Rio was just under two hours, so I planned to remain awake for this leg of the journey, and sleep during the next leg as the aircraft crossed the Atlantic overnight to Spain. I was seated with my honorary wife, Gillian. 'Wiggy' was in the row immediately behind and Pete and his partner were in the row immediately behind 'Wiggy'. The first few minutes of the flight were uneventful, but it was not long before our peace was rudely disturbed. Spain was the venue for the 1982 football World Cup, with the first round scheduled to start in a little under three weeks. Unfortunately, members of the Chilean press corps covering the World Cup were passengers on the flight. Shortly after the aircraft had levelled in the cruise and the Captain had switched off the seat-belt signs, some passengers started moving around in the cabin and it was not long before 'Wiggy', Pete and I were recognized by some of the journalists, a few of whom had attended our press conference. A number of them asked for interviews and wanted to take photographs of us. I politely refused them permission and asked one of the air hostesses if I could speak to the Captain as a matter of urgency.

Her response was to ask, 'Are you the three British airmen?'

To which we replied in unison, 'No signorita, we are tourists'. Yet another 'Allo Allo' moment. My request was granted and the three of us were invited onto the flight deck to meet the Captain. When I explained our situation to him and our reluctance to be exposed to the press he was very understanding and invited the three of us to remain on the flight deck for the remainder of the flight to Rio.

After nearly two hours the crew started manoeuvring the aircraft for its approach prior to landing. From our privileged position in the cockpit we were able to appreciate fully the magnificent scenery around Rio. The aircraft was flown in a descending circular approach pattern all the way around the city revealing to us the whole of the built-up area nestling on the sides of the many hills and the immediate surrounds as the aircraft closed the distance to the airport. Although dark, the vista was nonetheless breathtaking. Backed by coastal mountains, forests and fronted by the Atlantic, Rio enjoys a marvellous scenic location. It was an unforgettable experience to fly under the floodlit, welcoming, outstretched arms of 'Cristo Redentor' as the aircraft made its final approach to the airport, immediately adjacent to the sea.

Safely on the ground, the aircraft was taxied to its stand. All of the passengers disembarked, whilst the aircraft was prepared for the overnight flight to Madrid, the three of us remaining in the cockpit during this period. An hour later, the other passengers rejoined the flight, the three of us returned to our seats in the cabin, the Captain started the engines and the aircraft taxied ready for departure. Five minutes later we were airborne once more and enjoying a last look at the lights of Rio as the aircraft was flown onto a north-easterly heading for Madrid. Two hours later we were served an excellent meal, after which there was nothing to do but relax and sleep for much of the remainder of the flight. As I stared out into the starlit, moonless night, my mind drifted from time to time to the Falklands War. My thoughts were a mixture of frustration at not having news of the progress of the war and feelings of unease at having deserted my comrades in the Task Force and being on my way home.

The next morning, Thursday, 27 May, whilst flying at an altitude in excess of 30,000 feet, sunrise over the Atlantic was a colourful and spectacular event, unspoilt by cloud. An hour after finishing breakfast, the aircraft started its long and shallow descent towards Madrid Barajas airport. It was a bright sunny morning in Madrid as the aircraft touched down and taxied to its gate. On the advice of the Captain, the three of us remained in the cabin whilst the other passengers disembarked. After about five minutes or so the cabin was cleared of passengers. We thanked the Captain and cabin crew for their kindness, understanding and hospitality, before leaving the aircraft and followed the long line of passengers making their way towards immigration.

With the formalities of immigration control nervously completed, the five of us made our way towards the check-in desks. Before departing the Embassy in Santiago, we had been briefed by the Air Attaché that we were booked on the British Airways flight to London Heathrow, departing Madrid at 1230hrs. Whilst loitering in the check-in area, Gillian told us that she had been briefed to collect the tickets from the BA desk on arrival in Madrid on behalf of the five of us and subsequently disappeared for several minutes. Meanwhile, seeing one of the female members of the Chilean press corps making a phone call from a public call-box, I moved closer so that I could overhear her conversation. She was speaking to a Reuters agent informing them that the three British aircrew from Chile were in Madrid and presumably booked on BA 455 flight to London, news that I did not want to hear. The prospect of having to run a gauntlet of press at Heathrow was not on my agenda for the day. But then I reasoned that if our arrival at Heathrow was expected by the MoD, then plans would have been made for our reception well away from the prying eyes of the British public and the media. After about thirty minutes, Gillian returned with news that the London Heathrow BA flight had been 'weight-listed' so there were no seats for us. I told her about the telephone conversation that I had taken steps to eavesdrop and she informed us that she had instead reserved seats on the later BA 2465 flight to Gatwick, departing Madrid at 1310hrs. So far so good.

Meanwhile, at my home in Crewkerne, Lorraine heard a news flash report on BBC Radio Bristol, early in the afternoon, announcing that 'Wiggy', Pete and I were booked on the BA flight to Heathrow and would be arriving in England later in the afternoon. Lorraine's emotions on hearing the news were mixed: on the one hand she was overjoyed to learn that I was safe and on my way home; on the other hand, angry that she had found out about my repatriation from a radio news report. So much for the efficiency of the MoD PR machine, or so she thought at the time. But as later events were to reveal, the communications failure could not be laid at the door of the MoD PR organization.

Back in Madrid, with the check-in process completed, the five of us made our way to the departure lounge to await our flight to Gatwick. Sitting in the lounge by the departure gate, I glanced around at our fellow passengers but there was not a hint that any of them knew who we were. This was a relief. With the Chilean press corps having departed the airport, we could at last relax for a while. At midday our flight was called, we boarded the aircraft and took our seats. Whilst walking through the business-class area, I managed to liberate a copy of an English daily newspaper. The front-page articles were about the sinking of HMS *Antelope* and two features about our operation in Argentina. One was headed 'Crash Helicopter on SAS Raid', and the other 'Mystery Mission Crew Handed Back', complete with a photograph taken of the three of us during the press conference the previous afternoon. It was sad to find out about the tragedy of *Antelope* and frustrating to read the speculation surrounding our operation. After several minutes of reading, it occurred to me that many of the passengers would be looking at the same newspaper and therefore the same photograph – I visibly shrank into my seat for fear of being recognized. At 1310hrs the aircraft took off for the two-hour, thirty-minute flight to Gatwick.

CHAPTER 24

Arrival in the UK – 'We're Not Expecting You'

After an uneventful flight, the aircraft landed at Gatwick at 1435hrs. Assuming that there would be an official reception of some kind arranged to spirit us away, we remained in our seats until all other passengers had disembarked. With the aircraft empty of passengers we vacated our seats expecting to be met by MoD officials as we arrived at the aircraft door; no such luck. We reasoned, therefore, that we would be intercepted at some point on our short journey to immigration; wrong again. Following the formality of immigration, we made our way to the arrivals lounge where we assumed there would be an official holding a board with our three names on it; wrong for the third time. No sooner had we walked through the doors into the arrivals lounge when we were confronted by a small group of press and photographers, most of them apparently freelance. At this point Gillian and Pete's companion managed to extricate themselves and continue on their own separate journeys, to return to Chile a week later.

'There they are,' shouted one of the press, whereupon many of our fellow passengers looked around at us in astonishment wondering who on earth we were and what was happening. We endeavoured to outpace the press as we made our way hurriedly to the exit.

'Typical bloody MoD,' I cursed under my breath. 'Can't organize an orgy in a brothel.'

I decided that we should make our way to the BAA Headquarters, a short distance from the terminal building, where we could seek sanctuary briefly whilst I made a telephone call to the MoD. With the exception of a very fit and determined young female journalist, we were soon able to put some distance between ourselves and the chasing press pack. I felt some sympathy for her – she was, after all, just doing the job for which she was paid. But in wearing a tight skirt and high heels, she was not suitably attired for hot pursuit and after a few minutes the inevitable happened: she tripped and fell. Being immediately to hand, and possessed of a gallant disposition, 'Wiggy' quickly helped her to her feet. She thanked him and decided to give up the chase. After a five-minute dash, we arrived at the BAA Headquarters. I explained who we were to the security staff and they obliged by readily granting me access to a telephone. I called the phone number that had been given to me by the Air Attaché prior to leaving the Embassy in Santiago. After a few seconds the phone was answered.

'Major Bruce,' announced the voice at the other end. I knew of only one Major Bruce – Bob – who at the time was the Grade II staff officer responsible for operations on the staff of the Commandant General of the Royal Marines.

'Is that Bob Bruce?'

'Yes, who's that?'

'Dick Hutchings.' There was a short silence.

'Dick, how nice to hear from you. Where are you?'

'Gatwick.'

'Gatwick?' Bob exclaimed, in a somewhat alarmed tone of voice.

'That's right, I'm phoning from the BAA Headquarters having arrived with my two chums half an hour ago on a BA flight from Madrid. The earlier flight to Heathrow was weight-listed, so we changed our tickets. I assume that you didn't get the message.'

'That's right, we're not expecting you. You'd better get in a taxi and come to the MoD. Make sure that you arrive at the Richmond Terrace entrance, not the main entrance – there are press crawling all over it.'

'We don't have much money.'

'Don't worry about that, just climb in a cab. Someone at this end will pay when you arrive.'

'See you in an hour or so.' With that I rang off, and told 'Wiggy' and Pete the gist of the conversation, after which we left the building and climbed into the nearest black cab.

The journey by taxi was uneventful, apart from being recognized by the driver and subsequently having to bat away a tiresome but understandable litany of questions. After several minutes the driver realized that he was flogging three dead horses and the conversation turned to generalities about the progress of the war. For much of the journey I was stunned by the apparent normality of life in England which I was witnessing as we headed towards London in the comfort of our taxi. I felt uneasy – the normality seemed vulgar and surreal when compared to the death, misery and hardship being endured by those who were still very much in the middle of a war 8,000 miles away. I found it hard to come to terms with; it did not feel right to be back in England. The normality of everyday life seemed misplaced.

It was late in the afternoon when the taxi arrived outside the MoD. Within a few seconds Bob Bruce came bounding out of the building clutching a fistful of bank notes with which to pay the driver. We were hurriedly ushered into the building, issued with passes, and taken to a small meeting room. Bob offered us coffee and we chatted for several minutes about our general experiences of the war, but not the specifics of our operation. After twenty minutes the door opened and we were joined by another man who was unknown to us. He introduced himself as Rear Admiral Tony Whetstone, a member of the Special Operations Group, or SOG as it was known in the MoD. The SOG comprised a group of senior officers from the three Services, headed by the Chief of the Defence Staff, Admiral of the Fleet Sir Terence Lewin. The SOG's role was akin to that of the SOE during the Second World War. Admiral Whetstone questioned us about the conduct of our operation. After thirty minutes of questions and answers the Admiral informed us that our arrival in London was quite unexpected, going on to explain that the plan had been for the three of us to be flown from Santiago to Madrid. During the immigration process at the airport, we should have been intercepted by Interpol and handed over to officials in the British Embassy. As soon as arrangements had been made, we were to have been flown in a military aircraft to Ascension Island for debriefing and a short period of rest prior to being returned to the Task Force. Depending on the urgency of the situation, our delivery back to the Task Force would have been by parachute if necessary, otherwise a slower journey by sea. Before leaving the Embassy in Santiago, Gillian had been briefed by the Air Attaché that our party might be met on arrival in Madrid. Now her disappearance for the best part of half an hour after our arrival at the airport began to make sense. Having been briefed to expect a police interest, she was subsequently at something of a loss as what best to do when Interpol failed to make an appearance and took the only sensible course of action by booking the three of us on the BA flight to Gatwick. I asked Admiral Whetstone why we had not been privy to the arrangements from the outset, to which the Admiral replied that it was for reasons of operational security. I was dumbfounded by the explanation. There was no way on earth that our knowledge of the plan for our repatriation could have been compromised by us between leaving the Embassy in Santiago and our arrival in Madrid; I was incredulous. The plan could have been rescued had Gillian or I been furnished with a telephone contact number for Interpol. There are times when an overzealous adherence to security can have negative consequences. I considered this to be one such occasion – yet more fog of war.

As the discussions with Admiral Whetstone progressed, it became clear to me that the unexpected arrival in London of three high-profile aircrew had rather wrong-footed the SOG. Our presence in the UK was clearly an embarrassment to the MoD. The explanation given for the breakdown in communications was that it had been an error or misinterpretation by staff in the MoD of a date/time group specific to our itinerary as outlined in signals between Santiago and the MoD – yet another example of the fog of war.

Towards the end of the meeting, Admiral Whetsone informed us that we were to be returned to the Task Force at the first opportunity. You could have heard a pin drop in the room in the seconds after he made the announcement. The three of us appreciated the logic and common sense in the original, but as it turned out, flawed plan for our return to the Task Force via Madrid and

Ascension Island. But with that plan consigned to the waste bin of failure, I told the Admiral that I felt strongly there was an urgent need for reflection on the errors thus far and that a new plan for our return to the Task Force needed careful consideration in the cold light of day – not the 'back-of-a-fag-packet' solution that was on the table, arrived at in haste and with a significant degree of one-sided expedient exigency. I concluded by adding that, having travelled this far, it made sense for us to rest and be formally debriefed in the UK prior to redeployment. Furthermore, although unbeknown to the three of us at the time, our families were aware that we were in the UK, thanks to the 'on-the-ball' media; how was the MoD to explain our sudden disappearance to them?

Having listened to my forthright entreaty, Admiral Whetstone left the room leaving the three of us to ponder our fate. Comments including, 'piss-up in a brewery' and 'lions led by donkeys', passed between us and summarized our feelings. We felt badly let down by the machinery of the MoD and the organization's apparent inability to manage the unexpected sensibly. We were appalled that MoD officials appeared to be treating us as if we were simply pawns to be disposed of at a whim. We were three human beings who had been engaged in operations for four weeks without respite. Although fatigued, we were nonetheless still capable of making a valuable input into the decision-making process about our immediate disposition. After twenty minutes the door opened and the Admiral re-entered the room accompanied by another man who was unknown to us. He introduced himself as John from MI6. I'll refer to him as John 'P' to save confusion later. John explained that he was going to arrange for our return to the Task Force, via a 'safe house', in the first instance, but gave no further details. The mystique and reputation of the SIS held no sway with me, so I reiterated my concerns to the Admiral, for John's benefit. Realizing that they were making no headway, John and the Admiral then left the room leaving the three of us to our own devices, yet again. An hour passed before Admiral Whetstone returned and announced that Admiral Lewin wanted to see us in his office. The four of us left the meeting room and took the lift to the fifth floor, the location of the offices of the MoD's senior management team.

As we arrived outside the office of the Chief of the Defence Staff, Admiral Whetstone knocked on the polished mahogany door and the four of us entered the office which was modestly furnished and softly lit. Seated at a round table were Admiral Lewin and Vice Admiral David Brown, Assistant Chief of Defence Staff (Operations), another SOG member. Admiral Lewin invited the four of us to sit at the table and immediately offered us a large malt whiskey. Over the next thirty minutes we were invited by Admiral Lewin to talk about our experiences during the war, in particular Operation Plum Duff. The Admiral was especially keen to hear our appraisal of the effectiveness of NVG. Having sung their praises, we recommended the immediate procurement of sufficient sets of goggles for the Sea King IV fleet together with a cockpit modification programme. Finally, I suggested that the potential for the wider application of

NVG throughout the entire military air fleet be investigated. Admiral Lewin concluded by informing us of the plan for our immediate management. We were to be taken to a 'safe house' where we would remain in the short term under the care of MI6, whilst our longer-term disposition was decided in slower time. At an appropriate juncture we were to be formally debriefed at a location yet to be decided. Having listened to Admiral Lewin, I felt that at long last a sensible plan for our immediate future, albeit germinal, was on the table. Having downed two large whiskeys and put the world to rights, it was time to leave CDS's office. As we departed, Admiral Lewin's final words were to remind us that it could be as long as thirty years before we would be able to tell our story, but that given the high level of interest, the MoD might put the story into the public domain somewhat earlier. As it turned out this was the case and details were published in the *Sunday Times* fourteen years later, albeit with several aspects of the operation misrepresented. Following our departure from Admiral Lewin's office, Admiral Whetstone led us back to the meeting room where John was waiting along with two colleagues, Angela and Roger.

CHAPTER 25

The 'Safe House'

We had been inside the MoD for so long, focused on just the one subject at the exclusion of all others, that we had lost all sense of time. When, eventually, we walked out of the Richmond Terrace entrance, accompanied by John, Angela and Roger, we were taken by surprise by the fading daylight. The frenetic pace of activity in the streets of five hours earlier had been replaced by an atmosphere of relative calm. There were two cars parked outside of the building. John suggested that 'Wiggy' and I accompany him and Roger in one car and that Pete travel with Angela in the other. He then issued instructions for Angela to make her way independently to a prearranged rendezvous at Membury Services on the M4, where the two cars would meet up and continue the journey to the 'safe house' together.

Progress along the streets of London was quick, facilitated by the hour of day. In no time at all we were out of town and speeding our way west along the M4. During the journey John asked questions of 'Wiggy' and me about our respective backgrounds and overall operational experiences. He was particularly searching in his questions specific to our experiences in the South Atlantic, Argentina and Chile. It was a while before I appreciated in part the motivation behind the voracity of his interest in the conduct of operations – it was the first opportunity for John to talk to any service personnel who had returned to the UK since the Task Force had deployed from Portsmouth two months earlier. In his position I too would have been all questions. What I did not know until some years later, when talking with a former MI6 officer, was the significant involvement of MI6 in many aspects of intelligence in support of Operation Corporate, particularly clandestine activities to prevent General Galtieri from procuring more Exocet missiles.

After two hours driving, we arrived at Membury Services where we were able to take advantage of a much-needed comfort break. After another thirty minutes, Pete and Angela arrived in the second car and the two groups of us walked around the car park for a leg stretch before departing on the final leg of the journey. For the next couple of hours there was less chat; so much had been said already. After a total of about four hours driving, we exited the M4 and drove along increasingly winding country roads as we approached our final destination for the night. During the last few minutes of the journey, John briefed us about where we would be staying for a few days and the identity of our hosts, which for reasons of privacy and security will remain confidential. However, five years later I was interested to read in the book *Spy Catcher*, Peter Wright's description of our host: 'MI6's best technical operator'.

It was in the early hours of the morning of Friday, 28 May, when the two cars arrived at the 'safe house', a large detached property in an isolated rural location, set in several acres of pleasant mature gardens and paddocks. As the cars drew up to the house, a man appeared at the front door. As we got out of the cars, our host approached enthusiastically and introduced himself as John. Hmm, another John, just how many spies are there called John? I wondered. I'll refer to him as John 'W'. As I was to discover in the months ahead, both of the Johns were genuine Christian names.

Our host invited us into his home and introduced his wife, who I'll call Sarah, and their two teenage daughters. I was surprised that the girls were still awake, but in excited expectation of our arrival, they had been allowed to stay up late so that they could meet and greet. All ten of us gathered in the large farmhouse-style kitchen where our hosts kindly offered us refreshments. Shortly afterwards the two girls disappeared off to bed leaving the two Johns and the three of us to talk over the plan for the next few days. In a nutshell, it was very simple – to stay where we were, out of the public eye, until it was either time to attend the venue for our formal debrief, or return home to our families. Having drunk his coffee, John 'P' undertook to phone John 'W' as soon as he had confirmation of our programme. With that he, Angela and Roger returned to their cars and set off on the long drive back to London. Aware that we were ready to drop, our hosts showed the three of us to the bedroom that we would be sharing for the remainder of our stay. Exhausted after the last forty-eight hours of travel, it was not long after my head hit the pillow that I was sound asleep.

The time was a little after 0900hrs when I awoke with a start from a deep sleep to the sound of our host, John, who had put his head around the door and was ordering, 'Come on you three, breakfast in thirty minutes.' None of us needed any further encouragement. After showering, we made our way to the kitchen where we were greeted by the sight of Sarah standing at the Aga cooking a traditional English breakfast. Having enjoyed a delicious and hearty meal, John suggested that we amuse ourselves by taking a turn in the garden and by helping the girls with their ponies. Although a welcome change to the type of activities that we had become accustomed to over the last month, I felt that adjusting to the normality of life back in England was going to take some time.

Meanwhile in Crewkerne, Lorraine was going about her daily routine of taking the boys to the local primary school, a half-mile walk from our home. On the way back she bumped into one of our neighbours.

'I should stay away from home if I were you,' warned Terry. 'The street is crawling with journalists and TV crews camped on you doorstep. They've blocked the lane with their cameras and lights.' Following the visit of Captain Nick Beyts a few days earlier, the MoD had released the names of 'Wiggy', Pete and me. As soon as the press knew that the three of us were back on English soil, it took them just a few hours of simple detective work to identify the locations of our respective homes and telephone numbers, in spite of being ex-directory. We were clearly hot news and they wanted to talk to our respective wives. Anxious to avoid the press, Lorraine stayed away from the house for the remainder of the day, seeking refuge with friends nearby until it was time to collect the boys from school. By late afternoon the press had given up on her and she was able to return to our home.

Meanwhile at the 'safe house', Sarah informed us that she was going to do a spot of shopping in the local town and asked if there was anything that the three of us wanted. Quick as a flash all three of us asked for the same items: replacement underwear and socks. Suffice to say that we had not had a change of underwear or socks for the best part of two weeks, so a change was long overdue! The three of us handed over to Sarah all of the sterling that had been issued to us whilst in HMS *Invincible*, sufficient cash to buy the clothing and contribute to our keep for a while.

Later in the morning John decided to cut the acre or so of grass to the rear of the house. Whilst 'Wiggy' and Pete became better acquainted with Sarah and the girls, I hijacked John's ride-on mower and spent the best part of an hour cutting the grass for him. As I steered the mower relentlessly up and down the garden, dodging the lines of fruit trees, I could not help but feel a sense of misgiving about the apparent normality of my new existence. My comrades in arms were still fighting for Queen and country 8,000 miles away and here I was cutting a lawn in the warmth of an English summer's morning.

After a couple of hours, Sarah returned from her shopping expedition clutching three sets of pristine new underwear and socks. Without further ado, the three of us took turns to shower again and change our clothes. Our old underwear was promptly and unceremoniously burned. Later that morning, John regaled us with stories of a couple of adventures from his very active life of derring-do as an intelligence officer in MI6. It was clear to all three of us that he was a truly remarkable man who had served his country with distinction. James Bond fans eat your hearts out! A few years later I bought and read a copy of Peter Wright's book *Spy Catcher*. Although a career officer in MI5, Wright was scathing about aspects of some MI6 operations and personnel, but lavished praise on John 'W' and one of his operations.

Early in the afternoon, John 'W' received a telephone call from John 'P' in London. Notwithstanding the intense press interest, the SOG had decided that the three of us were to be reunited with our families the following day, but at locations away from potential press interest. For the early part of the afternoon, we each made telephone calls to our families to make provisional plans for the weekend – the first time that the three of us had spoken to our families in two months. The conversations were not without emotion. Preliminary arrangements had to be made with third parties for accommodation, so there was a succession of phone calls over the next couple of hours. With provisional plans for the weekend agreed with our families and third-party hosts, we briefed John 'W' and he in turn phoned John 'P'. By late afternoon we had heard back from John 'P' that all our proposals had been approved by the MoD – we were to be reunited with our families the next day. During the evening we were treated to John's cooking over a barbecue, washed down with copious quantities of Pimms: the perfect end to a perfect day.

CHAPTER 26

The Aftermath

The morning of Saturday, 29 May was warm and sunny, ideal conditions for travelling to be reunited with our families. After an early start, John 'P', Angela and Roger arrived in two cars from London. Having said farewell to our generous and delightful hosts, and promising to keep in touch, Pete and I set off with John 'P' and Roger by road for the four-hour journey to west London, where arrangements had been made by Lorraine for us to meet at a friend's house. Having been dropped off close to my destination, the car then took Pete to King's Cross railway station where he had made arrangements to meet his parents who had travelled to London from Scotland. 'Wiggy' was driven by Angela to a nearby railway station from where he caught a train to Taunton to meet his wife, Sarah, who had driven from their home in Dorset, untroubled by the press. From Taunton they drove to Dartmoor and spent the weekend at the Forest Inn, Hexworthy, where they had first stayed for a few days three years earlier during their honeymoon.

After a long weekend of leave relaxing with our families, we returned to our homes in the Yeovilton area and went back to our respective places of work to await the decision as to whether or not we were to return to the Task Force. The following week the three of us were invited to the headquarters of the Flag Officer Naval Air Command at Yeovilton for formal debriefing. The MoD had decided to launch an internal secret investigation to establish the cause or causes of the failure of Operation Mikado; our statements would form a crucial piece of evidence. The debrief was conducted by a Royal Marine officer from the SBS, Major 'C', and Squadron Leader David Niven, a RAF officer with considerable Special Forces flying experience, who ultimately rose to the rank of Air-Vice Marshal. During a two-hour period of questioning, we described the chronology of events from the time of leaving *Hermes* on 17 May, to our arrival at the home of the British Consul in Santiago. The sequence of events after that was already known to them and of no relevance to the investigation. Major 'C' and David's aim was to establish exactly what took place following our arrival in Argentina to the period immediately after the destruction of the aircraft.

With the debrief process completed, each of us returned to our duties. 'Wiggy' returned to 702 Squadron to finish the Lynx conversion course from which he had been 'hijacked' by Simon Thornewill on 1 April. Prior to the Falklands War, 'Wiggy' had been training to be the Flight Commander of HMS *Ardent*, now lying at the bottom of Falkland Sound as an official war grave. Following completion of his Lynx conversion, 'Wiggy' was appointed Flight Commander of HMS *Arrow* which was in refit at the time. Not one for kicking his heels, he took his flight to Gibraltar prior to joining HMS *Battleaxe* to gain small-ship flight experience before rejoining *Arrow* and deploying to the Falkland Islands in 1983. This was the first time that 'Wiggy' had seen the Falkland Islands in daylight, something I have yet to achieve. In 1990, in the rank of Commander, 'Wiggy' took command of HMS *Alacrity* and again spent some time in the vicinity of the Falkland Islands. In September 1991, his ship paid a courtesy call to Punta Arenas. Whilst there, 'Wiggy' visited the headquarters of the local Police Chief and was amused to see one of 'Victor Charlie's' rotor blades adorning the wall of the reception area. He was able to visit the beach where nine years earlier the Sea King had been destroyed and its remains buried. Whilst scratching around in the sand 'Wiggy' managed to unearth three of the aircraft's components as souvenirs for himself, Pete and me. 'Wiggy' kept the gyro, Pete has the forward spotlight and I have a CASS box (communications control panel). At the time of writing, 'Wiggy' is a Commodore and is the Naval Attaché in Washington.

Pete's immediate future lay with 772 Squadron, based at HMS *Osprey* at Portland where he was employed as a SAR aircrewman for a short while. After a few weeks he returned to Yeovilton on secondment to 707 Squadron to assist in the training of commando aircrew. In 1987 Pete received a Special Duties Commission and, at the time of writing, is a Lieutenant Commander serving on the Admiralty Interview Board, as part of the panel selecting candidates for Commissions in the Royal Navy.

In the short term, I returned to my duties at Yeovilton where, a week later, I heard the news that the Argentine forces in the Falkland Islands had surrendered. The three of us were subsequently informed that we would not be required to return to the Task Force. With 846 Squadron not due to return to Yeovilton until July, there were no flying duties for me, so the CO of the Royal Naval Air Station (Captain Peter Williams) decided that I should be seconded to the Public Relations team until the return of the Squadron. When he broke the news, I did not know whether to laugh or cry – the one thing I wanted was to keep out of the public eye and away from the press. Instead, I was placed firmly in the public eye and had to deal with press enquires and arrange press facilities on a daily basis for the best part of four weeks!

One of the saddest moments for me was attending a memorial service at Yeovil for 'Doc' Love. I spent a long time that day with 'Doc's' parents and relatives. I hope I managed to bring them some comfort as I talked about him and his irrepressible sense of fun and humour. As the programme for the homecoming of the Task Force became public knowledge, press facilities for the Squadron's return to Yeovilton started to take shape. I was surprised to be asked to provide a second-by-second commentary for the Radio 4 'PM' programme to cover the arrival at Yeovilton of 846 Squadron. The commentary was in the form of an interview with Peter Hobday in the minutes leading up to the return of the aircraft, and continued as they flew past the watching press corps and families. The formation of helicopters was a magnificent sight, led by Simon Thornewill and Pete Rainey, flying the two Augusta A109 helicopters (AE334 and AE331) captured from the Argentine forces by the Squadron. The interview and commentary was broadcast on Radio 4 on 13 July.

Over the coming days and weeks there was plenty of time to reflect on events of recent weeks and months. It seemed almost incomprehensible that the Squadron had embarked in *Hermes* as recently as just over 100 days earlier. During that short time, a war had been fought and won over 8,000 miles from home. Very brave men had lost their lives, some of whom were friends and colleagues. I had witnessed many acts of selflessness and acts of gallantry. Families had been superbly supportive throughout the conflict. After the challenges of the war, the normality of life at Yeovilton and being back with my family required considerable readjustment. I was brought back to the reality of life in the Royal Marines with a bump when I received my June pay statement. I was both bemused and annoyed to see that the princely sum of £40 had been deducted from my pay to recover the advance that I had received whilst in *Invincible* to cover operational expenses during operation Plum Duff. Without delay I called on Commander Supply and explained the circumstances leading to the payment and its eventual expenditure whilst staying at the 'safe house'. Commander Supply was understanding and authorized a one-off payment of £40 to reimburse my expenses. One's deeds may have been considered distinguished, but at the end of the day, the system is a great leveller! So finally, with the paperwork completed, it was all over.

Epilogue

With 846 Squadron's programme as busy as ever, life at Yeovilton resumed a semblance of normality come the autumn. That was up to the moment when one morning, during the last week of October, I received a phone call from Colonel John St J. Grey, Colonel Operations, on the Staff of the Commandant General Royal Marines. Colonel Grey invited me to meet him in the MoD the following week, but could not discuss the purpose of my visit on the phone. How mysterious, I thought.

The following week I dutifully travelled to London and called on the Colonel who informed me that I was to receive a short briefing from an Air-Vice Marshal in preparation for returning to Chile at the invitation of the Chilean Government. Colonel Grey accompanied me to the meeting with the Air-Vice Marshal, an encounter which can best be summarized as businesslike and frosty. The Air-Vice Marshal wasted no time on pleasantries, but instead launched into a tirade criticizing the Royal Navy's conduct of NVG flying operations during the Falklands War. He concluded by informing me that it was a role of the RAF to support Special Forces and not the Royal Navy, and that the RAF should have flown the NVG operations in support of Special Forces and not the Royal Navy. When I pointed out that two sets of NVG had been loaned to the crew of the one Chinook to have survived the attack on SS *Atlantic Conveyor*, and the helicopter promptly hit the surface of the sea whilst the crew were flying with goggles, Colonel Grey intervened and politely asked the Air-Vice Marshal to finish his briefing.

In a nutshell, President Reagan was planning a round of visits to Latin American countries to 'mend fences' and 'build bridge's after his government's support to the UK during the Falklands War. I was to return to Chile in November to locate and destroy all equipment that had been buried at our last location on top of the hill overlooking Punta Arenas. The Chilean Government was keen to pre-empt the possibility of any embarrassment that would arise should an inquisitive civilian happen to stumble across British military equipment in Punta Arenas at the time of President Reagan's visit to Chile.

On Tuesday, 16 November I flew to Miami on a BA flight arriving early evening. Following an overnight stay in an airport hotel, I flew on a LanChile flight to

Santiago via Lima, Peru, arriving late on the Wednesday evening. On arrival, I was met by Sid Edwards who briefed me on the programme for the remainder of my time in Chile. Early the next morning, we flew on a LanChile flight to Punta Arenas where we were met by two officers from Chilean Air Force Intelligence, one of whom introduced himself as Ernesto. We drove to a lay-by close to the Carabineros headquarters, where I had been six months earlier, where the vehicle was parked. The three of us then set off on foot to walk up the hill, retracing my steps from several months earlier. After thirty minutes we arrived on top of the hill and I quickly found the location where, on 25 May, I had buried the bergens containing spare clothing, sleeping bags, a tent and, most importantly, the fifty ampoules of diamorphine. Alas, someone had got there before us. It was readily apparent from the maturity of the growth of vegetation in the immediate area that the site had been discovered many weeks earlier, perhaps within a few days of 'Wiggy', Pete and me vacating the position at the end of May. There was no kit to be recovered and no diamorphine. Without further ado, my Chilean minders and I walked back down the hill, got into the car and drove to the home of Ernesto.

That evening my hosts treated Sid and me to an evening in a local fish restaurant where a good time was enjoyed by all. Later that night we returned to Ernesto's home where I awoke during the early hours with severe stomach pains. It was not long before the contents of my stomach were down the loo and I spent the remainder of the night emptying the contents of my digestive system from both ends, sometimes simultaneously. Later that morning, somewhat the worse for wear, it was time to bid farewell to my hostess and travel to the airport to catch the flight to Santiago, a journey that I was dreading. I was accompanied on the flight by Ernesto. Once airborne, no sooner had the Captain switched off the seat belts sign, than I was occupying one of the lavatories, where I remained for the duration of the three-hour flight. Following our arrival in Santiago on the Friday afternoon, I was barely able to walk through severe dehydration. Ernesto arranged for a military car to collect us from the airport and I was driven immediately to the military hospital where I was diagnosed with acute food poisoning and admitted for a few hours, during which time intravenous drips were administered via both arms and legs simultaneously. Fully rehydrated, I was discharged later that night and was driven to an hotel in the centre of Santiago.

At 0900hrs on the Saturday morning, I was collected by car from the hotel and driven to the airport where I boarded a LanChile flight for the return journey to Miami, arriving at 1900hrs. There were no flights to London until Monday, 22 November so I spent the Sunday relaxing as best I could, nursing very tender insides. On the Monday I flew to London on a BA flight departing 1930hrs, arriving at Heathrow on the Tuesday morning at 0900hrs. Within a few hours I was back at my desk.

I was to reflect on my recent experiences over the next few days. The Falklands War had been an action-packed, short-lived and close-run adventure. The return visit to Chile had also been a short-lived adventure, characterized by mystery, excitement, disappointment, frustration and pain – was this to be the norm for me from now on I wondered?

As the months turned into years, the interest of journalists in Operation Mikado gathered pace. From time to time I received phone calls from newspaper journalists and other writers asking me to reveal aspects of the operation, but I maintained my silence. It was not until 1996, with the publication of the *Sunday Times* article, that the story was placed in the public domain on the authority of the MoD. Whereas the account of events in Argentina, as briefed by the SAS to Nigel West, was a misrepresentation, the account of events in Argentina as written in this book is definitive.

In recent years I have had the opportunity to walk the ground in the vicinity of the Rio Grande airbase and have been privy to the ground defence plan that was in place at the time of the Falklands War. The Argentine military command was acutely aware from the outset of the potential devastating impact on the Task Force of their Exocet missiles, and anticipated the possibility of raids by land, sea and air against the Super Etendards. They had planned accordingly. From early in the conflict, a brigade-sized defence force of over 3,000 marines and infantry surrounded the airbase in depth, to include minefields, and frequent patrols were conducted into the surrounding area – penetration of the base by the Special Forces team to conduct a close target reconnaissance would have been all but impossible. The only high ground close to the airbase, from which flying operations could be observed, lay within the defended cordon of the Argentine troops, rendering impossible stand-off surveillance of air operations by Special Forces. Nearly three weeks before the execution of operation Plum Duff, the Argentine command had moved the Super Etendards from the airbase to a number of heavily defended sand-bagged emplacements in car parks along Highway 3, close to the coast, so in effect had the SAS got there the cupboard would have been bare. The airbase's anti-aircraft defences had been reinforced early in the conflict with additional anti-aircraft artillery units, SAMs and long-range surveillance radar. Furthermore, two destroyers, ARA *Piedra Buena* and *ARA Hipolito Bouchard* were stationed close by off the Argentine coast. It is therefore probable that a Special Forces raid by C130 onto Rio Grande airbase would have resulted in failure and numerous casualties.

The SAS is a regiment with a noble and distinguished history, although 'Who Dares Wins' did not prove to be an apposite motto for Operation Plum Duff. With the benefit of hindsight, however, the nickname given by many in the SAS to Operation Mikado and its preliminary reconnaissance mission, Plum Duff, almost certainly was: Operation Certain Death.

Glossary

AAEE	Aircraft and Armaments Experimental Establishment – the military Flight Test Centre at Boscombe Down, Wiltshire, since 2001 a QinetiQ facility.
ACRB	Aircrew Refreshment Buffet.
AEO	Air Engineering Officer.
AFCS	Automatic Flight Control System – an autopilot fitted to the Sea King.
Aircraft	Used generically to describe both fixed-wing aircraft and helicopters.
AS12	A first-generation, wire-guided, anti-ship missile.
ASW	Anti-submarine Warfare
AWI	Air Warfare Instructor.
Baralt	Barometric altimeter.
Bivvy	Describes a temporary shelter or bivouac made from man-made and/or natural materials.
CAP	Combat Air Patrol.
Carabineros	Chilean uniformed national Police Force & Gendarmerie.
Chaff	Small strips of aluminium foil used as a radar countermeasure.
CO	Commanding Officer – the officer in command of a military unit, for example a Naval air squadron.
Conventional night flight	Flight in darkness without recourse by the pilot to image intensifier or thermal-imaging devices.
Crabs	Armed Forces slang for the RAF.
CTF	Check Test Flight.
CSI	Combat Survival Instructor.
CWP	Central Warning Panel.
DAEO	Deputy Air Engineering Officer. Each Naval air squadron is complemented with a number, each deputizing for the AEO.
DLP	Deck Landing Practice.
Dockyard 'Maties'	Civilian personnel employed in the dockyards as maintenance staff.

Downwind	An aviation term denoting the position of an aircraft either in the landing circuit or when preparatory to landing.
DPM	Disruptive Pattern Material – camouflage clothing worn by military personnel.
DS	Directing Staff.
Exocet	A French-built, radar-homing, sea-skimming, anti-ship missile.
FAA	Fleet Air Arm.
Fast jet	Pseudonym for a military fighter aircraft.
FDO	Flight Deck Officer.
Flyco	The aviation control room alongside the bridge overlooking the flight deck on a carrier.
FOB	Forward Operating Base.
FONAC	Flag Officer Naval Air Command. Administrative headquarters of the FAA.
FOO	Forward Observation Officer – an artillery officer who directs artillery fire.
GPMG	General Purpose Machine Gun – a belt-fed, 7.62mm weapon. Can be mounted in a number of ways depending on the role.
G	The force of gravity. Can be expressed as being either positive or negative in its effect.
Goofers	The naval equivalent of 'rubber-neckers' – those with no official involvement who wish to watch interesting events.
Goon suit	A rubberized, neck-to-toe, waterproof garment worn by aviators when flying over cold water.
GSI	Ground Speed Indicator.
Harrier (SHAR)	Fighter, reconnaissance strike aircraft.
HDS	Helicopter Dispatch Service – a routine helicopter flight between ships carrying stores, mail and passengers.
HLS	Helicopter Landing Site.
HWI	Helicopter Warfare Instructor. Competent to train other pilots in the use of helicopter weapons and tactics.
Icing condition	Freezing meteorological conditions which form ice on aircraft.
IFF	Identification Friend or Foe – an active electronic identification system fitted in all military combat aircraft.
ILS	Instrument Landing System – a passive electronic system linked to an aircraft's instrument and navigation systems that facilities landing at ILS-fitted airfields in poor visibility.
IMC	Instrument Meteorological Conditions. When the level of visibility and lack of external references render visual flight impossible.
Instrument Flying	When a pilot uses the flight instruments as the principal reference for controlling the aircraft during flight.
IRI	Instrument Rating Instructor.

Island (ship)	The superstructure above the flight deck on the starboard side of a carrier housing the ship's bridge, Flyco, funnels.
Junglies	Nickname for naval commando helicopter aircrew.
Lepus flare	A six-million-candlepower flare, dropped or tossed from fast jets to illuminate targets.
Limers	A cold drink made with water and fruit juice in powder form.
'Little F'	Nickname of Lt Cdr Flying, the second-in-command to 'Wings'.
LPD	Landing Platform Dock – amphibious assault ship. In 1982 these were HMS *Fearless* and HMS *Intrepid*.
LPH	Landing Platform Helicopter.
LSL	Landing Ship Logistic – roll-on, roll-off amphibious assault ships operated by the RFA.
Lynx	A small-sized helicopter used by the RN in the ASW, anti-ship surface search and battlefield support roles – replaced the Wasp and Scout helicopters.
MI6 / SIS	Secret Intelligence Service.
MAUM	Maximum All Up Mass – the maximum mass for an aircraft.
MLA	Minimum Land On Allowance.
NGFSO	Naval Gunfire Support Officer – an artillery officer provided to control naval gunfire.
NOE	Nap of the Earth. Flying at extremely low level.
NVG	Night Vision Goggles – passive image-intensifier goggles worn by pilots that amplify the ambient light.
NVIS	Night Vision Imaging System.
OAS	Organisation of American States.
OC	The officer in command of a military sub-unit, for example, a company.
OP	Observation Post – a small concealed position from which to observe.
Pickle	A button on the cyclic which when operated by the pilot operates the SACRU to release an underslung load.
Pipe	Ship's public address system.
PNG	Passive Night Goggles.
Port	Left.
Pucara	Argentine-built twin turbo-prop ground-attack fighter armed with guns, rockets and bombs.
Puff-jet	Naval slang for a Harrier.
QHI	Qualified Helicopter Instructor. Competent to train other pilots.
Radalt	Radio Altimeter.
RFA	Royal Fleet Auxiliary – civilianized naval logistics vessels.
RNAS	Royal Naval Air Station.

ROE	Rules of Engagement.
Rotary Wing	Helicopters.
RV	Rendezvous.
RWR	Radar Warning Receiver.
SACRU	Semi-Automatic Cargo Release Unit – an electro/mechanical hook suspended underneath a helicopter to which loads are attached.
Safe house	A house which through its anonymity is safe for purposes of concealment from the media and public in general.
SAR	Search and Rescue.
SARBE	Search and rescue beacon – a two-way emergency radio and distress beacon carried on aircrews' life preserver.
SAS	Special Air Service.
SAVO	Staff Aviation Officer. A member of the Admiral's staff appointed to advise on aviation matters.
SBS	Special Boat Service.
SCA	Ship Controlled Approach.
Sea King	Medium-sized helicopter with a number of derivatives including AEW, ASW, Commando, SAR.
Senior Pilot	Otherwise known as SP, or 'Splot' – second-in-command of a naval helicopter or fixed-wing squadron.
Sidewinder	Air-to-air missile.
SOG	Special Operations Group.
Special Forces	The SAS and SBS.
SS11	A first-generation, wire-guided, anti-tank missile.
Starboard	Right.
Super Etendard	French-built surface attack fighter armed with the AM 39 Exocet missile.
TANS	Tactical Air Navigation System – an inertial navigation system compatible with Decca.
Task Force	A group of ships with a designated commander.
Task Group	A group of ships with a designated commander subordinate to the Task Force commander.
Time	All times in this book are local to the country or area concerned. The official time used throughout the Falklands War was 'Zulu' time (Greenwich Mean Time) which is four hours ahead of the local time in the Falkland Islands.
TEZ	Total Exclusion Zone.
Vertrep	Vertical replenishment – the movement of logistics when slung underneath a helicopter.
VFR	Visual Flight Rules. Applied in non-IMC flying conditions.
VipTax	VIP Taxi service.

Wasp	A small-sized helicopter, no longer in service, used in the ASW anti-ship and surface search roles.
'Wings'	Nickname for Commander Air – the officer responsible to the Captain of a carrier for all aspects of aviation.
Wessex	A medium sized helicopter, no longer in service, used in the ASW, SAR and Commando roles.
Wet	A hot drink.

Index

Advance Force Operations, 26, 39, 41, 44
Augua Fresca, Chile, 153
Augusta 109 Helicopter, 196
Ajax Bay, 55
Alacrity HMS, 82, 93, 101–2, 195
Albion HMS, 4
Alferez Sobral ARA, 74
Anaya, Adm, Jorge, 16
Andrew, HRH, Prince ('H'), 138–9
Angela, (MI6), 189–90, 195
Antelope HMS, 173, 184
AN/TPS 43 Radar, 91, 96, 139, 147, 149–50
Antrim HMS, 38, 49–50, 53, 173
Ardent HMS, 173, 195
Argentine
   Air Force, 44
   Government, 15, 28
   Mainland, 123
   Radar, 61
   Special Forces, 3
Argonaught RFA, 173
Army Air Corps, 41
Arrow HMS, 81–2, 100–1, 195
Ascension Island, 10, 21, 26–8, 30, 36–41, 43–4, 49, 51, 60, 80, 87, 113, 160, 164, 187–8
Atlantic Conveyor SS, 173, 197
Auld, Lt Cdr, Andy, 47

B Squadron SAS, 130–1, 160, 164
BAA Headquarters, 185–6
Bahia Inutil, Chile, 149, 151, 159
Bahia San Sebastian, Chile, 144–6, 150

Ball, Flt Lt, Ted, 123
Barras Airport, Madrid, 183
Barron, Brian, 181
Batt, Lt Cdr, Gordie, 83, 93
Battleaxe HMS, 195
BBC
   'PM' Programme, 196
   Radio Bristol, 184
   World Service, 43, 54, 59
Beagle Channel, 59, 175
Belfast Aircraft, 19, 37
Belgrano ARA, (see *General Belgrano*)
Bennett, Lt RN, ARC, 'Wiggy', 6, 15, 34, 44, 50, 55, 66, 72, 81, 85, 90, 105–6, 109, 114, 128–30, 134, 136–9, 142–4, 146–9, 151–6, 158–9, 161–5, 167–71, 177–82, 184–6, 190, 192, 194–5, 198
Bennett, Sarah, 194
Berkley Sound, 49, 78
Beuchene Island, 143
Beyts, Capt RM, Nick, 164–5, 192
Black, Capt RN, J.J., 23, 54, 139–41
Bluff Cove, 55, 67
Boeing 707, 47–8, 54, 77
Bombilla Hill, 66, 76
Boscombe Down, 8, 140
Branch-Evans, Lt RN, Simon, 'Radar', 55–7, 132–5, 137–9, 142–3, 154
Brandt, Lt, 175
Brennan, POACMN, Alfie, 38
Brenton Lock, 76
Brilliant HMS, 49, 53, 60, 71, 74, 102, 107–8, 144
British Consul (see Cummins)

British Embassy Santiago, 154, 169, 174, 177–9, 183, 186–7
British Forces Support Unit Ascension Island, (BFSUAI), 38
Broadsword HMS, 93, 111–13
Brown, VAdm, David, 188
Brown, Capt, Chris, 114
Bruce, Maj RM, Bob, 186
Buenos Aires, 3
Bulwark HMS, 4, 29
Burnett POACMN, Richie, 34, 46, 54, 72, 94, 112, 114

C130 Hercules
  Argentine, 107
  RAF, 126, 130–1, 164, 174–7, 199
Cambridge University, 129
Cape Dolphin, 67, 72–3, 101, 105–6, 109, 116, 126
Captain 'A', 129, 131, 137–8, 140, 142, 147–9, 152–3, 156, 159, 164, 174
Captain 'C', 41, 49, 68
Captain 'H', 174–5
Carabineros Chile, 171–2, 174, 198
Carina Gas Field Argentina, 145
Carrington, Lord, Peter, 14, 15
Carpenter, Sue, 15
Casey, Elly, 55
Casey, POACMN, 'Ben', 24, 51–5, 134
Chaff, 33, 57, 59, 79, 82–5, 150
Chile, 59, 129–30, 140, 147, 149–154, 160–2, 164–5, 169, 171–5, 179, 181, 183, 190, 197–9
Chinook, 197
Choiseul Sound, 116–17
Clapp, Cdre, MC, 38
Combat Survival, 14, 44, 47, 49
Commodore Amphibious Warfare (COMAW), 5
Concordia Rock, 66, 73
Conqueror HMS, 75
Cook, Maj, Ian, 160
'Corporate' (Operation), 190
'Council of War', 38,40
Coventry HMS, 74, 77, 82, 93–4, 144, 173
Craig, Cdr, Chris, 101

Crawford, Lt RM, Ron, 24
Crewkerne, 164, 176, 178, 182–5, 187
Culdrose, RNAS, 4, 7, 10, 19, 138
Cummins, Gillian, 177–9, 182–5, 187
Cummins, John, 177–8
Curtis, Lt RN, Allan, 86

D Squadron SAS, 60, 111, 134
Darwin, 55, 73, 76
Dawson Island, 153
Defence Review 1981, 12, 14
Delves, Maj, Cedric, 134
de la Billiere, Brig, Peter, 125, 160
Dockyard
  'Maties', 6
  Royal, 6–7, 10–13, 19
Douglas, 55

Eales, Sub Lt, Martin, 29
Edwards, Gp Capt, Sid, 179–80, 198
Ellerbeck, Lt Cdr, Tony, 53
Endurance HMS, 3, 50, 178
European Economic Community (EEC), 59
Exocet missile, 79, 82–4, 123–4, 130–1, 136, 162, 173, 190, 199
Eyton-Jones, Lt Cdr, John, 86

F5 Aircraft, 168, 175, 177
Falkland Islands, 3, 7, 16, 23–4, 27, 38, 43, 47–8, 58, 60, 65, 67, 73, 85, 124
Falkland Sound, 101–2, 105–6, 117, 195
Fanning Head, 116–17
Farnborough, Royal Aircraft Establishment, 8, 12, 21,25
Fearless HMS, 10, 38, 40–1, 49
Fieldhouse, Adm, Sir John, 38
Fitzroy, 55, 66, 73, 127
Fleet Air Arm, 5
Flight Deck Officer (FDO), 18, 99
Forrest Inn, Hexworthy, 194
Fort Austin RFA, 126
Fortuna Glacier, 49, 53
Forward Operating Base (FOB), 9, 17
Foul Bay, 127
Fox Bay, 76, 101

G Squadron SAS, 41, 60
Gallipoli, 112
Galtieri, Gen, Leopoldo, 16, 59, 175, 190
Galves, Lt Col, Horaldo Carrusco, 172, 174
Garrett, CPO Art, 9
Gatwick Airport London, 184–7
General Belgrano ARA, 75, 134
Geneva Convention, 30, 99
Glamorgan HMS, 34, 71, 111–13, 115
Glasgow HMS, 74, 77, 98-9, 102, 107–8
Goose Green, 55, 60, 68, 70, 83-4, 108–9
Gordon, Robert, 179
GPMG, 5, 17, 26–7, 55–7, 96, 109, 117, 127, 140
Grey, Col, John St J., 197
Grundy, Flt Lt, 8, 12, 29, 44, 50–3, 57, 85, 109, 125
Grytviken, 53

Haigh, Gen, Al, 42
Hamilton, Capt, John, 115
Hammond, CPOACMN, Wally, 85
Hanrahan, Brian, 12, 15–16, 71
Harden, Lt Cdr, Richard, 7
Harrier (see Sea Harrier)
Havers, Sir Michael, 124
Helicopter Dispatch Service (HDS), 43, 54, 87–8, 112–13
Heath, John, 174, 179
Heathrow Airport London, 183–4, 186, 198
Heavy Lift Ltd, 10, 37
Helicopter Warfare Instructor (HWI), 8, 26
Hereford, 19, 42, 124, 131, 139, 147, 159–60, 174
Hermes HMS, 3, 5–7, 9–13, 16–17, 20, 23, 26–7, 31–4, 37–44, 47–50, 52, 55–6, 68–73, 75–9, 82, 84–6, 88–92, 95, 100, 102, 105–6, 108–18, 123, 126–7, 129–31, 136–8, 140, 146, 155, 162, 180, 194, 196
Hesketh, Bernard, 16

Hoddinott, Capt RN, Paul, 99
Hodgson, Lt Cdr, Tony, 18
Horton, Lt RN, Bob, 8, 12, 26, 43–4, 50, 56, 68, 72, 78, 100, 114
Humphreys, Sub Lt, Paul, 44–5, 50, 56, 68, 72, 78, 109, 114, 125
Hunt, Lt RN, Phil, 57
Hunt, Sir Rex, 3
Hutchings, Lt Cdr, David, 50
Hutchings, James, 8
Hutchings, Justin, 9
Hutchings, Lorraine, 17, 23, 86, 102, 125, 132, 136, 164–5, 176, 178, 181, 184, 191, 194
Hutchings, Lt RM, Richard (Dick), x, 15, 35, 128–9

Identification Friend or Foe (IFF), 4
Illustrious HMS, 138
Imrie, LACMN, Pete, 37, 40, 57, 94, 128–30, 132, 136–9, 142–3, 150, 152, 156, 158–9, 161–9, 171, 177–82, 184–6, 190, 192, 194–5, 198
Instrument Landing System (ILS),4
Instrument Rating Instructor (IRI), 44
Interpol, 187
Intrepid HMS, 10
Invincible HMS, 3, 5–6, 23, 26, 31, 38, 43, 48, 52, 54, 70–1, 74–5, 85–6, 95, 97, 99, 100, 129, 131, 135–40, 142, 144, 146, 151, 153, 155, 168, 178, 192, 196

Jablex Float, 154
Jockel, John, 16
John 'P', 188–93
John 'W', 191–93
Johnson, Capt USMC, Dale, 8
Joint Intelligence Committee, 124
'Junglies', 4–5, 18, 78, 90, 104

King Neptune, 34–5, 103
Klepper canoe, 105
Knott, Sir John, 3, 12, 14–15

Lafonia, 76, 116–17
Lami Dozo, Brig, B., 16
Lawrence, Lt RAN, Ron, 8
Leach, Adm, Sir Henry, 3
Lewin, Adm, Sir Terence, 139, 187–9
Lewis, POACMN, Ken, 176, 178, 181
Lieutenant 'R', 95–6, 98
Lima, Peru, 198
Lively Island, 85
Locke, Cdr, John, 22, 71, 75, 79, 85
Lord, Lt RN, David, 29
Love, Cpl RM, 'Doc', 17, 43, 45, 47–8,
    50–1, 55–6, 65–7, 72, 75, 85, 90, 94,
    96, 98, 109, 111–12, 116–17, 126, 128,
    173, 195
Lynham, RAF, 10, 37, 160, 164, 175
Lynx Helicopter, 6, 74, 77, 81–2, 195

Madrid, 182–4, 186–7
Major 'C', 194
Major 'E', 41, 49, 68, 101, 129
Malaya, 29
Malvern (see RSRE)
Mare Rock, 105–6
Mather, Sgt, Joseph, 67
Membury Services, 190
MI6 (SIS), 188–92
Miami, 197–8
Middleton, Capt RN, Lyn, 23, 31–2,
    94, 124, 131
Middleton, Lt RN, John, 'Stumpy', 44,
    50–1, 77, 85, 109, 116, 118
'Mikado' (Operation), 130–1, 147, 160,
    164, 173–4, 194, 199
Miller, Lt RN, John, 14, 23
Milner, Cdr, 'Dusty', 23, 139
Mirage aircraft, 70, 113, 150
MoD Form 700, 57, 140
Moody Brook, 102
Moran, Lt, Cesar Pradenas, 172
Morgan, Flt Lt, Dave, 9, 31–2, 47–8, 56,
    59, 75, 77–9, 86, 90, 93–5, 123, 135
Mortimer, Flt Lt, Ian, 23
Moss, Maj, John, 160
Mount Brisbane, 85
Mount Kent, 116
Muller, Lt, 175

Nap of the Earth (NOE), 38, 148
Narwal (Arg trawler), 94–7, 100, 112, 134
Naval Air Squadrons
  702 Sqn, 195
  705 Sqn, 139
  706 Sqn, 139
  707 Sqn, 195
  772 Sqn, 195
  800 Sqn, 6, 31, 36, 47, 54, 60, 69, 70,
    83
  801 Sqn, 6, 23, 70, 74, 80, 138
  820 Sqn, 52, 95,138
  826 Sqn, 15, 58, 74
  845 Sqn, 5, 37, 49
  846 Sqn, 4–6, 40–1, 44, 140, 169,
    195–7
Naval Gunfire Support Officer
  (NGFSO), 41, 114, 117
Naval Party 8901 (NP8901), 23, 68,
  102
Nicholson, Michael, 12, 15
Night Vision Goggles (NVG), 4, 8, 12,
  20–2, 24, 26, 29–30, 32–3, 38, 43–5,
  47–8, 50–1, 55, 57, 59–61, 65, 85,
  90–2, 105, 155–6, 161, 188–9, 197
Niven, Sqn Ldr, David, 194
North, Lt RN, Nigel, 8, 12, 19, 27,
  29–30, 32–4, 39, 43–4, 50, 55, 57, 68,
  72, 77, 85–6, 94, 97, 100, 105–7,109,
  114, 137
Northwood, 123–5
Norway, 7

O'Connor, Lt Cdr, Rod, 23
Oerliken guns, 43, 93
Ogilvy, Lt Cdr, Tony, 43, 47, 54, 57, 69
Olmeda RFA, 52
Omega (see Radar Warning Receiver)
'One Hundred Days', 100, 147
Organisation of American States
  (OAS), 59
Osprey HMS, 195

Parachute Regiment, 42
'Paraquet' (Operation), 49, 50
Pebble Island, 101, 106–7, 109, 111–13,
  115, 123–4, 134, 137–8

Penfold, Flt Lt, Bertie, 15, 113
Peninsula de Brunswick, 153,
Piedra Buena ARA, 199
'Pingers', 78
Pinochet, President Augusto, 174,
    177
Pita, Brig, Miguel, 148, 150
'Plum Duff', Operation, 143, 147–8,
    188, 196, 199
Plymouth HMS, 49, 53
Pollock, Lt Cdr, Bill, 6, 40–3, 45, 49,
    51–2, 60, 68, 73, 76, 81, 85, 87, 90,
    92–100, 105, 116, 118, 123, 125–6,
    128–30, 132, 135, 137, 140
Port Howard, 76
Portland, Royal Naval Air Station, 176
Port Salvador, 76
Port Stanley, 3, 43, 49, 55–6, 67–8, 70,
    78, 80, 91, 93, 101–2, 109, 126, 144
'Prelim' (Operation), 110–11
Preston, Col, Richard, 41, 43, 49, 68,
    73, 76
Pucara Aircraft, 68, 96
Puma Helicopter, 8, 12
Punta Arenas, 129, 152–4, 158–9, 164,
    167, 171, 173–5, 181, 195, 197–8

QHI (Qualified Helicopter Instructor),
    8, 30

Radar Warning Receiver (RWR), 61,
    66, 68, 74, 83–4, 87, 144, 148–51
RAF, 8–9, 15, 41, 60, 168, 175, 197
Rainey, Lt RN, Peter, 8, 12, 19–22,
    24–6, 31, 44–8, 50, 55–7, 65–8, 72–3,
    75–7, 85, 100, 109, 116–18, 126–7,
    137, 196
Reagan, President Ronald, 197
Resource RFA, 52
Reuters, 183
Rio de Janero, 182–3
Rio Gallegos, 124, 150
Rio Grande Airfield, 124, 130–1,
    146–50, 164, 199
Roger (MI6), 189–90, 194
Roland, Surface to Air Missile, 43, 93,
    150

Rose, Lt Col, Mike, 41
Royal Marines, 3, 13, 17, 23–4, 102,
    104, 128–9, 142, 196
    A Coy, 25
    Dept of CGRM, 186, 197
    M Coy, 53
    3 Cdo Bde, 4–5
    42 Cdo, 29
Royal Navy, 5, 7, 12, 14, 17, 25, 34, 84,
    195, 197
RSRE Malvern, 56, 150

'Sailing', Rod Stewart, 13, 134
Salt, Capt RN, Sam, 82, 90–1, 100
San Carlos, 49, 55, 67, 82, 101, 116, 129
Santa Fe ARA, 53–4
Santiago, 154, 173–5, 177, 181–2, 187,
    194, 198
Schmitt, Lt, 175
Sea Cat Missile, 21, 33, 57
Sea Dart Missile, 81, 83, 107, 108
Sea Eagle
    Bird, 168–9
    Missile, 84
Sea Harrier (SHAR), 5–6, 13, 15,
    18–19, 23–6, 31, 36, 38, 43, 45, 47–8,
    54–6, 58–9, 68–71, 75, 78, 80, 83–7,
    89, 93–6, 107, 113, 123, 130, 138, 144
Sea King Helicopter, 5–7, 9–10, 13, 15,
    18, 23, 28–9, 44, 51, 55, 57–8, 66, 68,
    71–2, 74, 76, 78, 81, 83, 87, 94–100,
    108, 111, 113–14, 116, 124–6, 128–30,
    132, 137–40, 143–4, 155–6, 158, 164,
    174, 188, 195
Sea Skua Missile, 74, 77, 91
Sea Slug Missile, 112
Sea Wolf Missile, 107–8
Seccion Miranda, 147
Sheffield HMS, 81–4, 90–1, 100, 103,
    124, 134, 162
Shercliffe, Cdr, (Wings), Robin, 18, 137
Sherridan, Maj RM, Guy, 53
Ship Controlled Approach (SCA), 19,
    29, 34, 87, 112
Short, POACMN, Terry, 27, 169
Sidewinder missile, 19, 26, 36
Sierra de Carmen Silva, 149

Sir Galahad RFA, 173
Sir Lancelot RFA, 173
SIS (see MI6)
Skyhawk (A4), 107–8
Snow, Jon, 180–1
South Georgia, 3, 38, 49, 53–4, 60, 84
Special Air Service (SAS), 41–2, 49–50,
   53, 65, 67, 72–3, 76, 78–9, 101, 105–7,
   109, 111–12, 114, 126–8, 130, 132,
   139, 142, 147, 152, 155, 159, 160, 163,
   168, 174, 179, 199
Special Boat Squadron (SBS), 41–2, 53,
   60, 72, 85–6, 93, 95–7, 99–100, 116,
   126, 142, 194
Special Operations Group (SOG), 139,
   187, 192
Special Forces (see SAS/SBS)
Spencer, Lt Cdr, Mike, 8, 12
Spense-Black, Lt RN, Peter, 10, 37
Stanley, Lt Cdr, Ian, 53
Straits of Magellan, 149, 153–4, 159–60
Suez Crisis, 13
Sunday Telegraph, 145
Sunday Times, 147–8, 189, 199
Super Etendard Aircraft, 82–3, 123–4,
   130–1, 136, 199
'Sutton' (Operation), 65

Tactical Air Navigation System
   (TANS), 32, 39, 43–6, 48, 50, 65–6,
   68, 73, 75–6, 81, 87, 90, 105, 116, 143,
   146–7, 149, 151, 153
Tamar Strait, 106
Tattersal, POACMN, Colin, 55, 66, 72,
   85, 105–6, 109, 114
Taylor, Lt RN, Nick, 83–4
Taylor, Claire, 83
Teal Inlet, 55, 67, 127
Thatcher, Margaret, 3, 14
The Secret War for the Falklands (see
   West, Nigel)
Thompson, Brig, Julian, 38
   newill, Lt Cdr, Simon, 5, 7, 23, 41,

     FA, 49, 53

Tierra del Fuego, 124, 129, 131, 149,
   154, 159
Torpedo Mk 46, 81
Torres, Capt, Marcos Moya, 172
Total Exclusion Zone (TEZ), 11, 58, 75,
   87, 113
Turner, LACMN, 'Topsy', 30
Type 965 Radar, 82–3
Type 1022 Radar, 82

United Nations (UN), 42
USA, 129, 145

Veinteccinco de Mayo ARA, 144
'Victor Charlie' (ZA290), 135, 137–8,
   140, 151, 195
Victor Tanker, 80
Villa Grimaldi, 172
Volunteer Bay, 49
Von Reinhart, Lt, 175
Vulcan, 60, 70, 80

Ward, Cdr, 'Sharkey', 23, 54, 70, 95
Wasp Helicopter, 9, 53
Wessex Helicopter, 4–6, 15, 29, 38, 44,
   49–50, 53
West, Nigel, 140, 147, 199
Whetstone, RAdm, Tony, 187, 189
Whirlwind Helicopter, 4
Wideawake Airfield, 28, 37–9
Wight, Capt, Aldwin, 67
'Wiggy', (see Bennett)
Williams, Capt RN, Peter, 195
Woodhead Capt RN, Peter, 90–1
Woodward, RAdm, Sandy, 34, 42,
   48, 50, 52, 74–5, 78, 101–2, 113, 124,
   128–9, 139, 147, 153
Wright, Peter (MI5), 191–2
Wykes-Snead, Lt Cdr, Ralph, 23

Yarmouth HMS, 52, 71, 74, 81–2, 90–2,
   100
Yeovilton, Royal Naval Air station,
   4–6, 9, 17, 79, 164-5, 194–7